I Trusted You

*Fully and Honestly
Speaking
Of
Gendered Assault*

&

The Way to a

Rape-Free Culture

Nadine Rosechild Sullivan, Ph.D.

Used by permission:

Good Boyfriend Material
Copyright © 2012 Angelique Owenby Craw

Was It Rape?
Copyright © 2012 Anonymous

Cover Art
Copyright ©2012 Sarah Boujais, Bugaroo Moments Photography
http://www.bugaroomoments.com/
https://www.facebook.com/BugarooMoments

Produced in the United States of America

ISBN: 0984822615
ISBN-13: 978-0984822614

1.Gender—Masculinity—United States. 2. Sexual Assault—
Rape—Prevention. 3. Abuse—Child Abuse. 4. Domestic
Violence—Intimate Partner Violence. 5. Healing—Recovery—
Survivor. I. Title.

Lifting Consciousness Press
Philadelphia

ABOUT THE AUTHOR

Rev. Dr. Nadine Rosechild Sullivan is a diversity and spirituality expert. Her education and life experience give her a breadth of knowledge and wisdom about gender, sexuality, ethnicity, race and their intersection with spirituality.

Dr. Sullivan works with **groups and individuals** (*communities, congregations, businesses, corporations, schools, families, and private clients*) **to reduce conflict and resolve misunderstanding** around issues of sexuality, gender, relationships, trauma, self-confidence, religion, spirituality, and multicultural (ethnic/racial) diversity.

As a public speaker and sociological consultant, Dr. Sullivan is **available for seminars, workshops, lectures, focus groups or consultation** to your organization, business, corporation, congregation, or group and can help you gain and retain members and/or staff that function more respectfully and cohesively as a team, lightening personal and interpersonal issues. She also conducts guided group visualizations to facilitate understanding, focus, achievement, and relaxation.

As an ordained (interfaith) minister, spiritual and sociological counselor, and certified hypnotherapist, Dr. Sullivan is available for individual, confidential, spiritual counseling sessions (*by phone, online, or in person*) to reduce personal pain, facilitate healing, and help you find clarity and direction.

Dr. Sullivan may be reached at:
www.nadinerosechildsullivan.com
drsullivan@nadinerosechildsullivan.com
twitter.com/@NadineRosechild
facebook.com/pages/Rev-Dr-Nadine-Rosechild-Sullivan-PhD/198930586828943

Acknowledgements

Heartfelt thanks to my editors,
Lisa Sullivan
and Brenda Murphy, Sr.,
and to my cover artist,
Sarah Boujais
of Bugaroo Moments Photography.
You have each been invaluable to this process.

Special thanks also to
Angelique Owenby Craw,
whose courage in penning & publicly presenting her story,
Good Boyfriend Material,[1]
inspired me with the courage, first, to pen my own,
second, to address this topic in the classroom,
and third, to more fully and honestly speak
through these texts.

May these texts help all who read them
come to see the Other
as the Self.

---

[1] Page 31

TABLE OF CONTENTS

Nadine Rosechild Sullivan, Ph.D., Rev.

MOVING FROM VICTIM TO SURVIVOR:
RECOVERY FROM SEXUAL
&
PARTNER ASSAULT

This book is a collection of narratives and poems, interwoven with sociological fact.

I do not write this book from the psychological perspective, in part, because I am not a psychologist, and in part, because I believe that these social issues also need to be addressed at the level of society.

Therefore, I write this text as a sociologist, because I believe that the sociological perspective has something to say on these issues.

I do not contend that sexual assault and relationship battery are individual-level problems, but rather, ones that are society-wide. And using the sociological perspective, we get the view of the forest, not a view of the trees. Sociology allows us to pull back the lens from cause and effect for the individual to look at cause and effect for a society as a whole. It allows us to look at large groups of people, to get a broader view of that which is going on.

Sociologically, we can see that gendered personal assault is epidemic in our society.

Anthropology also, allowing us an overview of multiple cultures, has something to say.

Anthropologically we can see that, since these kinds of interpersonal violence are NOT a given in all human societies across time, they cannot spring from an intractable component of human nature. It is NOT that – biologically – we cannot and have not ever been less sexually and interpersonally violent.

Both sociology and anthropology will speak in the following pages. However, they do not subtract from, but rather, add to, the generally psychological perspective from which these topics are commonly addressed.

But I also write this book as a survivor.

And as a survivor – I write from the personal perspective of having done my own internal work to move past having been a victim into becoming a survivor.

As a matter of personal experience I assert that it is both possible and desirable to make that transition – to heal from sexual and partner assault.

I do not subscribe to the belief that there is *anything* inherently wrong with the individual who has been victimized. The victim has not caused her or his own victimization.

ANYONE can have the misfortune of being victimized.

Bad things sometimes happen to good people in this often scary world.

Having been victimized tells you *nothing* about me (or any other victim).

It casts NO aspersions on MY (or their) character.

All it tells you is that I had the random misfortune of being in the presence of one or more perpetrators in a setting in which the perpetrator/s felt that he/she/they had opportunity – and then, acted swiftly and without forewarning to take that opportunity.

It tells you no more about my character than it would if I had been the victim of a mugging or some other violent crime.

All it tells you is that I'm human, and that some of the crap that *can* happen in this world *has* happened – to me.

On the other hand, my telling you that I am a survivor does tell you something more than my telling you that I have been a victim.

By sharing that I am a survivor, I intend to communicate with you the thought that I have worked toward and attained some level of healing. Blessedly, inside of me, the pain (or almost all of the pain) of sexual assault, rape, and partner violence is gone.

How do I make this claim?

I make this claim because I have processed my experience and come out on the other side.

The experience itself is in my past.

On the other hand, my present – while altered in some measure from the fairy tale life I was led to expect – is, nonetheless, full and rich and sweet.

The assaults no longer reign in the core of my psyche, or trouble my solar plexus.

In large measure, this is true because I have come to know individually, personally, that I was not at fault – for any of it.

I was the victim, not the victimizer. [1]

Also, I have come to know as an established, internal truth, that I am not alone.

That which happened to me has happened to uncounted – and uncountable – others, who also did not deserve it. Sometimes, it even happened to those who perpetrated against

---

[1] There are times when someone who has been victimized, learns how to victimize, and then victimizes others. However, even then, it is not the initial victimization for which that one should feel shame. We will talk more later about topics like body betrayal (a physical response to pleasurable stimulation in the midst of an undesired situation) and other effects for which victims sometimes internalize guilt or shame.

us – causing them to be at fault in the role of abuser – after having first, through no fault of their own, been abused.

Moving from victim to survivor is a process. It is not a single step, and it is not accomplished overnight.

The unconscious mind INSISTS on facing our experiences, then categorizing, and filing them. If we have repressed memories, they will haunt our dreams until we recover them and face them and process them. Memories, whether repressed or never forgotten, must be faced and thought about and grieved.

When we suffer loss – and the loss of innocence, autonomy, and inviolability (our sense of safety) is devastating – we must grieve.

When we lose a loved one, we grieve. We must grieve. The stages of grief carry us along to a day when we can go on, when life can recover its joy, and we can continue our journey. When we lose (or suffer an alteration in) our sense of self, we must go through the stages of – process – our grief just the same. It is a kind of death – and a very real theft. But we are not without resources for recovery.

~~~

She needs to forget,

and one day, she'll need to remember . . . .

One day she will break down

and build herself back up again.

We all do.

Angelique Owenby Craw[2]

~~~

---

[2] From *Good Boyfriend Material* by Angelique Owenby Craw, a memoir included in this book.

Our memories must be cognitively slotted.

Whenever possible, it is good to do this work with an understanding and supportive therapist who has experience working with victims of trauma, helping them transition from victim to survivor.

The goal is to understand the psychological effects of trauma, recover the memories (little by little, as you are ready, as your unconscious is willing), and work toward self-affirmation.[3]

We need to release the false shame and guilt that attach themselves to violations which are this personal, and to work toward rebuilding a sense of self that is whole and self-actualizing.

You move from victim to survivor – inside – when you cognitively reframe – when you recognize that YOU did not, at least initially, assault anyone – rather, you were the one assaulted – and that does not make you *bad*.

As an alternative therapist,[4] there is a guided imagery exercise I sometimes use in which I may ask the victim of assault to imagine a time before the assault when s/he[5] was good and whole and clean. I encourage hir[6] to see hirself[7] BEFORE the assault (however young that may be), and – in hir mind's eye to comfort and affirm the person s/he was before the assault. This may require hir to move back to childhood or even early infancy.

This can be difficult for victims.

---

[3] Sometimes anger can be a tool of self-affirmation, a stage of grieving along the path of recovery (Kubler-Ross & Kessler 2007)
[4] I am an interfaith minister with three decades of experience in pastoral counseling, a certified hypnotherapist, and hold a doctorate in sociology with a concentration in sexuality and gender.
[5] A gender-inclusive personal pronoun
[6] A gender-inclusive personal pronoun
[7] A gender-inclusive personal pronoun

For some of us, our sense of self was damaged so early that it can be hard to remember, or even imagine, a time before the initial violent or sexual assault[8] – to re/construct a time in which we felt clean and worthy.

My experience is that there is a core deep part of me that feels the same no matter what my age. I have a sense of self as the observer of the world around me that feels unchanged by time. That part of me felt the same as a young adult as it did as an adolescent, as it did as a child, as it did as a toddler and, as best I can recall, as it did as an infant. In a sexual assault, that core observer of the human experience still *feels* empowered. Assault victims often internalize their sense of guilt around that core observer – having the sense that they "could" have/"should" have been able to stop the assailant.

But that core sense of agency is entirely out of sync with the realities of victimization.

The child, the adolescent, or the older victim taken by surprise or overpowered (etcetera) is rarely in the position – whether physically or cognitively – to have agency – to have been able to stop the assault.

I have known victims who, in their 30s, 40, 50s, 60s, 70s, still felt as though they had some blame in being assaulted yet, when they recovered the memory of the initial assault, it happened while they were still too young to stand up in a crib. In their unconscious minds, in their emotional sense of self, they were at fault because they *"didn't stop it,"* yet they were physically too young to stand or speak, let alone fight off an inappropriate adult or teen.

Other causes of self-blame include body betrayal (the body's pleasurable response to touch despite the emotional/mental violation), promiscuity (often a sign that one has been prematurely and inappropriately sexualized by the

---

[8] This includes verbal, mental, and emotional violence as well as physical and sexual violence.

sexual attentions of a perpetrator), and the sexual double standard (slut bashing the female for actions considered socially appropriate for a male).

All of these sources of self-blaming must be cognitively reframed – which is to say that part of moving from victim to survivor, from injured to healed, is putting your response to your experience back into context: the context of your age and/or physical capabilities and training, of your gender and the gendered ways in which you were socialized to think and behave, of the social setting (the times and history effects of the world around you), of your position in your family and/or other group structures, and more.

A realistic view of what you should have/could have done looks at the big picture – the whole picture – and looks with the kindness of understanding at the many ways in which one's own agency may have been, at the time, constrained.

We hear a lot about forgiveness, and forgiveness has its place, but even if forgiveness may be an appropriate place to end up, forgiveness is not always an appropriate starting ground for healing.

Anger can be an appropriate starting ground and response to being assaulted. Anger directed at the other who inflicted the harm is a part of the healing process – a form of self-affirmation. Misdirected anger – anger directed at the self – anger turned inward – leads to depression, which serves no one and nothing but the sense of false guilt. But the anger that arises out of a recognition of your own vulnerability at the time of attack, and that is then directed (internally) against the assailant who caused the pain and confusion may be a necessary step toward healing.

When you do the work of remembering *AND* of putting your experience back into the context of its time, and you recall and face the realities that made it hard/impossible to resist the assault,[9] you are able to get rid of the blame that is not rightly yours,[10] and to come out (at least to yourself) about your experience and defy the world to judge you. You are free because you refuse to judge yourself any longer.

The following narratives, poems, and interweavings of sociological and anthropological fact are sobering, but they are also liberating.

My intention in offering them is that,

- if you have never been victimized, they can serve to enlighten you to the realities that are/have been experienced all around you by family members, neighbors, and friends – as more than a third of the population nationally and globally[11] experience rape, incest, and/or interpersonal (partner/family/"domestic") violence.

- if you have been victimized, you will find healing in reading the experiences of others – letting them increase in you the knowledge that you are not alone, help you recover and process repressed memory, and encourage you to seek out the supportive help that is available. There is healing – and life and light and love – after recovery from assault.

- if you have ever (knowingly or unknowingly) perpetrated, or are thinking of perpetrating, I hope that you will hear the hurt, the damage, that such actions cause, and abandon the sense of entitlement that justifies such actions, and do the work of finding a better way to be (sexually and relationally) human in the days and years you have ahead. There is good evidence

---

[9] People who are assaulted, and who are so positioned that they are able and do successfully resist, are still traumatized by having been attacked at all. They may be less traumatized than if they were attacked and were unable to successfully resist, but even with the fortune of successful resistance, there is a remnant of post-traumatic stress.

[10] And if you still find some blame to be rightly yours, better able to face it, though I recommend double-checking the reality of your sense of self-blame with an understanding therapist, well-educated about the aftermath of sexual and relationship trauma.

[11] UN 2012, 2008

that perpetrators harm others *because* they *think wrong about* those they victimize. I hope you will hear – and recognize – the shared humanity of your victim – and find the path to your own healing – so that you may add to and bless those around you – rather than take from and harm them. You have a right to have your legitimate needs met, but no need is legitimate if it can only be met at the cost of devastation to another. I encourage you to seek the help you need to really know that women/children/partners feel even as you feel, think even as you think, can bleed even as you can bleed, and have every human right to health and happiness that you have. I hope you will seek and find the help that you need to heal from any of the ways other perpetrators have harmed you. You can transition from being a perpetrator to becoming an advocate, an ally for all. You are fully human and can change the way you think, the way you see others.

This book will address both the root – and the solution to – the problem of sexually and physically violent gendered assault in our modern, Western, U.S. society.

We can heal.

We can change how we think, how we see each other, and how we interact.

We are thinking beings. We can – one by one – heal the world.

Disclosure:

Throughout these texts, the essential details and emotional truths shared are true. Except when another author's name or pseudonym is credited, the following work is mine.

Narratives designated as *memoir* (and without another author's name) are from my own experience.

Narratives designated as *retellings* are recreations of *the experiences of combined others.*

No direct resemblance to any one individual (living or passed) is intended

As narratives, the included works (memoirs and retellings) all remain essentially and emotionally true, but throughout, names and significant identifying details have been changed, and overall, details have been at least partially fictionalized, to protect the privacy of the survivors and of those important to them.

The poetry in this volume is the work of Nadine Rosechild Sullivan, publishing pseudononymously as *N. D. Rosechild.*

SOCIAL – NOT BIOLOGICAL
RAPE-FREE
VS.
RAPE-PRONE SOCIETIES

The United States today is what social scientists call a *rape-prone* society. We have very high levels of gender-related and sexual violence. Oftentimes, in discussions of rape and gendered violence, I am told that the disparities between women and men, and the social sexualization of violence, are *inevitable, biological.* I am told that what we have today – socially and culturally – both in the United States and around the globe – is simply the outworking of *human nature* as it manifests through gender. I am told that we (human beings) have always been *brutal,* and therefore, *will always brutalize (be like this).* I am told that this is *how it has always been* and *how it will always be.*

When it comes to men's violence against women (here and elsewhere), I am told that it is simply testosterone.

I am told that male hormones make men *aggressive* and *violent* and *predatory.*

I am told that female hormones make women *passive* and *non-violent* and *prey* (easy to victimize).

The problem with that argument is that it is simply not true.

We – human beings – have not always been *like this* – at least not in all times and places.

And even now, *this* (violent, brutal, rape-prone) is not all we are.

As one author rightly points out, despite our frequent bad behavior, *human history is a history **not only of cruelty, but also of compassion, sacrifice, courage, kindness.***[1]

---

[1] Zinn 2004

1

The same author also notes that for things to become better, *We don't have to wait for some grand utopian future*, because *the future is an infinite succession of presents*. And **to live now, as we think human beings should live**, *in defiance of all that is bad around us*, **is itself a marvelous victory**.[2]

In an undergraduate gender studies class, I asked students for possible alternatives to gender roles based on male dominance and female submission.

One male in attendance answered, *"Well, if men didn't dominate women, then women would have to dominate men."*

I queried, *"Is there any other alternative?"*

The class fell silent – a long silence.

One woman ventured, *"There is no alternative. This is human nature. It's the way it's always been."*

To which I replied, *"There is solid anthropological evidence that this is not the way it's always been.[3] Can anyone think of any other way things could be? Of any other way we could "do" gender?"*[4]

Finally, more as a question than a statement, one brave young woman hesitantly ventured the thought, *"Mutual respect? We could have egalitarian relationships?"*

We have not always been – in all times and places – brutal and prone to using sex as a form of violation.

There is solid anthropological evidence that there have been, in the history of humankind, cultures in which gender has been done very differently than we do gender here.[5]

There were, in fact, pre-modern societies (before Western imperialism colonized and globalized the world, increasingly

---

[2] ibid
[3] Coltrane 2005, chpt.7
[4] West & Zimmerman 1987
[5] ibid

homogenizing culture) in which it was the women who were aggressive and the men who were passive.

There were also cultures in which both females and males were aggressive or in which both males and females were passive. Both the anthropological and the archaeological records show, there have also actually been *rape-free* cultures. Perhaps, even cultures without war or intertribal conflicts.

I tell the narratives that follow – not because I want to wallow in my pain or the pain of others.

I share these memoirs, retellings, poems, and sociological facts, because I have rational, anthropological, reason for hope.

Human nature has demonstrated the ability to manifest differently in different times and places – even, to manifest the best in itself. Therefore, we humans possess the ability to move a culture, any culture, from one that is rape-prone to one that is rape-free.

The key is ideology.

The (generally male) violence of our (rape- and domestic-violence prone) culture is based in world-view, and ideology (or beliefs) can be changed – in this case, for the better.

We began this process of cultural change in the 1970s (and since), when those who had been sexually-victimized and silenced (young/old, child/adolescent/adult, female/male/transgender/ intersex, White/Black/Asian/Latino/First Nations) began to stand up and tell their stories.

We began this process – of moving our culture from victim to survivor – when we began to affirm that the victim is not at fault (that the victim did not/does not "ask for" or "deserve" to be abused), and to demand redress of sexual grievances.

Our anger has been healing – for ourselves – for each other – and for a culture that is still learning not to sweep sexual assault – and all forms of interpersonal violence and abuse – under the proverbial carpet.

I am not looking for a new society in which women dominate men (or in which children dominate adults, etc.).

I am looking for the *mutual-respect* that that one smart young female undergraduate student theorized – those interpersonal egalitarian relationships based on equity – built not so much on our differences across gender but on our similarities within gender – on people of all genders (and gender presentations) being recognized as fully equal members of the human race.

If we were to take all known facts about males and females, and chart them on a bell curve – one for females and one for males – and print those curves out on transparency film – the bell curves (the distributions) would overlap.

Almost all of each curve would lie atop the other.

Little tails would extend at either end, giving social scientists the chance to argue that males are "better at" this and females "better at" that.

But in arguing about the tails of the distribution (the far ends of the curves), they would miss the point – the overwhelming evidence of the curves themselves: that each gender is overwhelmingly similar – that almost all of each distribution overlaps the other.

Any given woman is likely to have more in common with any given man than with another woman.

Put another way, even though I am a woman – I think, I feel, I hope, I dream, I long, I suffer – just like the man next to me.

Or addressing cultural stereotypes, perhaps I should say, "Females also think. Males also feel."

Our culture marks, and divides, human characteristics into binary gender camps. They say logic is male and emotion is female. They say courage is masculine and nurturance is feminine. Yet, there are brilliant and logical women and warm and emotional men. We all know men who nurture and women of courage.

It has been argued that biology is destiny.

For women who cannot control their reproduction (heterosexual women who hold anti-contraceptive theologies or for women whose access to contraception is limited: women in much of the Third World, women in poverty, women with controlling male partners who prohibit or complicate their access to contraception), biology can be destiny.

But for women with unimpeded access to (and finances for) contraception, and for women not in sexually-active, fertile, heterosexual relationships, the simple fact of being biologically female does not, of necessity, determine the mountains they can undertake to climb or the heights they may attain.

After one of my lectures on human sexuality, as the class was discussing the inequalities between men and women, a male in attendance exclaimed, *"But why would I want to change that? I benefit from that!"*

He spoke the truth.

But he was wrong.

The destiny of women IS the destiny of men (the destiny of each is the destiny of the human race [all ages, genders, races, socioeconomic classes] as a whole).

The world will be a better place for you, when it is a better place for me.

The Rev. Dr. Martin Luther King, Jr. argued, "We are caught in an inescapable network of mutuality, tied in a single garment of destiny. Whatever affects one directly, affects all indirectly."

Our destiny – female or male, child or adult, socially dominant or socially subordinated – is interconnected – is "indivisible."[6]

We may be human animals, **but we are thinking animals**.

We make our sociocultural milieu.

We can change our sociocultural milieu.

It is with my recognition of the ability of human nature to define, and redefine, itself, that the following texts are offered.

Important:

Readers for whom these texts bring up (perhaps repressed) memories or issues should seek the help of a counselor experienced in dealing with issues of sexual or physical assault.

Colleges and universities generally provide counseling services for their students.

A list of national resources may be accessed in: *Appendix C – Resource Links for Victims & Survivors.*

---

[6] Rev. Dr. Martin Luther King, Jr.

I TRUSTED YOU:

FULLY AND HONESTLY SPEAKING OF GENDERED ASSAULT & THE WAY TO A RAPE-FREE CULTURE

~~~

As long as rape is deemed unspeakable,

and is therefore not fully and honestly spoken of,

the public outrage will be muted as well.

Geneva Overholser[1]

~~~

My Best Friend's Uncle
A Memoir

I was twelve-years-old. My mind was twelve-years-old. My body would have passed for eighteen. But I was not eighteen. I was twelve.

I had gone with my best friend, Regina,[2] to her extended family's celebration of the Easter holiday. We were all Catholic. I was Austro-Hungarian and Irish. She was German and Italian, but what happened that day, happens in all religions and ethnicities. It happened then. It happens now.

---

[1] Overholser 1992

[2] As previously stated, names have been changed, throughout, to protect the personal privacy of those who lived through these narratives.

I was a baby boomer. I was growing up in a post-World War II, U.S., suburb, north of Philadelphia, and I had a very protected childhood. It was unhappy in its own way. I was often quite lonely. But, prepubescence, I was, indubitably, protected.

I had lived my twelve years in a very asexual space. No one mentioned sex. No one had ever touched me inappropriately – or even insinuated that such a thing was possible.

In my own family, the twelve-year-old me had more than a decade's evidence that my father respected my mother, my grandfather respected my grandmother, and my great-grandfather respected my great-grandmother. I grew up in a family where *"never was heard a discouraging* [or a sexually-explicit] *word."*[3]

I had needled and begged until I had gotten permission to go with my best friend to her family's Easter celebration. The food was fabulous. I was having a great time. We were just at an age when music and dancing was beginning to seem important. The high school we would be attending in a year or two had a weekly dance, and we were seriously working to learn to perform the fast dances and the steps of the line dances we watched on Dick Clark's American Bandstand. Another friend's older sister had taught me how to find the rhythm in a song the year before. We spent hours listening to our local pop radio stations, WIBG and WFIL. Regularly cutting the carpet in Regina's family room was, to us, serious business.

Regina suggested we go downstairs to the finished basement, in the home where the family party was being held, and turn on the radio and dance. I was amenable, as were a stream of younger children who happily followed us down the stairs. A few minutes later, we were also followed by one of Regina's many uncles. At one end of the room, there was a set of drums. Uncle Tony[4] took a seat and began to keep time to the music. Thinking nothing of it, Regina and I continued to dance.

---

[3] Higley 1876
[4] This name has also been changed.

A few songs later, a slower song came on the radio. Suddenly, there was an arm on my elbow. Uncle Tony had left the drums. He pivoted me around and began to slow dance. I don't remember whether or not I fell into step, but within seconds, he planted his right hand on my left breast and his mouth on mine.

I froze.

They say there are three response mechanisms to danger or assault – flight, or fight, or freeze ('playing dead').[5] They say it is the primitive brain that responds immediately, at a level beneath conscious choice.

He intended the element of surprise.

And in the unexpectedness of the moment, in my utter confusion about what was going on, my brain stem – inadvertently – without my forethought or cognition – responded by freezing, and I became rigid, like a statue.

With time on pause, I remember puzzling, *What is he doing?*

I became aware of the slime of his tongue, that it was extended beyond his lips, and in response, clenched my mouth tightly closed.

I had never even heard of French kissing, and I remember wondering, *Why is he licking my lips?*

I was, literally, so actually innocent that I had no conceptual idea of either his actions or the fact that someone so much older than me – who KNEW I was a child – could be directing those actions toward me.

In the very definition of the term, I was blindsided. You *cannot* **see** *what you cannot* **believe**.[6]

And I could not have foreseen this that I could never have imagined.

---

[5] Bracha et al. 2004
[6] DeBecker 1997

Intellectually, I'm sure the entire event lasted only seconds.

In memory, however, it is as frozen still as I was then, and it stretches out as a span between innocence and devastation.

I'm sure it only took moments for Regina's little brother, Frankie, to begin to sing-song, *Uncle Tony's kissing Diane! Uncle Tony's kissing Diane!* in the lilting tones of the 7-year-old.

Regina's Uncle Tony let go. He turned on his heel and sped up the steps.

Regina demanded, *Did he touch you?*

I shook my head, *No.* Maybe I said it too.

We went upstairs. As was common for preteen girlfriends, we went into the bathroom together. I started to sob. Regina exclaimed, *He did touch you!*, threw open the door, and went in search of her father.

Regina's father went in search of the offender, who had already hurriedly gathered up his pregnant wife and two-year old and fled.

Regina's father was apologetic. It was his brother.

We left the party.

Regina's mother was wonderful. She told me it was not my fault.

She told me how wrong he was, and how they would make sure he was not allowed at family gatherings in the future.

They drove me home.

Once home, I ran to the bathroom and began to scrub my mouth with the Comet cleanser I found under the sink, hoping the chlorine bleach in it would take away the dirty feeling, kill the germs.

I kept scrubbing my lips, but the feeling didn't lessen.

I crawled into bed, under the covers, way under the covers.

When I woke the next morning, for just a second I felt fine.

But then the memory (and with it, the confusion and an overpowering sweep of dirtiness) flooded back in, and I was overwhelmed with nausea and the desperate desire to simply go back to sleep, where I could escape both feeling and memory.

I pulled the covers back over my head.

Through my window, from the backyard, I heard the sound of a basketball dribbling on the asphalt court my father had installed and knew it meant that my brother's friend,

Jesse, was there, playing ball. Jesse had given me my first kiss just two days before, on that very basketball court. I should have been ecstatic with anticipation at the sight of him.

I pulled the covers over my head tighter.

As the day wore on, my mother came looking for me.

I pled illness, and retreated even further.

It was months before I began to feel normal again, and that, only with the help of Regina's mother, who brought up the topic periodically, reaffirming my worth and reaffirming her in-law's error, opening a space for me to process the assault.

Not much happened to me physically that day – an uninvited hand on a breast, an unwelcome and intrusive kiss . . . .

Physically, it was not the stuff that alters your perceptions of sexual acts. It was not the kind of assault that requires stitches or time for the body to mend.

But my world changed.

Until that frozen moment, I thought I mattered.

I thought men respected women.

I was an American. I thought my mind mattered – to the men around me. After all, they (*males - my father, male religious leaders*) were educating me!

I thought my character mattered. I was being given a religious education, and I was being *churched.*

I was surrounded by women of piety and faith: my mother, grandmother, great-grandmother, Regina's mother. .

My grade school teachers were women with a religious vocation who dedicated their lives to their faith, to their God, and to the education of children – even girl children.

But Uncle Tony, and many of the boys and men who followed (most of whom played by the rules and at least sought to date me before they sought to touch me), changed that perception.

Regina's uncle was merely the start of a parade. From that day forward, I began to feel, not respected like a person, but disrespected – like a random body.

I began to notice what sociologists call "the male gaze" – the sense and reality of being scanned by each male I passed for the acceptability or unacceptability – for the sexiness or lack thereof – of my body – of being primarily a body.

I began to recognize that, in many of their eyes, I was merely a walking vehicle for a pair of breasts (breasts to which they often talked when addressing me, instead of meeting my eyes) and an available vagina.

Breasts which even a random man might walk up to, and, without invitation, reach out and touch – like the guy whose hand I had to knock off as I descended a subway stair while he ascended the other side.

Regina's Uncle Tony began my sense of betrayal.

The world I had been sheltered in those first twelve years was a fairy tale of my mother's careful construction.

She never warned me, but she kept me safe as long as she could. And not warning me was (for her) a part of keeping me safe, of not letting me know there was a world out there that would treat me poorly.

But once I, as a girl, was out beyond her view, the fact that there were perpetrators in the world came home to roost.

~ ~ ~

I Trusted You

N. D. Rosechild

I trusted you.

Trusted life.

Walked free with the breeze combing my hair,

   head erect,

   shoulders square,

Facing future.

I was a warrior inside;

   vast, enormous, capable.

The source of Spring –

Ruler of the Galaxy –

Wild, strong, and full of dreams.

Through me,

    morning glories turned their faces to the
sun.

Through me,

    flowers bore their fruit.

Through me,

    ice crystals formed

    on the skin of virgin snow

And God heard – me –

    on High.

I was strong,

    compact, vigorous, alive.

My body, my own,

    free of vulnerable parts,

    muscles powerful.

Victor in every contest,

I bested each brother,

    time and again.

Won,

    brought them down,

    received their cries of "uncle,"

    magnanimous.

Let them go,

I Trusted You

showed compassion.

I studied tadpoles,

    collected snakes,

    scaled trees,

    ate dirt, even worms –

    chased you with the large and hairy bug.

Studied dinosaurs.

    Knew the names of clouds

        brisking my blue and open terrain.

Noted trade winds,

    sleuthed mysteries,

    created secret codes,

    played spy.

Ran the woods,

    waded streams,

    unearthed fossils.

I was large,

    and the world revolved around me.

I was pretty.

Dresses of taffeta and lace

    graced my form;

Ribboned pumps

> and tiny purses of real patent leather.

I wore lace,

> reveled in the feel of my hair
>
> curling 'round my face.

Life lay before me

> - open -
>
> a realm of possibilities
>
> oozing promise.

But then you came

> and in a moment
>
> put out the sun,
>
> muted the song of birds,
>
> took the warmth
>
> > from the air.

I trusted you.

I didn't know you.

I trusted everyone

> trusted life.

And so, I went with you,

> off,

I Trusted You

alone.

No reason to suspect,

no forewarning,

no knowledge of evil,

an innocent.

And with your hand

and with your mouth

and with your misplaced lust

You took that which should have been,

and all that had always been,

And never gave it back.

~~~

Nadine Rosechild Sullivan, Ph.D., Rev.

THE GLOBE
VS
THE UNITED STATES

The Globe

Teaching gender and sexuality, I am continually aware that women around the world face a host of horrors – just because they are women. Two waves of women's activism (from 1848 to 1920 and from 1963 until the present) have made continual improvements in the status of women in the United States.

In other geographic and cultural settings, women may be killed ("honor" killing) by their family members for perceived violations of their family's honor – for being found to have a broken hymen,[1] for getting pregnant outside of marriage,[2] for marrying outside of culture/religion/tribe, or even[3] for falling victim to rape.[4]

In some settings, women may be burned to death by their husband (or mother-in-law), so that their husband (or his family) may receive a new dowry, because by her death he is again made single and available for a second marriage. In India, over 8000 women per year are burned in dowry deaths [22 per day in 2007].[5]

"The most common form of violence experienced by women globally is physical violence inflicted by an intimate partner ("domestic" violence). On average, at least one in three women is beaten, coerced into sex or otherwise abused by an intimate partner in the course of her lifetime."[6]

---

[1] By choice, by force, or by accident
[2] Again, by choice, by force, or by accident
[3] No matter how young, unable to give consent, or resistant
[4] Souad & Cuny 2003; Jan Goodwin. 1994; Kristof & WuDunn 2009
[5] UN 2012; Young 1995
[6] UN 2012, 2008

Also, "it is estimated that, worldwide, one in five women will become a victim of rape or attempted rape in her lifetime."[7] And according to World Bank data, "women aged 15-44 are more at risk from rape and domestic violence than from cancer, motor accidents, war and malaria."[8]

Further, according to the World Health Organization, "several global surveys suggest that half of all women (depending on location, 40-70%) who die from homicide are killed by their current or former husbands or (male) partners."[9]

Around the globe, women are forced to work in *sweatshops* for pennies a day;[10] or forced by economics to migrate to seek domestic labor far from their homes and children.[11]

60 million girls worldwide have been forced (given or sold) into arranged marriages as children, being given into marriage so young that they face increased and inordinate risk during labor and childbirth (including dramatically increased rates of infant and maternal mortality and obstetrical fistula).[12]

Not including other forms of prostitution, "a conservative estimate" indicates that at least "3 million women and girls (and a very small number of boys) worldwide" have been kidnapped, deceived, or sold by their families and *trafficked* as slaves ("in effect . . . the property of another . . . [who] could be killed by their owner with impunity") for *sex work in brothels*, often servicing 17 or more men per day – with no respite, not even after a birth or an abortion – until they die (still often children or teens) of HIV/AIDS.[13]

---

[7] ibid
[8] ibid
[9] ibid
[10] Blodget 2005; Women and Global Human Rights 2012 [accessed]; FMF 2012; campaign for the Advancement of Women 2012 [accessed]; Black 2001
[11] Ehrenreicht & Hochschild 2002; Human Rights Watch 2011b; Human Rights Watch 2000
[12] Primarily in South Asia and Sub-Saharan Africa (UN 2012); See also: UN 2008; Human Rights Watch 2011a; Inbaraj 2004; LITA 2008; Muhsen & Crofts 1991; Kristof & WuDunn 2009
[13] Kristof & WuDunn 2009, p10; See also: Nazer & Lewis 2003; Muhsen & Crofts 1991; Bales 2007; UNICEF 2011; Varia 2011

And in many places, millions of girls, between their toddler and teen years (generally without anesthesia or antiseptic) have their genitals permanently mutilated: their clitorises removed, their labia removed, and, sometimes, also, their vaginas sewn shut in the practice of female genital mutilation.[14]

~~~

I Am the Japanese Picture Bride

N. D. Rosechild

I am

The Japanese picture bride

Given in marriage

To a stranger

I am

The five year old girl

Bleeding anguish

As her genitals are

Cut away

I am

The twelve-year-old

Pregnant by her father

---

[14] Kassindja & Bashir 1998; Dirie & Milborn 2005; Dirie & Miller 1998; Nazer & Lewis 2003; Walker 1992

Too stunned for weeping

Too numb to tell

I am

The disappointed wife

At forty

Blessing herself

She only has two to feed

As she throws husband

Out the door

I am

The immolated bride in India

Ashes melted at husband's mother's

Request

The smoke of all

Rejection

I am

The ten-year-old

Giving birth all week

'Til genitals rip

And fistula makes

A leper

I Trusted You

I am

The disenfranchised worker

Chipping fingers 18 hours a day

Back hunched, eyes dimming

Stitching designer labels

For 80 cents

A day

I am

the sex worker on her knees

Head pushed down on penis

Or thighs spread

Riding out

Its thrusts

These

All these

Live inside me

Breathe my air

Digest my meat

All these become

ME –

The United States

By comparison, the lives of women in North America seem sweet, and when assigned a paper on the status of women in the United States, most undergraduates[15] I have known over the past decade and a half have written glowing reports proclaiming mainstream[16] American women's successful and complete emancipation. *Students give reports claiming situations regarding gender are*

The overriding thesis of these papers is that – here – in regard to gender, it is – now – "all better."

And yet, the lives of women – here – are still complicated by the ongoing legacy of gender discrimination and a range of issues that are simply *not* actually "all better" yet.

It is true that – here – now – because of women's movements – mainstream, native-born, American women have relative freedom to pursue their own happiness. Prior to the first wave of the women's movement, women were perpetual minors by law, the legal property of either a father or a husband or the wards of their nearest male relative. Subsumed into father/husband's identity, they had no rights to own property, to sue or be sued, to serve on a jury, or to be tried by a jury of their (female) peers. No matter how ill, or how tired, or how pregnant, or how postpartum, or how menstrual, or how menopausal, a woman had no right to say no to sex in marriage,[17] or no to a husband's request for her domestic service. If a woman took time off to care for extended family members, even her own aging parents, her husband could sue the estate/s of his in-laws for remuneration for the wifely services lost to him

---

[15] all genders

[16] white, middle-class, straight, cisgendered, generally secular but culturally Christian

[17] A wife was considered to have given her husband standing sexual consent in the wedding ceremony. Therefore, despite the use of violence or coercion (or her perception or experience of the act), it was a *legal* impossibility for a husband to rape a wife until our consciousness of a woman's right to her own body began to change in the mid- to late-1970s.

during that time. In widowhood or divorce, a woman had no right to custody of the children to whom she had given birth and that she had been raising. If she fled an unhappy or abusive marriage, her husband could advertise for her return (and the return of "his" children), in the same the way that an "owner" could advertise for the return of a runaway slave or indentured servant. Oh, and . . . because they had no legal standing as citizens . . . no woman, of any race or socioeconomic status, could vote.

The first wave[18] of women's activism won women the right to own property, the right to enter into contracts and to legally dissolve them (including the right to sue for divorce), the right to consideration in child custody disputes, and the right to vote. Women also began to press into the workplace, and in small numbers, into the professions.

Because of the second strong wave[19] of women's activism, women gained reproductive rights (including contraception), and the legal recognition of a right to say no to sex within a marriage (the right to her own body). They also made a mass entrance into college, the workforce, and the professions.[20]

But an invisible ("glass") ceiling remains, restricting how high the mass of women rise within institutional and career settings[21] and contributing to an ongoing and significant gender

---

[18] 1848 to 1920

[19] 1963 through the late 1970s/early 1980s

[20] Rosechild Sullivan 2012

[21] Because of the efforts of the first wave of women's activism, for almost a hundred years women had been able to be secretaries, teachers, and nurses. Also already open to women at the start of the second wave of women's activism were positions as health aides, cashiers, customer service representatives, bookkeepers and auditors, receptionists, retail personnel, domestics, waitresses, teacher's aides, and social workers. Forty+ years after the second wave, secretary, teacher, and nurse are still at the top of the list of jobs women hold (DOL 2010). And while it is more common, post-second wave, to find a woman manager (office or retail sales), the fulltime jobs most women still hold are exactly the same (cashiers, retail salespersons, restaurant servers, customer service representatives, maids, receptionists, childcare workers, bookkeepers/accountants and auditors, teacher's aides, personal and home care aids, and cooks (DOL 2010)). When women hold jobs with the same duties as male employees, for the most part, employers enforce occupational segregation

wage gap.[22] And *the legacy of gender ideology* continues to affect the ways we share household work and childcare[23] and, even more, *the ways we interact in interpersonal relationships* – most especially, heterosexual ones.[24] Forty years after the second wave of women's activism, sexual violation and intimate partner assault remain overwhelming and concrete realities for millions of women in the United States today.

(handwritten margin note: shows how ongoing problems regarding gender, etc. aren't resolved)

---

by giving women different titles and lower income (Acker 1990; Bielby & Baron 1986). See also: Padavic & Reskin 1994; Williams 1995

[22] This phenomenon is markedly complicated even further by race and class. For many reasons, in 2010, women overall still earned only 77.6 cents to every dollar earned by men (Day & Rosenthal 2011; Bishaw & Semega 2010; Getz 2010; Jones & Smith 2001), with Black women earning 61 cents on the overall male dollar and Hispanic women earning only 52 cents on the male dollar (WOCPN 2011; NWLC 2007). This increase is connected to the second wave. In 1969, women overall only earned 56 cents to every male dollar (Blau 1998).

[23] We need measures of the realities of women's lives within those marriages and as mothers. Housework sharing is one such measure. Within the multiple ways men do masculinity (Connell 1995, 1987), men are reporting increased housework and childcare participation (Coltrane 1996). Hochschild & Machung (1990) reported that only 18% of the wives she interviewed had husbands who "shared the second shift" (p259). An overwhelming majority of men (82%) still thought of parenting their own children as "babysitting," and of housework as something with which they "helped" their wives. While this has improved (Hochschild & Machung 2010), we are not yet nearing the egalitarian ideal of the second wave of women's rights activism in the 1960 and 70s. Second wave women envisioned men conceiving of the cleaning their own homes and the parenting their own children as their own responsibilities, equally shared with their wives/live-in partners/co-parents. While it is likely that an increasing number of men of diverse masculinities do co-parent, Press (1998) argues that, on average, husbands now overreport their actual housework hours, and that once that overreport is accounted for, the reported increase disappears. Louis (2007) also found that changes in housework reporting were attributable – not to more actual housework done – but to a redefinition of what is called "housework" – with more men reporting their traditional male household chores (mowing the lawn, taking out the trash, fixing hinges) *AS "housework,"* without actually contributing more to the tradition female household chores (laundry and cleaning and dishes, etc.).

[24] Connell 1995, 1987; Faludi (2011)

SEXUAL ASSAULT

Sexual assault covers a broad range of violations. Sexual assault includes, but may not be limited to, acts we call: coercive paraphilias (e.g. nonconsensual exhibitionism), molestation (forced sexual touching), sexual harassment,[1] sexual abuse (of adults, children, the disabled, the elderly), and rape (forced penetration – oral, anal, or vaginal – by an object, hand, tongue, or penis, including date rape, stranger rape, gang rape, rape in war, and rape with the intent of genocide).

Primarily, the victims are female, whether adult or children; but also include males of all ages, even if in vastly disparate numbers.

1. Statistics

We do not know the exact number of individuals injured each year, either through physical violence by intimate partners or through sexual violation. Both sexual violation and relationship violence are overwhelmingly *under*reported.

The actual meticulous frequency of sexual assault cannot be precisely kept because the humiliating nature of, and the complicating legal questions surrounding, the crime, obscure record keeping. But the actual magnitude of the problem can be estimated – can be extrapolated – **from the known**. The statistics we can gather are based on incidents reported to law enforcement. (The counts are reduced even further when the criminal justice system *unfounds* a report or when, for a number of reasons, a victim "recants" a charge.[2])

---

[1] Roughly 40% of all employed women report that they have been sexually harassed at some time on the job. (NOMAS 2012a)
[2] See Appendix A

Nevertheless, we know that, while "more than two-thirds of rape/sexual assaults . . . remained unreported,"[3] given the number of reported incidents, rape and all other forms of sexual and interpersonal assault are epidemic in American society.

In an attempt to more accurately count the real incidence of sexual assault and intimate partner (domestic) violence, two surveys (the *National Violence Against Women Survey* and the *National Women's Survey*) asked respondents about incidents they had suffered that they did not report. The findings of these surveys indicate that far more violence and violation occurs than is reported to (or accepted into the record by)[4] law enforcement. Still (given the fact that many victims internalize a sense of guilt, and given the socially-conflicting definitions of rape/domestic violence), even in these two surveys, it is expected that respondents underreport the actual incidence of interpersonal and sexual violence.

Department of Justice statistics record that approximately one quarter of a million women are raped or sexually assaulted in the United States per year.[5] Because of the problems gathering accurate figures, the actual incidence of rape of females after puberty is thought to be much higher. It is believed that approximately:

- **Three quarters of a million (or about 700,000) U.S. women are raped per year**[6]
- The National Victim Center estimates that approximately 1,871 rapes occur daily.
  - On average, 1.3 women are raped[7] per minute, or one every 45 seconds.[8]
- **Before puberty**, the number of girls and boys assaulted is relatively close[9]

---

[3] Ringel 1997 p3 (National Crime Victimization Survey)
[4] See discussion of unfounding and recantation below.
[5] DOJ 2008
[6] Tjaden & Thoennes 1998; AMA 1995; NOW 2012 - with the majority of victims being under age 24; Rosechild Sullivan 2000; Kilpatrick et al. 1992
[7] by the legal definition of unwanted penile-vaginal penetration
[8] Kilpatrick et al. 1992 (National Victims Center)

- o **25-33-%** (1 in 3 or 1 in 4) **girl children**[10]
- o **17-20%** (1 in 5 or 1 in 6) **boy children**[11]
    - 61% of victims (3 out of 5) are **under age 18**.[12]
    - 29.3% of victims (3 out of 10) are **under age 11**.[13]
- **After puberty**, the likelihood of a female being victimized continues, while the likelihood of a male being victimized sharply decreases[14]
- Stranger rape accounts for only 22% of all rapes[15]
- Acquaintance[16] rape accounts for 78% of rapes[17]
    - o 11% of rapes are committed by fathers or stepfathers
    - o 29% of rapes are committed by acquaintances/dates
    - o 10% of rapes are committed by boyfriends/ex-boyfriends
    - o 9% of rapes are committed by husbands/ex-husbands
    - o 16% of rapes are committed by other relatives
    - o 3% of rapes are committed by persons unspecified[18]
- When it comes to those who are transgender:
    - o "The . . . data of transgendered and intersexed individuals gathered by the *Gender, Violence and Resource Access Survey* found that 50% of

[handwritten: i find it interesting that people more often by have are raped by people they know & connected to]

[handwritten: I can't help but wonder if it's because these men feel ownership over women due to relationship]

[handwritten: — felt entitled]

---

[9] DOJ 2008

[10] ibid

[11] ibid

[12] Kilpatrick et al. 1992 (National Victims Center)

[13] ibid

[14] ibid

[15] Tjaden & Thoennes 1998 pp2,5 (National Institute of Justice) ; Kilpatrick et al. 1992 (National Victims Center)

[16] committed by someone known to the victims (an acquaintance, friend, intimate partner, family member)

[17] Tjaden & Thoennes 1998 pp2,5 (National Institute of Justice); Kilpatrick et al. 1992 (National Victims Center)

[18] ibid

respondents had been raped or assaulted by a romantic partner."[19]

- o "Intimate partners, often appalled to discover the gender transgression, [often] verbally, psychologically, physically and sexually abuse the person."[20]
- o "Transgendered people are often sexually targeted *specifically because of* their transgendered status. The sexual perpetrator will stalk them, or attack them, infuriated by their cross-gender behavior."[21]
- o In "a longitudinal study of violence against the transgendered community . . . the preliminary data clearly show[ed] physical and sexual violence perpetrated on those who express cross-gender behavior."[22]

2. Long-Term Effects

The psychological aftermath of sexual assault, in any form and for any victim, is over-whelming. Victims suffer weeks, months, or even years of post-traumatic stress symptoms. These include shock, disorientation, depression, nightmares, nervousness, sexual dysfunction, and disassociation (including dissociative identity disorder).

> A rape survivor often fears [hir][23] dreams because s/he[24] relives the attack. S/he sees again the look of hatred in [hir] attacker's face, smells his odor, hears his degradation. S/he is frozen in fear and awakes, drenched in a cold sweat, gasping for air. Sleep, with its vulnerability and loss of control, becomes

---

[19] Lev & Lev 1999; Courvant and Cook-Daniels, 1998
[20] Lev & Lev 1999
[21] ibid, emphasis mine
[22] Lev & Lev 1999; Eyler & Witten 1999
[23] A gender-inclusive, gender non-specific third person singular pronoun
[24] Also, a gender-inclusive, gender non-specific third person singular pronoun

something to be dreaded and feared. Recurrent daytime flashbacks also are common. The victim may run in fear from any man on the street who resembles [hir] attacker. S/he may search desperately for a rest room in which she can regurgitate. An unexpected touch on [hir] shoulder prompts a startle reflex, and the wo/man braces for an assault and possibly death. The rape survivor cannot escape from [hir] own mind . . . . Once pleasurable activities are forgotten as though they existed in another lifetime. S/he withdraws from [hir]self and is alone . . . held prisoner by someone unseen for months, maybe years. The terror may never leave. Certainly, s/he will never be the same.[25]

These same trauma-induced symptoms plague female and male survivors alike – whether perpetrated against as children, adolescents, or adults – whether their assailants were male or female.

Good Boyfriend Material

Preface

Rape. I feel as if I should apologize for being so impolite. It's such a harsh word, both a verb and a noun. Perhaps it is those heavy consonants, the subtlety of the vowel *a*, caught between the *r* and the *p*. Maybe it's the way the *e* remains silent, unobtrusive, making the lips sputter to a stop, yielding abruptly to the letter *p*.

Or, maybe it's just the fear of the implications, accusations, insinuations, behind such a simple, one-syllable word. Although worthwhile, the after-school specials never fully explain the mess it leaves.

---

[25] Madigan & Gamble 1991 p5

I have been trying to write this for years – trying to get to the truth of the matter – without glossing it over, without making it sound better, without making it more believable – so I'm not to blame.

Please excuse me if my villain is not as clearly defined as you might like. Let me apologize in advance, if the moral of the story is unclear, or the ending leaves you dangling, or the climax makes you uncomfortable. Such is not my intention.

My purpose for writing is basically selfish, but perhaps someone else may read this and walk away feeling somehow cleansed. I hope I do.

Good Boyfriend Material
A Memoir

Angelique Owenby Craw

It was six days before my sixteenth birthday, Veteran's Day, to be exact. At the time, the only thing I wanted was a Harlequin Hero, a boyfriend who would erase the poodle-permed, freckle-faced, overweight girl I saw in the mirror.

All of my friends had a man, and I didn't.

Their boyfriends weren't that nice to them, but at least they provided a hot topic of conversation during lunch and study hall.

Boyfriends were a prized commodity in high school. Even if you were a nobody, a partner made you a somebody, because it meant you were someone worth having.

At that point, my romantic interludes consisted of three pecks on the lips during church camp, and one almost French kiss in seventh grade, from Sherman Kline at the back of the classroom, while we were watching, *A Tale of Two Cities*. We "went out" for a week, which meant that we talked on the phone once, when my mom wasn't home.

32

My best friend, Sabrina, was determined to find the man of my dreams and hand-deliver him to me for my sixteenth birthday: a man whose face belonged in between the posters of Luke Perry or the guy in the latest Calvin Klein commercials that adorned all of our bedroom walls.

Instead, she decided that I would settle for a senior. Her boyfriend, John, brought his friend, Steve, over to her house that night to meet me. It worked out perfectly, because her parents were working the graveyard shift and wouldn't be home until morning. Steve and John snuck through the back door just as her parents' car rolled out of the driveway.

Sabrina and I had already decided that Steve was good boyfriend material. He was a senior, and because we were mere sophomores, that automatically made him cool. He had good teeth and nice skin. His last name sounded good with my first name. He was a drummer in a band. All that was left was to get him to like me.

Steve and John had brought over a case of beer. Sabrina and I didn't like beer at the time – most girls didn't. So, we had a few wine coolers we stole from her mother. We played poker. The boys won. I smiled a lot. I had just gotten my braces taken off. I really didn't say much. I was afraid of sounding stupid, afraid of showing my age.

Steve, John, and Sabrina suggested that we play *Tune-In Tokyo* – which I had never heard of. Steve brought me into the living room and told me to lift up my arms. He proceeded to fondle my breasts, which were easily found underneath my oversized tee-shirt that ironically stated, in neon, block-sized letter, *Leave Me Alone*. That was the first time anyone had actually "felt me up." I had kept them cuddled in C-cups and hidden underneath baggy clothing since the fourth grade. I remember feeling more embarrassed than angry. I simply walked away, muttering, "Real funny, ha, ha."

I didn't want to seem too uptight.

This was my future boyfriend after all.

As the night went on, Steve became more attentive. He was telling me how beautiful I was, and how he couldn't understand why he'd never noticed me in school.

I had not yet mastered the art of flirting, but I was trying my best. I smiled. I smiled so much my cheeks ached. I never mustered up enough courage to look him in the eyes for more than two seconds at a time.

Sabrina took me aside and whispered in my ear that John told her that Steve really liked me. I was excited and scared and desperate to believe that this was finally it. A real boyfriend! Someone to take me to the movies, to hold my hand in school, to make me feel special.... My first romance....

Sabrina and John went into her bedroom, and that left me and Steve – alone. He put his hand on my knee, and I jumped up. I told him that I had to go to the bathroom. I was nervous. I was petrified. I wanted the moment to be perfect. I remember smiling at myself in the mirror. I remember quickly brushing my hair. I remember reapplying mascara, so much mascara that it smeared the lenses of my big, green glasses. I had just started brushing my teeth when Steve walked into the bathroom. I wagged my frothy toothbrush at him and mumbled that he should learn to knock first.

He shut the door and took the toothbrush from my hand. He asked me if he could have a kiss. I thought, *This is it, the big moment. Don't screw it up. Just follow his lead.*

I let him kiss me. I remember cringing at the mixture of toothpaste, cigarettes, and beer. I remember his tongue plunging in and out of my mouth as rapidly as a dog wags its tail when excited.

I watched him lock the door. I felt a little uneasy, but relatively safe.

He was *good boyfriend material*. He had a nice, good-boy smile.

I hoped the kiss would be better the second time.

The butterflies were there, but I wanted them to flutter with passion, not fear.

I wasn't scared of him. I was scared that I would mess things up, and he would leave.

He grabbed a handful of my hair and pushed his mouth against my lips so hard, that it felt like he was going to grind the enamel off my teeth.

This must be passion, I thought.

His cheekbones were scraping the side of my jaw.

I pushed against his chest. I looked at his face. I can't remember what I saw there, but I will never forget what I failed to see.

He turned off the lights. I tried to move around him. The butterflies were in my throat. I thought he was playing.

I said, *"C'mon, Steve. Stop Fucking around. Turn the light on. Unlock the door."*

He grabbed my arms, leaned down, and whispered in my ear, *"You know you want me. You've been batting your eyes at me all night. Don't be a dick-tease."*

Instantly, I felt stupid, immature, disappointed that the fairy-tale was not what I'd imagined.

I thought, *He just wants to kiss some more. Don't be a baby. It'll get better.*

The next thing I remember, he pulled a maneuver that I assume would be called a *leg sweep*, and I was on the floor, wedged between the bathtub and the sink.

I remember being thankful for the cushion of the dark, blue bathmat that was still damp from whoever showered last.

He had his full weight on top of me. He had both wrists in one hand, above my head. His mouth was covering mine, so that his upper lip grazed my nostrils, making it hard to breath. His ribs were jutting into my breasts.

I arched my back, in the attempt to buck him off.

His knees were pressing into the insides of my thighs. Every time I tried to move, pain registered through different parts – my spine, my wrists, my thighs, my breasts.... I concentrated on lying still.

His hands seemed to be everywhere all at once – squeezing my breasts, scraping between my legs, then back to my wrists – holding them in place.

I started pushing with the heels of my feet – trying to get his knees off my thighs – so at least I could squeeze them together.

He stopped.

I thought it was over.

I was going to tell him that I was tired, and then I was going to lock myself in Sabrina's brother's room.

He asked, "*Why are you fighting me? I'm giving you what you want.*"

His voice was low and soothing, as if he were talking to a frightened child.

He was.

I whispered that I was scared.

I whispered that I just wanted to kiss.

I whispered that I didn't think this was a good idea.

I whispered, *"Please...."*

He stared at my lips, as if he were trying to see the words.

He laughed.

I noticed my tears only when they reached the edge of my upper lip.

I grew numb.

I thought about screaming, as he lifted up my shirt and started to suck on my nipples as if he were trying to drink frozen ice cream through a straw.

I gulped in air, just before his mouth covered mine again. I'd like to say that he swallowed my scream, although, I know it's not true.

I should have screamed while he was talking, but I was listening.

Each word has registered slowly, across the years.

I lost control over my mind and my senses – much like the feeling you get when you've been out in the snow too long and you know your nose if running, but you can't feel the snot on your upper lip – or the feeling you get when you stand up too quickly when you've had too much caffeine and not enough food – or the feeling you get when you go down a water-slide a little faster than you expected and plunge into the water and think you're going to drown.

I gave up. I gave in, and let both wrists dangle in the palm of his hand.

I was in the doorway watching this happen in the mirror in which I'd primped for him.

He pulled my shorts down to my knees. He pulled my shirt up, so that it was just above my head, binding my arms.

At one point, he rose up over the sink and cupped some water in his hands. He splashed it on my stomach. I still don't know why.

I just lay there during his failed attempts to get it in.

When he finally succeeded, I had disowned my body – just in time – so that all I felt after he pushed through the dry folds of flesh was the dampness of the rug beneath me, my back teeth grinding together, and the rips in my palms from my jagged, chipped, red nails.

I remember the sound of his breathing in tempo with the steady drip of the faucet, the toilet's quiet gurgle, and maybe…I was whimpering.

There might even have been a point when I tried to convince myself to enjoy it, but by that time, he'd already finished and sprayed his victory all over my stomach and the deep blue bathroom rug.

He erased my virginity like yesterday's lesson on the blackboard.

He got up quickly, as if some alarm were going off, and he was late to class, late to work, late to dinner.

I was surprised that I was still crying.

The good-boy smile was back.

He gently wiped me off, pulled my shirt down, pulled my shorts up, and held me in his arms.

He whispered, *"That wasn't so bad now. Was it?"*

I remember the throbbing between my legs, the throbbing in my head, the drip of the faucet.

He kissed away my tears.

He said, "*I should go before her parents get home. I'll be talking to you soon.*"

Suddenly, it was all better. He was still going to be my boyfriend. Everything was going to be okay.

My thoughts were erratic.

I wondered why there was no blood. Wasn't there supposed to be?

He left.

I got into the shower and tenderly washed my body. My breasts were swollen. My nipples were visibly bruised. My thighs still bore the imprint of his knees. My wrists were blotted with thumb prints. My skin simply ached.

I worried that my mom would see the bruises.

I threw away my underwear.

Sabrina and John woke the next morning and asked what had happened. I told them we had sex, and it was great, and he was going to call – even though he never asked for my phone number.

The weeks went by. He never called.

Sabrina said, "*Maybe I gave it up too soon.*"

Then we found out that he got back together with his ex-girlfriend. Then, and only then, did I get angry.

I was angry for believing that the first time would be special.

I was angry with my mother for being right about boys.

I was angry at myself. *I didn't scream. I was a slut. I didn't really say no. I batted my eyes at him.*

I didn't tell anyone what really happened until two years after the fact.

I finally got a boyfriend, someone I still thank for being tender – if not with my mind, at least with my body.

He was the first person I told. I had to tell. After several weeks of heavy petting, and the first flutters of real passion, I finally had sex with him. I had to explain why I started crying when he went to grab my arms in the attempt to hold my hands.

He listened. Then he asked two questions,

"Did I lead him on?"

"Why didn't I scream?"

I forgave him for not saying what I wanted to hear.

I still don't know what I want to hear.

I've gotten to the point where I can control the wince when someone asks me if I want him.

I laugh at the look on their faces when I scream like a Siren during orgasms. I laugh even harder at the women who fake them.

I've never really figured out if I'm damaged goods.

I know I like sex, and I'm not sure that's allowed.

Through the years I've punished many men for someone else's sins, and I've almost self-destructed. I've had sex in bathrooms. I've watched movies about rape. I've read articles and stories about rape that seem vaguely familiar.

I feel lucky I was not held at gunpoint or severely beaten.

I feel lucky that I'm alive.

I don't hate men. In fact, I've almost begun to trust them again.

But more importantly, I don't hate myself.

I didn't try to get my friend to tell the cops when she got raped. I know that she needs to forget, and one day, she'll need to remember. We don't talk about it, but sometimes I hug her for no reason, and I think she knows why.

Sometimes I look at my other friend, who was raped at a younger age and more violently than I. I know why she cheats on men she says she loves. I know why she was labeled a slut in high school. I know one day she will break down and build herself back up again.

We all do.

I don't wonder where he is now or if he's sorry.

I don't feel guilty for not telling. I don't think about whether he's done the same thing to others.

For years, I've tried to explain why I'm the lover who is not afraid to be on top, but who's hard to please underneath. I'm surprised when I come when I'm not on top. I smile at their surprise when I hold their wrists above *their* heads.

For years, I've tried to find a voice, an outlet, for this very long, belated scream.

I don't think of myself as a victim. (Sometimes, I'm not even sure if it really happened.)

I refuse to believe that I'm a victim. I've been trying **not** to write this as if, somehow, I've been a witness to my own crime.

Every day that I don't bite my tongue for fear of being impolite or unladylike – every time that I don't hide my anger when I've been taught that aggressive displays are bad habits for women – is a small victory.

And every day – when I look at my mother – who was beaten by her parents, raped by her uncle, and beaten by her husband (who happened to be my father) – I thank God she never found out.

I could never tell her, so please, keep this quiet....

~ ~ ~

Some still consider rape an act of male sexuality gone awry,

rather than an act of violence.

But we know different,

just as we know that if a person hits another person over the head

with a frying pan,

we don't call that cooking.

Christopher Kilmartin[26]

~~~

3. The Rapist

Female perpetrators do commit a small, but nonetheless, real percentage of the sexual assaults against children and adolescents.

However, rape is "highly correlated with gender, with males commit[ting] nearly 100% of forcible rapes," especially adult-on-adult.[27] Therefore, whether through nature or nurture, the female perpetrator of rape is rare, with (not all, but) almost all sexual assault being committed by males.

~~~

---

[26] Kilmartin 2012
[27] NOMAS 2012b

**What percentage of rape is
committed by women?**

Is it 10 percent, 5 percent?

**No. Less than1 percent of rape is
committed by women.**

Let's state this another way:

**over 99 percent of rape is perpetrated
by men.**

**Whether the victims are female or
male,**

**men are overwhelmingly the
perpetrators.**

Jackson Katz[28]

~~~

Along with being male, most often, rapists are not strangers. While 20 to 22% of the time, the rapist is unknown to the victim before the attack, 78 to 80% of the time, rapists do not represent "stranger danger."[29] Most rapists are known to their assailants before they attack.

Also, generally speaking, rapists are not mentally ill and are unremarkable in appearance. Most rapists look "normal." Rapists do not *look like* Hollywood-typecasts of "the rapist.[30] They look like, and are, in many ways, ordinary guys.

Therefore, targeted populations cannot take comfort in the false hope that they are safe with someone, just because they

---

[28] Katz 2006
[29] Crooks & Baur 2002
[30] ibid

know them, or in the thought that they can tell a rapist, from afar, by the way they look.[31]

Rapists do, however, differ from other men in one significant way – they generally hold detrimental beliefs about their victims (often, about the overall "place" of women in society) and about what constitutes "rape."

Most rapists are males who buy into a hyper-masculine ideology, a series of rape myths, and sometimes, religious ideologies, that greatly increases the likelihood they will feel *justified* in violating others – or will justify their own acts as *not* violation.

In their minds, they are able to justify the social inequality of women (or of children) and are encouraged to disrespect all things deemed "feminine" (or innocent) through teachings of male dominance and female submission.[32]

~~~

Most rapists **don't consider** what they've done

to be rape.

Jack Straton [33]

~~~

Gender ideology is foundational to rape – belief systems about men and women (and/or children).

Rape is – **not so much the psychopathy of the individual perpetrator** – but the **systemic sociopathy** of a **rape-prone** society in which **masculinity is constructed as oppositional to all things "feminine"** (or empathetic) and in which **male violence is made to appear normative**.[34]

---

[31] Cowan 2000 p809
[32] Crooks & Baur 2002; Kilbourne 2000, 2010
[33] Straton 2008
[34] Crooks & Baur 2002; Reeves Sanday 1981; Katz 2000; Coltrane 2005; Connell 1995; Messner 2004

Rape is so commonplace in our society, that women are "many times more likely to be raped" here, in the United States, than in many other societies.[35]

In fact, the "United States has the highest incidence of rape among all Western nations."[36]

Rape is so common in the U.S., that "many researchers and clinicians view rape more as a product of [the] socialization processes that occur within the fabric of" our "society than as a product of the individual rapist's pathology."[37]

Not all societies are rape-prone. Rather, there are societies that are virtually rape-free.

In "rape-free" cultures, **the "relations between the sexes"** are constructed differently than in "rape-prone" cultures.[38]

An anthropological comparison of rape in 95 cultures indicates that "the frequency of rape in a given society is influenced by "the nature of the relations between the sexes, the status of women, and the attitudes that boys acquire during their developmental years...."[39]

"Rape-prone" cultures are **stratified** (socially and economically) **by gender**, glorify ... **violence" as manly**, and **"encourage[e] boys to be aggressive**."

In rape-prone cultures, men "have greater economic and political power," "remaining aloof from "women's work" such as child-rearing and household duties."[40]

In "rape-free" societies, the sexes "share power and authority and contribute equally to the community's welfare."[41] Also, in rape-free societies, both sexes "are raised to value nurturance and to avoid aggression and violence."[42]

---

[35] Reeves Sanday 1981
[36] Crooks & Baur 2002; Contemporary Sexuality 1996
[37] Crooks & Baur 2002; Hall & Barongan 1997; Hill & Fischer 2001; Simonson & Subich 1999
[38] Crooks & Baur 2002; Reeves Sanday 1981
[39] ibid
[40] ibid
[41] ibid
[42] ibid

For rape "to occur," the rapist must "**lack ... identification with the victim.**"[43]

Rapists often come from, or belong to, "all-male social groups that are disrespectful" of women. This sets up the ideological underpinning of rape – "**view[ing] women as being different from and less valued than men.**"[44]

~ ~ ~

I challenge you to tell me one way in which the sexes are opposite.
Calling men and women opposites is like calling an IBM computer the opposite of an Apple.

And "battle of the sexes" implies that men and women are at war.

We will never solve this problem until we work together and emphasize our commonalities rather than our differences.

I see research studies reported in the popular press: "a recent study proves what we have suspected all along - that men's and women's brains are different." And **what they do is find some infinitesimally small portion of the brain that has some minor difference that accounts for 5% of the variance in a population with wide variability, completely ignoring the fact that men and women's brains both have frontal cortex, amygdalas, thalmuses, hypothalamuses, and on and on.**

---

[43] Kilmartin 2012
[44] Kilmartin 2012

And at the end of the story, the anchorman on the news says, "Well, that explains why I can't understand my wife at all."
(If you can't understand your wife, I recommend the much-overlooked method of **listening** to her).
Christopher Kilmartin[45]

~~~

smart & fast witted.

In rape-affirming, all-male peer groups, women are seen as simply "**here for men's pleasure**," and the men in these groups "bond around" a "**shared masculinity" in which they "don't ... deal with women as human beings**, but instead, see them "as *lower status others*."

This, distancing allows them "to justify mistreating" women, "including [treating them with] violence."[46]

So, while not mentally ill, the rapist is highly likely to be influenced by a woman-demeaning all-male peer group or social setting in which women are constructed as "enemies."[47]

Such "all-male enclaves[48]...**implicitly and subtly** [create an "atmosphere" that] **condone[s] violence against women**," validates "**demeaning jokes" or even "calling [women] by animal names or [by] the names of their genitals**." There may be "an **unconscious, implicit conspiracy ... to keep women *in their place*....** by causing them to feel perpetually fearful of being physically attacked...."[49]

In such settings, "**men rarely confront each other for fear of being attacked or ostracized**.[50] Yet, research indicates **that 75% of college men are uncomfortable when their male peers display these kinds of attitudes.**

---

[45] ibid, emphasis mine
[46] ibid
[47] Whether or not the men in the group are "married" and "raising children with" these "enemies." Kilmartin 2012
[48] These include: some workplaces, country clubs, college dorms, athletic teams, fraternities, corporations, corner bars, social groups, some families
[49] Kilmartin 2012
[50] ibid

"Most men don't like" demeaning women, and that men "need to let other men know" when they don't like it. [51]

~ ~ ~

Along with changing our attitudes toward women, we've … got to **change our attitudes toward ourselves**….

"**Boys will be boys**" not only provides a measure of excuse for violence against women, **it is a very disrespectable attitude toward men, as if we are animals, with absolutely no control over ourselves**….

[T]here's an irony here. Self-control is another hallmark of traditional masculinity, but aggression and sexuality are considered to be completely out of control ….

I want men to have more dignity than that.

It's a sad state of affairs when so many men have behaved so irresponsibly that the rest of us have to carry the burden of understandable suspicion from women.

So, besides becoming more respectful toward women, we have to regain our self-respect.

(handwritten margin note: man speaking of how they need to take control of their actions)

---

[51] ibid

We are human beings who are capable of caring for others. We are not animals who lash out instinctively, poisoned by testosterone.

Violence against women is a men's issue, and men have to take **a leadership role in building a more positive male community**.

Christopher
Kilmartin[52]

~~~

Tears . . .

N. D. Rosechild

You roll off

and they roll out

silent

unnoticed

down my cheeks

So strange

this aloneness

within another's arms

This sense of *being* "service"

- uncommuned

~~~

---

[52] ibid

4. The Victim

The victim of the rapist can be anyone – any child, any early teen, any woman of any age (or any degree of compliance/non-compliance with the media standard of beauty), or (in various circumstances) any male.

Yet, adult victims are overwhelmingly female. Ninety to ninety-five percent of adult victims are female.[53] And about "one fourth of all women in the U.S. can expect to be raped in their lifetime, and the rate is increasing.[54]

In many years of pastoral counseling, personal experience has led me to suspect that, if we were to include all types of sexual assault in the counts, instead of finding that one out of four women have been raped,[55] we would find that as many as three out of four women have been molested or sexually assaulted – either as children, as adolescents, and/or as adults.[56]

Males also, frequently relate sexual abuse experiences, though generally, they were children or early adolescents at the time they were assaulted.

And again, law enforcement was unlikely to have been called in, even if the child or adolescent told parents or other authorities.[57]

5. Cultural Myths

It is widely believed that

> 1) only women get raped, that
>
> 2) only certain types of women get raped, and that

---

[53] Five to ten percent of adult victims are male (CMHC 2007)
[54] NOMAS 2012a; Globally, U.N. statistics indicate that 1 in 3, or one third of women, will be raped, incested, or beaten in her lifetime.
[55] experience forced penile-vaginal intercourse
[56] whether or not they would call it by name and although few incidents involve legal authorities
[57] "Most rapes (and sexual assaults) are never reported." (Straton 2008)

3) those types of women only get raped when they are involved in certain *"foolish"* activities – like picking up strangers at bars, or flirting while wearing mini-skirts alone, late, on a dark night.[58]

We have already noted that while women are the predominate victims of rape – men – and certainly children – also suffer rape.

It is a myth that only certain "types" of women are vulnerable to rape.

Further, any woman can be the victim of rape, no matter what "type" of woman she is.

While the primary victims of rape are young women, unfortunately, it is not uncommon for even very old women to be raped.

And it is **not valid** to separate women into "types."

Seeing women as either "madonnas" or "whores," is sexist, misogynistic, and downright erroneous.

Sexually, and in every other way, women are as complex and complicated as men.[59]

Women are, after all, **also human beings**.

Women get raped in all walks of life.

Virgins get raped.

Mothers get raped.

Sisters get raped.

Grandmothers get raped.

---

[58] Gilbert et al. 1991; Malamuth et al. 1980; Crooks & Baur 2002
[59] Like men, women have sex drives and a right to their sex drives.

Women enclosed in "protective" cloisters or harems get raped.

And on and on, ad infinitum....

Women do not only get raped while engaging in "risky" activities, like drinking in bars or going to parties.

And most of the time that women get raped, they get raped by men they know, who have access to them in all sorts of locations, times, and situations.

Women get raped in their homes, sleeping in their beds.

Women get raped in the course of their work or school life.

Women get raped in nursing homes.

Infant girls (and boys) get raped in their cradles.

It is a myth that women who get raped are "asking for it."

When, as women, we dress *sexy*, we are more likely to be doing so for the sake of other women (of being thought well-dressed by other women) as to be found enticing by men.

As women in a consumption-dominated culture, like men, we internalize the societal images of what constitutes looking *good*. Attempting to be well-dressed, whatever that means for our age, peers, and momentary mental state, IS NOT about ***asking to be*** violated by a male we ***don't want***. (After all, when we **want** someone, and **give clear consent**, the sex is **not** rape.)

It is a myth that a woman can't be raped if she doesn't want to be.

Rape is an opportunistic crime and rapists are opportunists – generally watching, calculating, and choosing "the time and place" of attack, so "the element of surprise" is often on their side.[60] Along with physical force, rapists may also use weapons to "coerce compliance."[61] Both stranger and acquaintance rapists may use "fear and intimidation,"[62] "verbal" and "emotional … manipulation," and "the threat of physical force"[63] to gain an advantage and dominate the victim.

The fact is, that even without the use of physical or emotional weapons, many women do not have the physical strength to resist many men. At puberty, as one of the male secondary sex characteristics, men tend to get greater upper body strength. It is also a fact that we further exaggerate that upper body strength differential by dating (and partnering) according to size, with heterosexual women socialized to be attracted to larger/taller men and heterosexual men socialized to be attracted to smaller/shorter women.[64] In addition, few women pursue physical strength training in adolescence or young adulthood, AND women are socialized to be "compliant and submissive," even as men are socialized to be persistent and aggressive.[65]

It is a myth that women want to be raped.[66]

No woman wants to be raped.[67] "The fact that some women have rape fantasies is sometimes used to support the idea that women want to be sexually assaulted. However, it is important to understand the distinction between an erotic fantasy and a conscious desire to be harmed. In a fantasy, a person retains

---

[60] Crooks & Baur 2002
[61] ibid
[62] ibid
[63] Ahterton-Zeman 2006
[64] Gilbert et al. 1991; Malamuth et al. 1980; Crooks & Baur 2002
[65] Crooks & Baur 2002
[66] Abel 1981; Muehlenhard & Rodgers 1998
[67] Crooks & Baur 2002 p518

control. A fantasy carries no threat of physical harm or death; a rape does."[68]

Women who say "no," do not mean, "yes."

In the BDSM (bondage/domination/sadomasochism) community, partners who want to participate in role playing games – and *pretend* to be forced – make an agreement ahead of time to enact a scenario – and they set up an agreed upon code word that means, *"Stop."* Unless your partner and you have pre-discussed such a scenario, *NO* means *NO!*[69]

Legally, and ethically, and in reality – women (and others) who **say** "no," **mean NO.**

It is a myth that victims tempt, tease, or entice their assailants.

Many rapists blame the victim, saying the victim "tempted" them.

Often, even perpetrators against very young children will claim that the child "came onto" or "seduced" or "teased" them.

Rapists may view their "acts as [just] . . . sex play." In interviews of college age males about acts that meet the legal definition of rape, many men responded with the question, *"Why doesn't she just relax and enjoy it? It's just sex."*

In one study "of 114 imprisoned rapists," over 80% did not see themselves as rapists."[70] They "used a variety of explanations to justify their actions, including . . . **claiming that women say "no" when they mean "yes,"** that women are **seducers who**

---

[68] ibid
[69] Crooks & Baur 2002
[70] ibid

"lead you on," and that most women eventually relax and enjoy it."[71]

Since *rape is an overwhelmingly under-prosecuted and under-punished crime, the very fact that these men were convicted and "imprisoned" for rape is strong evidence that they were quite wrong.*

~~~

I[f]…I get out of control….

How does that work, physiologically?

Prostate exerts pressure on the spinal cord,

cutting off oxygen to the brain?"

Christopher Kilmartin[72]

~~~

Every man is a "human being…capable of caring for others … NOT [an] animal "poisoned by testosterone."[73]

No child, no girl, no woman – no boy or man – has so "tempted" a rapist, that the rapist lost all control and couldn't help him[hir]self.

To rape – or not to rape?

It is **always** a **choice**.

---

[71] Scully & Marolla 1984: Crooks & Baur 2002
[72] Kilmartin 2012
[73] ibid

It is a myth that women cry rape falsely.

Another myth about rape is that the victim cries rape falsely. While not impossible, there is such a cost in our culture to reporting rape – that crying rape falsely is generally, highly unlikely. "False accusations of rape are quite uncommon, and they are even less frequently carried as far as prosecution."[74]

"Given the difficulties that exist in reporting and prosecuting a rape," even were someone with a vendetta who desires to besmirch the character of an enemy to report rape falsely, "few women (or men) could successfully proceed with an [untrue] rape case...."[75]

The much more likely, and common scenario, is that (female and male, adult and child) victims "suffer rape victimization" and do "not report the crime to any authorities."[76]

Reporting is further complicated when no physical bruises or wounds are immediately apparent, or the rapist was an acquaintance. In such situations, "many victims/survivors blame themselves." [77] Or, if they have the presence of mind to properly assign fault to the perpetrator, find themselves disbelieved (or "unfounded"[78]) by the legal system.[79]

Justifying the perpetrator while blaming the victim.

Our cultural rape myths both justify and forgive the perpetrator, while blaming and holding the victim to account.

The female victim is blamed for her morals, dress, poor judgment, and/or social activity.[80]

---

[74] Crooks & Baur 2002
[75] ibid
[76] Lonsway & Fitzgerald 1994 p136
[77] Ahterton-Zeman 2006
[78] See Appendix A
[79] Ahterton-Zeman 2006
[80] Madigan & Gamble 1991 p105

Since even little boys must *be men*, and men must, at all times, be both invulnerable and inviolate, the male victim – when he is acknowledged at all – is blamed, no matter his age or size – for his failure to successfully resist.

Even child victims are quickly blamed – questioned about their "truthfulness," their level of resistance (as demonstrated by their failure to get away), and their speed of report (waiting to tell).

Along with these rapes myths, other societal attitudes (attitudinal dinosaurs left over from an era in which women and children were legally property), hinder much needed change.

Where women are still viewed as legitimate prey for the male hunter, and males are encouraged to exalt violence and to persist until they win, either the relationship with the "good" girl, or the one-night stand with the "loose" girl, young men often report sexual activity, that they believe to be legitimate, that meets the definition of rape.[81]

Meanwhile, the sexual double standard – that gives kudos to a man who scores sexually but labels women who are freely sexual in negative ways – is still firmly in place. "Slut" bashing of females and harassment of males who do not womanize often begins in middle school. This double standard persists – in many locations – throughout the college years.

In undergraduate classes, I am routinely told that there are "two kinds of girls," the kind you bring home to family and marry and the kind you use for an evening or a few sexual escapades, and then discard.

Even within marriage, women who admit to having desires, or who initiate sex based on those desires, may be negatively labeled by their spouses.

And certainly, women of all ages (whether or no men are held to the same standard) must abide by the rules of monogamy (or male ownership of their sexuality) or suffer the social consequences.

---

[81] Boeringer 1996; Schwartz & Nogrady 1996; Reeves Sanday 1990

~~~

**In the case of rape, it can be argued that the
"victims were not having sex . . ."**

- the "perpetrators were not either."
Christopher Kilmartin[82]

~~~

Internet Predator
A Male Retelling

Jack started messaging me on Facebook. I was excited. He looked sooo hot!

I knew I was gay since I was like 6, maybe 5. But you could never say that out loud in my house.

My moms would 'a worn me out.

She was really my aunt. My bio mom had left out about eight years back with her latest man, leaving a string of us farmed out to different family.

My moms who had raised me was a sister-in-white at her cousin's church, and there, 'bout as often as she blessed Communion, Pastor Maddie railed against the fairies and the sin that had turned God's hand against us.

A number of the brothers in the congregation (and their wives) had the virus, and that was always her object lesson to the little ones.

It was the plague unleashed on us from our own wrong doing – God's loving chastisement to save the sinner before the judgment – a conviction of the Holy Ghost – a chance to turn before we burned.

---

[82] Kilmartin 2012

There was no way I could do what some of the celebrities were starting to do. I could not of "come out." There was no way I could date, or even suggest to one of my friends that we try something.

Jack asked, so I held my phone up in the bathroom mirror and sent him a shot of my chest.

Then he sexted me a pic of his jewels.

I got hot just thinking about them. His looked like all those dicks I downloaded late at night when moms was safely snoring in her room. It was rough not having a room to myself – always having to stroke it under the covers quietly, hoping she didn't wake up and catch me on her way to pee.

I got a lot of good action out of his sext. More than once a day in the shower.

Moms was always on me for staying long in the bathroom, or showering so much, but a man's gotta' do . . . .

When she let me go out, which wasn't that often, I'd play ball, just to be near some male flesh.

I couldn't let on, but Drew really turned me on. He was 6'2" next to my sprouting 5'11," and his sweat glistened in the sun as he bit his upper lip, all serious while making a shot.

But I could never of moved on him. I'd of got my ass whooped, and I wouldn't have won against him neither. And the boys would a known. Couldn't do it.

Jack kept sending me pics, and he didn't look too bad for someone that old. I guessed 40 wasn't *sooo* bad....

And he said he had some money, a real job, a house, a nice car. Wanted my address to send me a gift, but I didn't dare . . . . Talked about takin' me places far away.

We made a date.

I told my moms I was going to Drew's, and just after dark, I started toward the place we set to meet. I slipped 'round the corner and a couple blocks away, to a side street where the lamps were burnt out. The car was a lot older and more run down than I expected, but it was the right color and make. Then he tapped the horn and waved me inside. I slipped in the back, like we'd agreed.

His baseball cap was slung low over his face, but I recognized his voice from our calls. My heart was pounding. *This was my first date with a guy! OMG, he wasn't a jawn!*

The familiar sound of his voice helped me relax. Suddenly, he pulled off the road and into the state park. I thought he was taking me for something to eat, but he had waited so long, he couldn't wait any more. He hopped out and slid into the backseat next to me, tearing at my clothes and pressing his mouth against mine. It was all going kinda' fast. I realized he slobbered, so I pushed him back, knocking his cap.

That's when I saw.

It wasn't him.

This wasn't the guy in the pictures.

This guy could have been my grandfather, or great-grandfather.

And it wasn't just that he looked way older than the pics. The pics weren't him at all – ever – at any age. Not so's I could tell, anyway.

He pulled his zipper down, and his dick popped free.

It wasn't the same dick either. It was small and pale and turned.

He began shoving at the back of my head, trying to push my head down to suck it.

He shoved me close, but it smelled like pee, old pee that had been around a while.

I started to shove back, to shove him off, trying to think.

Where was I? I wasn't far from home. What turns had he made?

I went for the door, *Man, I'm outta' here*, when he grabbed me. I caught the flash of the blade in the moonlight, before I felt it, sharp, against my neck.

Low and mean, his voice said, *You're gonna do what I say now. Drop . . . your . . . drawers.*

I thought of grabbing it, but wasn't sure how to get a good hold on the handle, or him, without getting sliced bad.

I felt the point of the blade drawing blood.

He was old, but not weak.

I followed instructions. He had me get out of the car. He bound my hands and feet with silver tape. All the while, I was steady talking. Telling him there was no need to do this. No need to do it this way. He tripped me forward, kicked me hard, twice for good measure, then rammed me in the grass.

When he finished, he said, *You'll never forget me*, adding, *If I ever get any trouble from this, if this ever gets back to my wife or kids, I know where to find you.*

He drew the blade down my ass. *For good measure*, he said. The warm red oozed down my thigh. *Or was it his stuff?*

He left me in the grass, pointed away from his plates, and sped away.

I struggled, but he had bound me too tight.

Next morning, two grade school girls in uniform found me on their way to school, pants down, blood crusted. I felt for them. Their first sight of a man's dick and ass were mine, hanging out, covered with morning frost.

At the hospital, they took his DNA from my ass, but it didn't make a match.

His internet profile had disappeared. It was bogus anyway.

I'm not sure how Moms felt at first. I don't know if she was more upset I'd been gone all night and worried her, or mad I'd been stupid enough to hook up online, or more horrified that I was gay. Now she tells me she, *knew all along,* since I was like *two-years-old.* And she had *found my internet porn months before.*

Now that I have the virus, everyone at Pastor Maddie's church knows too. They put in a prayer request for me .You know, the *prayer request gossip grapevine.*

They all still *love me* though. They tell me, too often, that they're sinners too. And they tell me how I have to *resist sin and not act out on it.* They say, *God doesn't give us permission to just go on and do any old thing we want. He has rules.* And the classic, *He doesn't give us more temptation that we can bear.*

I just wonder why God would give us temptation at all.

Yeah, they love me, but they watch me, real close, especially around the little boys.

I'm not allowed to sit in youth group anymore. I have to sit in sanctuary with the grown sisters and brothers. And every so often everyone goes to clucking their teeth when Pastor gets to preaching on gay folk, whooping, *Gender lines are being crossed! Do you hear me? God is not happy with this nation! Gender lines are being crossed!*

~~~

**There are no consequences for men
as a result of being objectified.
Men don't live in a world in which they are likely to be**

raped, harassed, or beaten.
Or at least, straight [cisgender] men don't live in such a
world.
Whereas, [all] women [and gay men and transpeople] do.

Jean Kilbourne[83]

Charmed
A Female Retelling

He was charming. Young. Handsome. Intelligent. Well-spoken. And so attentive.

At first, all of his attention was mine. I reveled in being treated that way. The look in his eyes made me melt. He looked at me with desire, like I was a cross between filet mignon and chocolate caramel cheesecake.

He made me feel witty and wise and brilliant. He made me feel pretty, even enticing. He made me feel special – better than the other girls around me.

He put his best foot forward.

But then, I did that myself.

I spent hours getting ready for my dates with him. Took extra time with my hair, my makeup, my outfit. Made sure I was always sweet and polite.

But you expect someone to be, essentially, who they say they are. You expect them to be the age they tell you they are. You expect if they say they went to a certain school, or earned a certain degree, that that will be true.

The same is true for their feelings.

You, also, expect someone who tells you that you're beautiful to be fairly happy with your looks – face, form, body.

---

[83] Kilbourne 2000, 2010

And you expect someone who tells you that they love you to have some level of concern for your overall well-being. You expect them to have some empathy toward you when your feelings are on the line, and you expect them to be able to consider your side in a conflict. Not to always agree with you, just to be open to the possibility that you could have a point or two.

I know (now) that some abusers can put their best foot forward for months, even years, if necessary. I know, now, that abusers can keep you from seeing who they really are – maybe 'til the engagement, or the wedding, maybe even 'til the first pregnancy – or maybe just 'til they're sure you've fallen "in love."

That's when their true selves, and self-centeredness, come out.

In retrospect, I can look back and see the shifts in his level of attentive consideration.

He changed a little when he was sure I was *in love* with him.

He changed a little more on the altar.

When he should have been making vows to me, something in his face and attitude sounded like he was commanding his vows *at* me – like he was telling me what I would do (even though I had already just vowed the same vow he was supposed to be making back to me).

He changed the rest of the way when I got pregnant.

Then, it became clear that this thing called love, this "relationship" I was fighting for, and giving my all to, was one-sided. The "two of us" was an illusion. He had earned himself a combination sex slave/maid.

But back to the beginning . . . . Back to when *I fell in love* . .
. .

He started with his jealousy.

I dismissed it at first. I thought, *Well . . . . Okay . . . . I'd be upset too if I thought a woman at his job were after him. He thinks Sam is after me. It's kind of a complement that it bothers him so much. I'll do my best to make sure he knows he has nothing to be jealous about.*

It was all very much like the frog in the pot.

The water starts out about the same temperature as the frog.

If the water were hot – not even scalding, just hot – the frog would jump out.

I would have jumped out too. But the water was comfortable, and I had no cause for concern.

He looked like everything I'd ever wanted in a man – every woman's dream – the perfect man with whom to build the perfect home and successful family.

As the heat grew ever so gradually warmer, I adjusted to his temperature all along the way.

I never knew I was being cooked until it was much too late.

He used his jealousy as a door to an ever-increasing control. He moved from being jealous of my coworkers, who were merely respectful to me at work, to concern about the male attention I might attract if I went anywhere but work.

He moved along a continuum from attentive to hypervigilant to jealous to hurt to obsessed, and finally, to enraged at the thought of any other man even noticing me – or me so much as saying good morning to any other man.

He started to take my clothes.

One day, after I left for work, he "pruned" my closet, getting rid of all but my most dowdy outfits. If it would have hidden the flesh of a Victorian woman, he kept it. Otherwise, he had already disposed of it before I got home.

But then, he got to where he wouldn't even let me wear my shrouds. Since he deemed the house "warm enough," at home, I was forced to go naked. It was his way of keeping me from going out.

He began to need my whole paycheck for bills.

When my annual vacation arrived, he declared that we would stay home that year. One, *we* didn't have the money, and two, so no other man could *look on* my beauty at a tourist resort. God forbid I should wear a bathing suit, even with a cover up. Or even with t-shirt and shorts.

I fought with him. I wanted some clothes for the day. Even though we weren't going away, I still had things to do, errands to run, and I didn't want to spend the whole week cooped up in the house.

So he locked me in the bathroom.

The last day before vacation, he installed a sliding bolt on the outside of the bathroom door. He said it was because we were trying to have children, and he wanted to childproof early.

The next morning, when I got up to use the toilet, I grabbed the pregnancy test kit on the top shelf.

It came up positive.

I heard him slide the bolt.

For the duration of the week, he held me captive.

He badgered me through the door. Told me, *Now that I was a mother, I was going to have to act right.*

I took a blanket and a pillow from the back of the linen closet and lay down in the tub.

About once a day, he made extra threats through the door, then opened it and slid a bowl of food at me across the tile floor. *I had the sink*, he said, *for water. I didn't need anything else to drink.* From the spigot I gathered water in my open palm. He let me out the morning I had to return to work.

After that, he started to hit me. (But at least, with pregnancy, he gave me my house clothes back. He *didn't want to see my ass, now that it was getting fat*).

He began to tell me *it was a woman's job to please her man*, and that, *if she didn't, he needed to teach her a lesson or two – or he wasn't any kind of man. Now that I was going to be the mother of HIS children, I would have to learn a thing or two – so they wouldn't be fucked up, like me.*

The first couple of times he hit me, it was in the midst of another one of his jealous rages. He wept so hard afterward, he was so sorry, that it melted my heart.

Part of me really thought he just couldn't live without me, that he was that threatened by his own demons that he couldn't help himself.

I found myself double-stepping to try to make sure I didn't trigger his issues or make him the least bit insecure. I cooperated in toning down my looks. I gave up wearing makeup. Stopped going to the hairdresser. Let pregnancy make me cumbersome and unattractive.

The times in the middle of his cycle of violence were good – like in the beginning – when he was so charming and attentive. But then, his anger would begin to build again, and the tension would nearly drive me crazy with the terror of negative anticipation. And then, sure as the night falls each evening, he would explode again.

As they got bigger, he went for my breasts, then my abdomen, raging alternately between how I was *a pregnant pig* and about how *I was a whore who turned other men on.*

Sometimes, in the good part of the cycle I would tell myself I had this.

I had learned how to please him and everything would work out okay. In those times, I would wonder if I didn't exaggerate in my own mind the horror of the look in his eye, the disdain in his voice, and the extremes of sadism to which he increasingly took his violence in the bad times.

I thought about our child. I wanted him or her to have both parents, to grow up in an intact home like I did.

I had read the newspaper reports of the studies. Children needed a mother AND a father. This baby would NEED him, they said.

I was glad when he was better, thinking it would work out for our child.

In the bad times, I also thought about our child. I wondered how he would treat her, or him. How his anger would play out on an infant with colic, or a toddler climbing a bookcase, or an adolescent with a mind of its own. And then I would worry that, if I got away from him, I couldn't support a child on my own – that I didn't and couldn't make enough, that I had no one to watch a child while I worked. I priced daycare and my heart sank. I knew there was no way out.

And then, I didn't want others to know what our marriage was really like. I had always wanted a "successful" marriage. Certainly, I didn't want my family (who had never treated each other like this) to know. And I didn't want the handful of people who respected me at work to know. I didn't want the cops involved. I didn't want to end up in family court, or to go through all those things you hear about second hand in life, those things only other families suffer through.

As the kids came, one right after the other, because he wouldn't allow me to use birth control and wouldn't wear a condom himself, I tried to shield them.

I walked on eggshells, not just for my own sake, but for theirs.

And I stayed, not just for my own safety and well-being, but for theirs.

With the passage of time, my financial desperation without him only grew. And I knew he had the money to fight me, he had relatives he could tap, even though I'd never have the money to fight him.

In the bad times, he would remind me that he knew high-powered lawyers who knew how to *clean a woman's clock*. He would say, *No woman will ever get the best of me in court!*

He would tell me what a bad mother I was and list the things he thought I did that the court would hold against me in a custody contest.

He let me know he was not above fabricating evidence and had friends who knew how.

Then, just as hopelessness sank deep to my very bones, he would describe how he would kill me, little by little, and the kids too, if *I* made it necessary, or if I ever got any judge dumb enough to take away his rights.

So I rode the kids, sometimes as hard as he did, to keep them in line, to try to keep them from triggering his wrath.

I told myself he didn't beat them — not quite like he did me.

He didn't kick the shit out of them.

But I cringed each time he got free with his hands, or his belt, or the nearest rigid object — each time they "got on Daddy's nerves."

They were so little and innocent, but I just couldn't see any way out. Deep down inside, I believed his threats.

I knew no cop could get to us in time to save us from his impulses. There was, literally, no place to hide.

Any one of his weekly rages could have turned murder-suicide. A couple came close. But I was certain sure that leaving him would guarantee it.

Once, for only a few hours, he thought I left him (I was simply out at the store with the kids). We returned to find the house ransacked like a band of thieves had searched the very floorboards for treasure. All the family photos were thrown down from the walls and smashed across the floor, and the framed wedding photo and padded headboard of the bed were slashed and shredded.

It let me know, beyond words, that a restraining order is, after all, only a piece of paper.

Someone at work said she overheard a domestic dispute in her neighborhood, then told how slow the cops were to respond to her reports of the woman's screams.

I heard they were even slower to respond if a wife made the call. They didn't want to risk their lives when she'd only take him back in the morning.

They didn't' understand. She had to take him back in the morning.

So, I never called the police. Half in fear for my life afterward, if I were ever so foolish (he called it, *the ultimate betrayal*). And half because the only sense of pride I had in the world was the way our family looked from the outside.

False as it was, it shielded me from the public scorn of being *the abused woman – the battered wife!*

Lord knows, I faced enough scorn at home.

I wanted also to shield the kids.

70

Perhaps, if no one knew, they could have friends from solid families, and when their turn came to marry, they might luck out, and get a man like the one my mother had – a man from a home where they didn't scream and punch and act out whenever they were angry or their humors were displeased.

I couldn't undo the fact that I had married an abuser. I couldn't make any difference in my own life now. I couldn't go back and stay in school and put a self-sufficient career ahead of love and romance. I had, as his grandmother said, *made my bed,* and now, I *had to lie in it.*

But while I blamed myself for my lack of insight into his character (for not seeing through him when he came on all warm and fuzzy in the early days, for believing in fairy tale endings and happily ever after), and while I blamed myself for not making the choices that would have kept me independent – I hoped their futures were yet unwritten.

And we were a church-going family. He was a deacon, and all dressed up on Sunday mornings. We looked the picture of satisfied domesticity. I was a little on the frumpy side now, and he made sure the girls were over-clothed in unfashionable and too-long dresses, but we appeared (even he appeared) God-fearing and upstanding; and many women in the church turned to me for advice on how to get their husbands to be as godly as mine. They would share, in furtive whispers as they asked for prayer in the church hallway about their husband's drinking or his quick temper. I would catch their bruises peeking out from under their cover up. And I would actually be grateful that my husband had the foresight to be careful to make sure he hit me where it wouldn't show – below the neck, on all that long space of torso and limbs he made me cover day and night.

But then, as the kids got older, I walked in one night after a long day on my feet at work to find him pressed up close in the corner next to our thirteen-year-old. As I came through the doorway, I saw his hand moving under her shirt.

71

In an instant, I found my fury, and the rage that started in me began in my toes, rose through that bruised torso he kept so carefully hidden, spread through my heart and chest, and erupted from my throat. I picked up the nearest heavy object, a frying pan (how stereotypic) and went after him.

He let her go, then laughingly held me at arms' length, his 6'1" frame more than long-armed enough to make a mockery of my 5'6" rage. He commanded the kids to retreat upstairs, but they had gone long before he began to speak.

With one hand, he continued to hold me back, as I did my best to throttle him, while with the other, he calmly dialed 911. When the police arrived, he showed them his irate, raging, out-of-control wife, and the damage I had managed to inflict on the arm with which he held me at bay. He indicated his willingness to swear out a protection from abuse order against me, and the police arrested me on charges of domestic violence.

I told them what I had seen, why I had gone off, but when they called the kids downstairs, they were so shaken, they just stood there silently, too terrified to either affirm or deny.

They left the kids in his custody – even the 13-year-old.

They did not see him as the initiator of a sexual assault against our daughter, or at least, not as long as she would not accuse him.

And they did not see him as the primary aggressor in our home across the years of our marriage. I had made no paper trail of his abuse – no prior police calls, no emergency room visits. I had weathered it, or nursed it, all at home. I had done a good job keeping our private business private. We were the upstanding family.

They handcuffed me.

When I got out, of course, I could not go "home." My husband and my kids were "protected" from me.

I was fortunate, in that the weather was neither too cold nor too hot. I spent the first few nights sleeping in my car at a nearby rest stop on the highway. But the state police began to notice the same car night after night, and to "check" on me, to see if I was "alright."

I was warned not to *live in my car*.

I finally broke down, and asked for help. I went to a woman in the church who seemed stronger, more autonomous, more in charge within her marriage than most of the rest of us — a woman we mocked for not being submissive enough, according to God's design.

She couldn't get her husband to allow me to use their guest room, but she did put her foot down and demand that he allow me to park my car in their driveway and sleep there at night. At least, there, the police would not wake me with their flashlights and questions.

She gave me two blankets to use, and after he went to bed each night, she slipped me out a portion of their leftovers. And in the daytime, when he left for work, she let me in to take a shower.

My husband kept the restraining order on me for six months, but let me back in after three weeks.

He had proven his power.

He had proven the system was on his side, or at least, that he knew how to use it. And the house needed to be cleaned. And the daily needs of the kids were getting on his nerves.

I've been home for a few months now.

My daughter won't talk about it. Not about what happened that night. Not about what happened when I was out of the house.

None of the kids will. They won't talk about their daddy at all.

And he's taken up a new hobby.

He got himself a permit and bought the first of his new *collection* of firearms.

BATTERING

1. Intimate Partner Assault (a.k.a. Domestic Violence)

The intimate partner violence we euphemistically call "domestic" is difficult to accurately count. "No nationwide organization . . . gathers information from local police departments about the number of substantiated reports and calls," and "there is disagreement about what should be included in the definition of domestic violence."[1] Therefore, as with rape – sexual assault, partner battery is severely underreported.[2] Because of shame that one (or one's family) is involved in this way, or fears about not being believed, much family/intimate partner violence goes unreported *even on surveys*,[3] and hospital records are not enough. As the *National Center for Injury Prevention and Control* finds, "less than 20 percent of battered women" seek "medical treatment following an injury."[4] Reports (and certainly, prosecutions) fall far below actual incidence. Nevertheless, the commonness of woman battering is incontrovertible.

Another complication in the data collection is the conflation of the figures for female victims with the figures for male victims, with police sometimes failing to identify the primary aggressor, viewing domestic violence situations as mutually perpetrated, and arresting the victim, or arresting the victim and perpetrator in a dual arrest.[5]

This criminal justice attitude fails to recognize that the overwhelming initiation of domestic violence by one gender,

---

[1] Newton 2001

[2] Neither are we able to accurately gather solid statistics on verbal and emotional abuse, on the terror of stalking, or on dating violence. Though dating violence is not less harmful, marital violence is more likely to be counted Osofsky 1999; Baum et al. 2009; 13% of college women experience stalking in a given year (DOJ 2001);

[3] Newton 2001

[4] NOW 2012

[5] Hirschel et al. 2007; Dual arrest rates are particularly high for gay male couples (Hirschel 2009)

males. (In interpersonal relationships, violence *against women* continues to be epidemic.)[6]

Women do, sometimes, perpetrate physical violence: in adult heterosexual relationships against male intimate partners and, within female-to-female relationships, against female intimate partners, and against children.[7] Also, not all victims of male intimate violence are women, as men may also perpetrate physical violence against male intimate partners.[8]

> Are there instances in which men are physically dominated and assaulted by their female partners? This does occur, often when a man has become weakened by a factor such as illness, injury, or old age. Even in these circumstances, abuse by a woman is unusual and when it does occur, it is most often motivated by self defense, fighting back and other protections. Even in these instances, the language "battered husbands" is not useful, especially in light of the thousands and even millions of women known to have suffered or been murdered at the hands of a male abuser.[9]

When female intimate partners kill male intimate partners, there is almost always a history (documented or undocumented) of physical violence perpetrated by the male, and the homicide is viewed *by the woman* as self-defense. Homicides committed by women against male intimate partners are most often "preceded by some kind of immediate or anticipated attack on the woman or [by] a long history of abuse" of the woman by the partner she killed.[10] In other words, while women do kill their intimate partners, the cause is very often immediate self-defense (or the perceived need for a proactive self-defense, because he has

— Reminds me of the jail scene in Chicago

---

[6] Heise 1997; NCVC 2011; NOW 2011
[7] NOMAS 2012b
[8] ibid
[9] NOMAS 2012b; Women are more likely to be murdered by their husbands than by any other person." (NOMAS 2012a)
[10] Sadusky 2010; van Wormer 2009

promised to kill her) after years of violence initiated primarily by the male partner.[11]

While domestic violence can be initiated by either gender and perpetrated upon either gender, and both heterosexual and same-sex and transgender relationships are fraught with contestations of power and interpersonal violence, heterosexuals constitute the majority sexual orientation, and in keeping with the ongoing stratification of gender roles within heterosexual relationships, most domestic violence is enacted, male-on-female, within a sexually intimate (or formerly intimate) heterosexual relationship.[12] Therefore, partner battery is "very highly correlated with gender...."[13]

> It is a simple fact that men are usually larger and physically stronger than their female partners. It is true that men are far more often raised to enjoy and practice fighting, boxing and wrestling skills. Far more significantly, we live in a world where men globally have dominated women, physically, politically and economically – a stubbornly-held patriarchal domination which is deeply rooted in history and pre-history. So it is hardly surprising that men are the perpetrators of controlling or violent partner abuse.... Some authors and agencies and legislators have sought to linguistically de-gender the crime, [but] describ[ing] it in phrases like "family violence"...obfuscate[s] the reality that [overwhelmingly], this is a crime that men commit against women.[14]

---

[11] The woman may know/believe that, if she does not strike first, her male partner will continue or culminate his years of violence with her (or their children's) ultimate death; Sadusky 2010; van Wormer 2009
[12] FMF 2012; DOJ 2001; Fisher et al. 2001
[13] NOMAS 2012b
[14] ibid

Underlying social factors . . .
contribute

to the pandemic of [men's] violence

Jackson Katz[15]

~~~

The overwhelming majority of *intimate partner* violence in the United States (including: physical assault, isolation from family & friends, verbal abuse, public humiliation, physical violence, and forced sexual intercourse[16]) is perpetrated by male intimate partners, and the overwhelming majority of victims are their female intimate partners.[17]

Adolescent and adult males are much more at risk of violence *from other males*[18] than they are *from females of any age and in any role.*

~~~

Violence by men against each other

– from simple assaults to gay-bashing –

is linked to the same structures

of gender and power

that produce so much [of] men's violence

against women.

Jackson Katz[19]

---

[15] Katz 2006
[16] The Hotline 2012
[17] deLaHunta & Tulski 1996; DomesticViolence.org 2009
[18] 76% of male homicide victims are killed by male assailants (Katz 2000)
[19] Katz 2006

Midnight Train Home
A Memoir

I followed Maureen from Pennsylvania to Indiana, not so much because I was "in love," as because when I met her I got to have my first sex ever, outside the auditory/authoritative range of parents.

She wasn't good-looking, but she was persistent, and though she was 30 and I, 19, I was willing to give her – and a relationship with her – a chance.

She was from there, and a few months into our relationship, she went "home." She invited me to follow, going first and reestablishing her job as a butcher in her father's meat shop and taking an apartment downtown. I never met her family. She wasn't "out" to them.

My first night there was overwhelming. In our first floor unit, our front window was at street level, and the cacophony of pedestrian voices, lilting in the local accent, sounded as foreign as if I'd gone overseas. I never felt so far from home.

But we resumed our sex life with vigor and passion. And alone in our bedroom, we exchanged rings and made promises.

I took up housekeeping.

She had one cat when I arrived. Soon there were four. I swept and washed and cleaned. I tended the box daily. She got a dog, and I fought the cat fur and dog hair and kept the bed and the couch fur free. I was so fastidious, she called me *Felix Unger*, from *The Odd Couple*, but the apartment never smelled.

She also mocked me as *Suzy Homemaker*. With no real funds, I tried to decorate out of nothing, and rounded out our furniture with tables and shelves I trash-picked, or found at the thrift store, and then refinished. And I painted each room. Later, in the bad times, it felt like painting my own mausoleum.

And I went job hunting.

With my high school diploma and mediocre typing skills, I turned up a series of poorly-compensated waitressing jobs that generally paid little more than my bus fare and cigarettes.

But I went to work each day and worked hard at getting good at serving.

And in my spare time, I tried to write.

Meanwhile, Maureen came and went from her real job and paid the rent and the utilities, and her car loan. And while we never once went grocery shopping, she brought home cuts of beef wrapped in butcher's paper.

Slowly at first, she began to change. It got where, even in a gay-friendly space, when I went to touch her arm or hold her hand, suddenly, she'd push me off, barking, *"Not here! You do that when I say you so, not when you decide."*

And she took to calling me names. Many made the list, but *Stupid* always seemed at the top. If she said it once, she said it twenty times a day.

I was stymied. I'd never known anyone who spoke poorly to friends or family. It was so far outside my experience, it simply did not compute – which made me wonder if she were right.

And she became jealous. Even though she had taken me along once or twice, she began to insist that she go to the bar alone. She said, *"All the other women"* were *"looking at me,"* and *"She wouldn't have her friends thinking her lover with a slut. She wouldn't be no fool."*

So, weekend after weekend, she left me home alone.

And she traded in her car, the automatic *that I could drive* for a stick-shift *that I couldn't.* I worried that if either one of us needed to go to the E.R., I wouldn't be *able* to drive us there. But it was as if I hadn't spoken. My words went as unmarked as if I were the wind whistling through the trees.

And her passion began to dwindle. She went from daily interest, to once a week, to twice a month, then to months of nothing....

And every Friday and Saturday night, she stayed out later and later, and when she did come in (even though, the rest of the week, she only showered in the morning), she began showering before coming to bed – or within olfactory distance of me.

And she became secretive.

In our apartment's floor plan, the middle of our bedroom floor *was* the path between living room, kitchen and bath.

She took to screaming if I passed through while she was on the phone (or answered the phone when she was home). And she took to whispering her calls.

Then there was the night she didn't come home at all, not 'til mid-morning, and the extra long shower she took that day.

I didn't know what to do. By this time I was 20, and this was my first *real* live-in relationship.

There was no one to tell, no one to talk to.

I couldn't call home.

My parents weren't even sure why I'd changed states, or why I'd chosen such an unlikely location. At least, we didn't talk about it.

And we didn't talk about the fact I wasn't dating men.

And we didn't talk about the fact the woman they'd met once, before I'd left town, looked a lot like a man herself.

In fact, they really weren't talking to me much that year at all. They were mad at me for leaving home. That's what my parents did when they were mad. They were angry at me for leaving home, and I was, essentially, getting *the silent treatment*. But how, when I was gay, could I live out their vision that I stay home until I married a man?

I couldn't talk to my straight friends from high school. They didn't know I liked girls and wouldn't have known what to say, or think, if they had known.

I couldn't talk to the boys I had dated. Each was, in his own way, brokenhearted.

And I didn't have anyone in the lesbian community. After leaving high school and the suburbs, I hadn't stayed long enough in Philly, out in the community, to make many friends before leaving town for Maureen. And Maureen hadn't *let* me make any new connections there, in Indiana.

I could walk around town, explore the neighborhood, get a cone at the local ice cream shop, stop to hypothesize about ancient astronauts at the New Age bookshop, and get to and from work, but I was, for all intents and purposes, *isolated*.

Oh, and the other waitresses at my job were 30 to 40 years old, married, had kids, and husbands who took their paychecks. They had not a clue that my life (or orientation) was not theirs. And I hadn't a clue how similar our *husbands* actually were.

Making my way each day, by bus and on foot, to my latest restaurant job, I passed a "family" services counseling agency. I turned in. They had a sliding scale, so for $2 a session, I saw a psychologist. Looking back, I presume now that he was Freudian. He simply sat at his desk, placed slightly behind me, and wrote as I talked. Never once did he offer an insight or a moment's feedback. He just wrote. I look back now and shudder. At the time, according to the American Psychological

Association's DSM-II, *homosexuality* was classified as a mental illness.[20]

After the third session, I decided that, for less money, I could buy Deborah a beer. Deborah, an acquaintance of a friend of Maureen's, had left her boyfriend with a basketful of possessions and moved in with Maureen and me, to crash on our couch). At least she would give me feedback.

I was right. Hers was a good ear to bend. She told me I *deserved better treatment. Anyone did.*

In my second year in Indiana, friends of Maureen's from Philly, Georgeanne and Cara, came to visit.

They stayed three days.

Leaving me home again, Maureen took them around town. She took them to the bar without me.

While they were out, I cooked beef. When they got back, Maureen called me *"Stupid Bitch"* for burning it. I cleaned up, while she took them out for pizza.

On the last day of their visit, while Maureen was at work, George and Cara sat me down, *"We want to talk to you,"* Cara started. *"We love Maureen, but clearly, you're being abused. We can't take you with us now, but if you can get your own way back to Philly, we have an extra room and straight friends who need daycare. You can use our downstairs to babysit in the daytime and rent our room."*

I didn't really answer them. I was too humiliated. But I knew they were right.

They left, but they left me with a plan.

A few days later, my wisdom teeth went bad. The whole two years I'd been there, they'd been brewing their abscesses. They were impacted too. The pain was so bad, I thought of

---

[20] Diagnostic and Statistical Manual of Mental Disorders (prior to 1973/74)

shooting myself with the small handgun Maureen kept for our protection. But I had no insurance and no real money, and the oral surgeon wouldn't operate without payment in full first.

I called home. Dad wired the money, but he needed it back in 12 weeks, for taxes.

I had my surgery, recovered, and week after week, I took almost every dollar and repaid him. I continued to scrape until I had enough for my ticket home.

Maureen was growing suspicious. My attitude had changed. I started calling her out more on her affair. She would respond, in her most forlorn way, *"I love you. I love her too. I don't know what to do. I can't choose. If you leave me, I'll kill myself."* Then add, *"If you leave, I'll kill you too."*

One Friday afternoon, she came home as I was talking to the neighbor across the backyard fence. I had been weeding and wrestling a patch of unwanted rhubarb, planted by long-since-gone tenants. She was empathizing on the impossibility of ridding a flower patch of rhubarb roots.

Maureen demanded I *get inside that instant.* In the bedroom, she wanted *"to know why"* I was *"having an affair with the neighbor."*

I denied and countered with new accusations about her affair, listing again her obvious behaviors.

The air heated up. Suddenly, she balled up her fists and lunged, knocking me on the bed and landing on top of me. Then she was above me, screaming, *"Bitch!"* alternately pummeling me and ripping at my clothes. She *"wanted to do it, NOW,"* and *"to teach me a lesson."*

I was taller than her (5'11" to her 5'4") – and heavier.

I blocked her blows and dumped her sideways, but in an instant, she was back, riding my resistance, drawing energy from the struggle.

She knocked my glasses off, started her mantra again, *"I hate you. I hate you! I love you. I can't live without you. I love her. I can't live without her. I love you. If you leave me, I'll kill myself. If you leave me, I'll kill you! I'll kill you . . . ."*

Her voice trailed off. She leapt off and reached under the bed, grabbing the box where she kept the "protective" revolver. It was in her hand, then suddenly, at close range, in my face. She was threatening and gesticulating wildly, pistol flailing in every direction, then pointing at me again, yelling, *"I'll kill you, You Bitch! I'll kill you!"* Then waving it toward her own temple, crying, *"I'll kill myself! I don't want to live. I'm outta here!"*

I remember thinking, as it pointed away from me, *My arms are longer than hers,* and reaching out and knocking her arm upward, holding her wrist above her head, pistol pointing toward the ceiling (the floor of the apartment upstairs), until – no longer resolute in her struggle against me – she broke down in shaking sobs, and I was able to slip it from her grasp.

I left her pounding the bed and struggling with a pillow, while I hid the pistol deep in a kitchen cabinet. Later, after she composed herself and went out, I moved it again, locking it in the glove compartment of a car out back that didn't run, and kept the key on my person at all times.

I still didn't have enough for the train, but about four weeks later, I hid the key in a green glass vase, and after she went out *that* Friday night, had the neighbor drive me to the train.

On the way, I mailed a letter. It told Maureen where to find her protective pistol and the hiding spot of the key.

As I boarded the train and made my way to a seat in the dining car, I shed tears for *Shohondo*, my Shepherd Collie, and *Tommy Tiger*, and nine other cats I'd never again see. They had listened when even Deborah wasn't around, and had often jumped on my lap or nuzzled my face in my darkest moments. When the train crossed out of Ohio, the *"Welcome to Pennsylvania"* marker had never looked so sweet.

I wanted to get out and kiss the ground, but the locomotive engineer neither knew nor cared, and Amtrak's *Broadway Limited* was moving too fast. I waited, and kissed the ivy-lined sidewalk of Philadelphia's *Pulaski Avenue*, between *Seymour* and *Manheim Streets*, in front of George and Cara's *lesbian collective* slash *rooming house* slash *my new independent daycare center*.

~~~

2. Statistics

Even though partner assault is underreported, using the science of statistics and what we do know, we are able to make educated estimates of the actual incidence of intimate partner physical assault. Our best educated estimations indicate that:[21]

The Genders Are NOT Equally Represented As Intimate Partner Assailants/Victims

- Intimate Partner Violence is about gaining and maintaining control[22]
- **More than 90% of** "systematic, persistent, and injurious" **violence,** and **90% of murders,**[23] **are perpetrated by men**[24]
  - 85-95% of batterers are male
  - 85-95% of (lethal and non-lethal) domestic violence is perpetrated by straight males against their overwhelmingly female partners/ex-partners[25]
  - 1 in 4 males in the U.S. will use violence against a partner in his lifetime[26]

[21] Statistics (and some text about these statistics) are from taken from: DVRC 2012 (Feb9) [accessed]; NCADV 2012 (Feb9) [accessed]
[22] Kimmel 2002
[23] NOMAS 2012b
[24] Kimmel 2002
[25] Katz 2000
[26] ibid

- "Women are **much more likely** than men **to be victimized by a current or former intimate partner**" [27]

  - o Females make up "about 85% of the victims of non-lethal domestic violence.[28]
  - o In all, women are **victims of intimate partner violence at a rate about 5 times that of males**[29]
  - o Wife assault makes up **25%** of **all crime**
  - o **Irrespective of race, religion, socioeconomic class status, education, marital status, or age**, between 25% and 37%[30] of women experience physical battery by an intimate partner in their lifetimes[31]
  - o 10%-15% of "all women" who live with men experience "**severe and ongoing**" physical abuse"[32]
  - o A woman is battered at least once every 15 seconds in the United States.
  - o Women experience two million injuries from partner violence each year"[33]
  - o Between 20 and 52% of women in their teens and twenties[34] have been physically abused by their boyfriends/male intimate partners

- Also, "transgender people are the targets of the most vicious and blatant forms of violence." They are "subjected to random street violence and domestic partner abuse" and "routinely abused by the police and medical professionals."[35]

---

[27] DOJ 2008
[28] Rennison & Welchans 2000
[29] ibid
[30] From 1 in 4 to *more than 1 in 3*
[31] Commonwealth Fund 2009; Rennison & Welchans 2000
[32] NOMAS 2012a
[33] CDC 2008
[34] From 1 in5 to more than 1 in 2
[35] Lev & Lev 1999

Source of (Often Long-term) Physical, Emotional, & Mental Injury

- Men's violence is **the single most serious health problem for women in the U.S.**[36]
- Battered women's injuries *are as serious as injuries suffered in 90% of violent felonies*
- Between menses and menopause (ages 14 to 45), battery at the hands of a male intimate partner (or ex-partner) is **the primary cause of physical injury to women** (3 to 4 million per year[37]
  - It causes more harm than accidents, muggings, and cancer combined. [38]
- Intimate partner physical assault is **the number one cause of emergency room visits by women**
- Women are **particularly unsafe in the window of time in which they first leave a violent relationship**
  - 73% of the women seeking emergency services for battery having recently separated from their abusers
- **25 to 45%** of battered women are **battered during pregnancy**
  - the **breasts and abdomen become "targets of assault"**
  - Battery cause many **fetal deaths** (miscarriage and stillbirth)
  - Battery causes many **maternal deaths**[39]
- **Rape** is **often a part of** a **partner's physical assault.**
- Battery **affects mental health**
  - "up to 64% of hospitalized female psychiatric patients" have been physically abused
- Battery **affects rates of homelessness and the feminization of poverty**

---

[36] Kilmartin 2012
[37] ibid
[38] ibid
[39] van Wormer 2009; See also: Sutton 2005; SWNI 2006; NDVH 2011; IDVAAC 2012 [accessed]

- o "50% of homeless women and children in the U.S." are homeless because they are "fleeing abuse"
- Battered women are often **coerced to stay** by **practical reasons**
  - o **fear for their own lives**
  - o **fear for the lives of their children**
  - o **a lack of resources**
    - **there is a reality to the gender wage gap**[40]
    - **More than 50% of women** report that they **stay because they cannot support their children on "their wages"**

~~~

One third of all the women who are murdered in our country

are killed by their male partners....

This is a terrible fact for all of us,

but **until we face it,**

we're not going to be able

to do anything about it.

Jean Kilbourne[41]

~~~

---

[40] Women overall still earned only 77.6 cents to every dollar earned by men (Day & Rosenthal 2011; Bishaw & Semega 2010; Getz 2010; Jones & Smith 2001), with Black women earning 61 cents on the overall male dollar and Hispanic women earning only 52 cents on the male dollar (WOCPN 2011; NWLC 2007).

[41] Kilbourne 2010

Partner Homicide and/or Murder-Suicide

- More than **90% of murder-suicides are intimate-partner homicides**
  - About 95% of "the offenders in murder-suicides" are current or former male intimate partners[42]
  - About 95% of the victims are female[43]
    - "Women are more likely to be victims of homicide at the hands of **their partners during" pregnancy**" (than when they are not pregnant)[44]
    - Women are **more likely to be murdered by their husbands/ partners than by all other types of assailants combined.**[45]
- Weapons are used in 30% of domestic violence incidents.
- In the U.S., women **murdered** by their current/former male partners average: [46]
  - one every six hours
  - more than 3 (and up to 4) each day
  - 1,200 per year
    - "Family violence kills as many women every five years as the total number of Americans who died in the Vietnam War."

---

[42] BOJ 2003
[43] VPC 2006
[44] van Wormer 2009; See also: Sutton 2005; SWNI 2006; NDVH 2011; IDVAAC 2012 [accessed]
[45] NOMAS 2012a; Browne & Williams 1989
[46] Kilmartin 2012; Catalano 2007; IBIS-PH 2011

High Kicking
A Female Retelling

I've known Gary since preschool. Dropping us off and picking us up, his mom and my mom became friends. So, really, we kind of grew up together. I remember his 5th birthday party. It was all *Darth Vader* and *the Force*. He and his mom have been a part of my world so long, they're like a part of my own family – part of my own nature. So, as we got older, and we got more and more attracted, and he really wasn't my brother, it just seemed kind of natural to get involved.

We were fifteen when we lost our virginity with each other. We didn't know much, but he asked his older cousin some questions, and then, he always made sure he pulled out. He also said we couldn't do it in the middle of my cycle. We were together so much of the time, he always kept a kind of eye on when that was. So it worked for a really long time. We didn't get pregnant for a while.

In fact, we didn't get pregnant until about the time I wanted to break up.

I didn't like the way he was being.

He wouldn't let me have any friends, and he was trying to tell me what to do. He *"didn't want me to join"* the cheerleading squad. Was *"afraid all the other guys would see my legs sticking out from under that short skirt."* So he said, *"No."* And I told him, he *"couldn't tell me what to do."* And he said, *"Yes,"* he *"could, because he was my man."* And I said, I was *"still a person with rights."* And so it went.

I stood up to him. Went for tryouts. Got on the team and everything.

And he was all sorry. *"Sorry"* he had told me *"no."* Sorry he had been *"so mean."*

So sorry, we ended up doing it again.

Only thing was, that time, he had an accident. And it was right in the middle of my cycle.

I was sweatin' it sooo bad when my period came. Just beads of sweat all over me until it showed up. Then I was relieved.

But he kept being bossy. Really overbearing. Like his dad with his mom. He started fights with me more and more. I kept trying to get back to how we used to be. And that made me careless too. A couple more times, he made up with me just at the middle of my cycle. And a couple more times, he got so carried away, he just lost it and forgot to pull out *"in time."*

I didn't really know how to break up with him. I mean, *How do you dump a man you've known since you were like two? How do you break up with a family? His mom? His dad? His sisters who are your best friends?*

But I was determined. I wasn't going down that road. I wasn't going to take what his mom took. So I was still telling him that I wouldn't put up with the way he was treating me.

And then, my period didn't come. And it didn't come. And then he got his sister to give him a couple of bucks for the pregnancy test, and she brought it over with him and went in the bathroom with me while I peed on the stick. And it turned into a blue cross. Positive. Pregnant.

He wasn't bad in helping me deal with the parents – all four of them – his and mine.

And his sisters were happy – happy as they could be that they were going to be aunts to their baby brother's baby when he was still just 17.

But that was the way it was, and everyone started adjusting.

I started adjusting too.

I had to quit the squad. No more hopping up on other girls' shoulders. No more being out there in front of everyone, a role model of the perfect teen.

The way things went down, about the end of my second trimester, I dropped out of school and moved into his bedroom at his parents' house.

There was talk of a wedding, and of what he could do without a college education that could make a living for a wife and kid.

He got edgier and edgier.

And then he started. Whenever people were out, he'd pick a big fight with me over something stupid, get carried away with himself, and punch me in the gut – or where my gut used to be.

He started to hit my boobs too – telling me they were too big, that all the guys were looking, that *all his friends thought* I *was just a whore* who *trapped him.*

It didn't do any good to remind him that he was the one who quit pulling out. Nothing did any good.

We were, pretty much, both miserable.

I was sick all the time. I missed my friends and my life. He missed his friends and his life.

He started to work for his dad, doing construction, but just then, the industry started falling apart from the financial crisis. No one was buying houses anymore and less and less people had the money to fix them up.

We didn't have anything. Not a crib or a playpen or a car seat or a car…. We didn't have diapers or formula or any way to get them. He thought breastfeeding was gross. He told me, "*He wouldn't have no kid sucking on me,*" then he'd punch me in my stretched boobs, extra hard, and I'd double over with the pain.

And he told me, "*I could never leave him now. No one else would ever want a fat bitch with a baby.*" I "*was his for good now, like a damn pair of handcuffs on his freedom.*"

My mom didn't want to hear it.

I tried to tell her how he was changing, but she was so mad at me for shaming her in front of the ladies at church and the women at her job, she barely managed a smile when she did her duty and came to the baby shower his sisters threw.

But after the shower, that's when he really had it. One day, he lost it good. No one was home. I was trying to make his dinner. I didn't know what I was doing. I was new to the domestic thing, and he started beatin' on me. Then he started kicking me. He pulled me down by the hair and went to kicking my stomach. I felt something give, and I started to gush. There was water and blood. I was about eight months. He didn't stop, not even when I started to make a mess on the floor. But then his mom came in. She took a broom stick and chased him off me and called 911.

I was in and out of consciousness pretty much the whole ride. In the E.R., I heard them asking what had happened. His mom was answering. She tried to steer them off of him. She didn't want to lose *her* baby to this mess, didn't want *him* in trouble.

And then I started into labor. The pains kept coming.

My head hurt a lot, but my back and sides hurt more. When they hooked up the monitor, the doctor got a solemn look on her face. There was no sign of life. No heartbeat. No movement on the ultrasound. She said she wanted me to labor through it, so that next time, I could still have a natural birth. She didn't tell me how much it would hurt.

I struggled through the pain for 17 hours, hoping against hope to hear her cry. Finally, she was born.

She had a tiny little head. She had Gary's hair and chin and my high cheekbones. And such a peaceful look, like she was all unaware of the rage that took her from me.

Placenta abruption. That's what they said. They said the placenta came detached. And they called it a still birth. It was true. She was very, very still. I last felt her kick just before I burnt his steak.

At the funeral, I could barely walk. I had to lean on his mother with each step. Both families had to come up with the money to open a plot.

Standing next to the tiny casket, he took my hand and wept. He wants to make it up to me.

~~~

Disparate Rates of Victimization

- **34% (more than a third) of female homicide victims** over age 15 are murdered by their current or former male intimate partner [47]
- **Only 3% of male murder victims are killed by their current or former intimate partner**
  - **those partners are also, generally, male**[48]
- **In 70-80%** of partner homicides, **the man physically abused the woman before the murder,** no matter which partner was killed

---

[47] SWNI 2006; Commonwealth Fund 2009; Rennison & Welchans 2000; It is also important to realize that of female homicides before puberty, a strong percentage of children murdered are murdered by fathers, step-fathers, mother's boyfriends, and other male relatives.; See also Paulozzi et al. 2001.
[48] ibid

Disparate Punishment & Legal Standards Across Gender Lines

- On average, **prison terms for women who kill their husbands are <u>twice as long</u>[49] as those given to men who kill their wives**
  - Yet, **93%** of women who kill their mates have been **consistently battered** by them.[50]
  - And **67% of women who kill their abusers do so to protect themselves and their children, as an act of self-defense, at the moment of the murder**

displays male priveledge

- Whether or not a homicide committed by an abused woman meets the legal standard for self-defense (a standard of *Equal Force* based on a male-on-male scenario), the abused woman views her act as one of self-defense, either for herself or for herself and her children.

- Even when the risk of death does not appear (legally) imminent at the moment of the homicide, the female abuse victim may view her action as self-defense, in that:

- the male abuser has often (intentionally) convinced his partner that she (and/or her children) will be killed if they try to leave

- The male-on-male **standard of equal force,**[51] applies to the male/female conflict the male-on-male question of

---

[49] Women's prison terms for murder of a spouse/partner are so much higher, in part, because if/when a woman kills, she is breaking gender norms that prohibit women from violence, while when men kill, they are not violating the norm of hegemonic violent masculinity.

[50] ibid

[51] Which cannot be realistically applied in most female-on-male homicides. Most men can kill most women with fists or feet alone. If a woman (or her children) are at imminent risk of being killed by a male partner, in order to stop him from murdering them, most women would be required to make use of a higher level of weapon. If he is using his fists, she would likely need a club or a knife. If he is using a knife, she would likely need a gun, etc. Most women cannot win in a physical contest with a man by using the same level of weaponry – say fist on fist. The male standard of Equal Force does not apply in a cross-gender physical contest in which only one will come out alive.

whether or not the survivor could have left the altercation with her assailant still alive.

- In male-on-male cases, murder is generally not considered to have been committed in self-defense if the survivor could have left the scene without committing the homicide

- However, many abused women are all but held hostage by their partners for years. [52] And:

- Their partners detail plans that – if they leave – they will stalk them, find them, and kill them before the police can save them.

- He will convince them of what is essentially true – that there is no one (*friend, relative, or legal authority*) who **CAN** stop him from finding them, bringing them back and/or finishing them off.

- In these cases, a percentage of abused women premeditate their actions, and commit homicide as their only way out (or the only way to stop his damage toward and save the lives of their children).

- Even though premeditated, from the perspective of a woman held hostage to abuse, it may be her only possible act of self-defense.

~~~

Over 85% of the people who commit murder are men, and **the women that do, often do so as a defense against men who are battering them.**

Ninety percent of people who commit violent physical assault are men.

---

[52] With the institution of women's shelters, which give female victims of domestic violence a means of escape (so that they are less likely to find that their only resort is murder in self-defense), the rates of male partners being killed by female intimates dropped significantly (DOJ 2008).

Ninety-five percent of serious domestic violence is perpetrated by males, and it's been estimated that 1 in 4 males will use violence against a partner in their lifetimes.

Over 95% of dating violence is committed by men, and, very often, it's young men in their teens.

Studies have found that young men are responsible for between 85 and 95% of child sexual abuse, whether the victim is female or male.

And 99.8% of people in prison convicted of rape are men.

What this shows is that an awful lot of boys and men are inflicting an incredible level of pain and suffering both on themselves and others.

And we know that much of the violence is **cyclical** – that many boys who are abused as children grow up and become perpetrators themselves.

[Up to] **81% of batterers grew up in abusive households**.

Jackson Katz[53]

~~~

---

[53] Katz 2000

Partial Profile of the Batterer/Effect on Children

- Batterers are likely to have **substance abuse** problem
- Batterers tend to **isolate their victims, including from immediate/extended family members**
- As an isolation tactic, batterers tend to be **jealous over their partner's relationships with others**
- Batterers are likely to **blame their partners** for their own violent/abusive actions
- **"Children are abused at a rate of 1,500 percent higher,"** in homes with spousal abuse
  - o **"30-70%** of men who batter their partners, **also** either **sexually or physically abuse their children."**
- More than **50% of child abductions** arise from domestic violence situations.
- **"Witnessing violence** between one's parents or caretakers is **the strongest risk factor of transmitting violent behavior from one generation to the next."** [54]
  - o *At least* **60% of men who batter** grew up in homes where
    - they were beaten
    - they witnessed a parent being beaten[55]
  - o "More than half of children who witness their fathers beating their mothers become abusers or victims themselves"[56]
    - boys become twice as likely to abuse partners and children
    - girls become twice as likely to take abuse and fail to protect children[57]

Abuse is not love. Real love doesn't actually hurt, at least, not in these ways.

---

[54] NCADV 2012 Feb9 [accessed]
[55] ibid
[56] ibid
[57] ibid

Intimate partner assault is not limited by class status.

- **Men of all socioeconomic strata commit partner battery.**
  - o "Approximately one third of the men counseled for battering are professional men who are well respected in their jobs and in their communities. These have included doctors, physiologists, lawyers, ministers and business executives."[58]
- Overall, **male perpetrators are much more likely** than female perpetrators **to engage in "stalking . . . severe violence, forced sex, threats to kill, and other coercive behaviors."**[59]
- **Our ideology of gender** – our construction of masculinity as tough and violent – contributes to males perpetrating approximately 90% of the violence in the United States in general:
  - o toward intimate partners,
  - o toward children,
  - o toward other men including in male-on-male *non-intimate* altercations, and
  - o in crime in general.[60]

As with all forms of *gendered violence,* and *violence against women* **because they are women**, partner battery indicates that the **task of the second wave of the women's movement is not yet complete.**

---

[58] Adams 1989
[59] Sadusky 2010; van Wormer 2009; DOJ 2001; Baum et al. 2009
[60] Katz 2000

You Bind Our Minds

N. D. Rosechild

You bind our minds

our hands

    our feet

Your honor

    by our deaths

    complete

Control

belittle

bully, abuse

Our bodies

with your own

    you use

A hundred years

and fifty more

Served not to even up

the score

The tally

    rises higher still

Mind, heart, and body

still you kill

Nadine Rosechild Sullivan, Ph.D., Rev.

This moment

in alone despair

a sister's scream

pierces the air

Your victim

in a crippling win

And it is she

you say has sinned

Upon your pyres

murdered still

As witch or wife

flesh lights the hill

Each time we trust

betrayed again

Our loyalty

our curse within

Like phoenix

rising from the dust

We seek recovery

from your lust

Pass again a century's

wealth

You still won't see us

as yourself.

~~~

3. The Ideology of Male Supremacy

There is an epidemic of male violence against women, in the U.S., and around the globe.

Overall, this violence is enacted by men against women toward whom they feel a sense of ownership, and perhaps, for whom they feel a sense of responsibility. Men who are violent, are violent toward the women with whom they are sexually intimate, or to whom they are connected by close relationship,[61] primarily wives/girlfriends and sometimes daughters/step-daughters.

Social attitudes have long crystallized around a cultural, and often religious, belief in male dominance and female submission – a doctrine of male supremacy (or male superiority)[62] – (still) often believed (even by those who are scientific instead of religious) to be biologically determined.[63] In many settings, a man was (or is) deemed responsible, not only to provide for partners and female relatives, but to control them as well.

---

[61] by birth or marriage or relationship
[62] patriarchy
[63] The anthropological record demonstrates, however, that our thinking has been much too narrow along this line. See Coltrane 2005, ch 7

Woman battering springs out of these underlying beliefs[64] about gender roles.

Women are not seen as (essentially) the same as men, and therefore, treating women differently is not shocking.

Some males may even rationalize that it is their duty to keep a woman in subjection – even as parents are held responsible for the behavior and discipline of their children.

Increasingly, U.S. society has come to recognize the adult female as fully autonomous and self-responsible, and the idea of disciplining women has come to be (at least legally) recognized as both absurd, and as the violent crime, that it is.

Yet, while the laws, at least in the United States, have been amended through social justice imperatives, and are now supposed to reflect a standard of **equal *justice***, remnants of their origins in a male-centered standard survive. [65] In largely unexamined ways, our laws continue to mirror the attitudes and traditions of male supremacy.

~~~

Most men are not violent.

Overwhelmingly, most men are not violent, but

many men

are **afraid to speak out against [gendered violence],**

are **afraid to support women,**

are **afraid to challenge other men**.

Jean Kilbourne[66]

---

[64] internalized ideologies
[65] androcentric
[66] Kilbourne 2010

4. The Experience of the Battered Woman

Women who are being battered live in a certain kind of hell.
Never relaxed, never sure of safety, physically and sexually
violated at every turn, emotionally reeling, they have no safe
haven in a non-comprehending world:

> It is always the same . . . . There is terror, yes,
> and physical pain. There is desperation and
> despair. One blames oneself, forgives him. One
> judges oneself harshly for not loving him
> enough. "It's your fault," he shouts as he is
> battering in the door, or slamming your head
> against the floor. And before you pass out, you
> say, *Yes.* You run, but no one will hide you or
> stand up for you – which means standing up to
> him . . . . Eventually you surrender to him,
> apologize, beg him to forgive you for hurting
> him or provoking him or insulting him or being
> careless with something of his . . . . You ask
> him not to hurt you as he does what he wants
> to you. The shame of this physical capitulation,
> often sexual, and the betrayal of your self-
> respect will never leave you. You will blame
> yourself and hate yourself forever. In your
> mind, you will remember yourself – begging,
> abject . . . . The violence becomes contextual,
> the element in which you try to survive . . . .
> You will be so frightened you think dying might
> be okay . . . . [I]f you do stay away and make a
> break, he will strike out of nowhere, still beat
> you, vandalize your home, stalk you. Still no
> one stops him . . . . *Every battered woman's life has
> in it many rapes . . . . Sometimes, one complies without
> the overt violence but in fear of it. Or sometimes, one
> initiates sex to try to stop or head off a beating. Of
> course, there are also the so-called good times – when
> romance overcomes the memory of violence. Both the
> violation and the complicity make one deeply ashamed.*

The shame is corrosive . . . . Why would one tell? How can one face it?[67]

Many observers blame the victim, and yet, "the heart of the problem [lies] in *male* violence."[68]

> [W]hat most people find troubling about violence . . . is the hideous nature of male violence against the rest of humanity. History doesn't recount the tales of Jacqueline the Ripper who stalked 19th century rent-boys because there is no *female* equivalent of Jack the Ripper and his penchant for slaughtering defenseless prostitutes . . . . No *female* psychopath has ever hunted down 16 little first graders and shot them like cornered animals . . . . There are [essentially] no dead men outside the family court shot by their vindictive wives . . . . [But] there are countless . . . victims [of male violence] whose names I [can't] remember because there are simply so many . . . . Let's move beyond the deceptively simple notion that women can be violent.[69]

> Compared to the frequency and severity of male violence, female violence is a side-show. The main game always has been, and should remain, asking men to tame their anger, lust and vindictiveness. Many men and all women have a stake in that.[70]

Woman battering is perceived to be the woman's fault. "Why does **she** choose *that kind* of man?"

---

[67] Dworkin, 1997 pp41-42, 46-47, emphasis mine
[68] Jones 1980 p306, emphasis mine
[69] And they can, but the frequencies and brutalities just don't compare.
[70] Moriarty 2000

One survivor writes, "I had been told by everyone I asked for help the many times I tried to escape – strangers and friends – that he would not be hitting me if I didn't like it or want it."[71]

Such finger pointing amounts to a societal level of betrayal.

> There are cases on record of men still harassing and beating their wives twenty-five years after the wives left them and tried to go into hiding. If researchers were not quite so intent upon assigning the pathological behavior to the wo**men, they might see that the more telling question** is not, "Why do the women stay?" but "Why don't the men let them go?"[72]

Woman battering is not a problem because women *like* to be assaulted, violated, and threatened. Violence against women is not a problem because girls raised in dysfunctional homes are psychologically deformed and therefore – ask for it – in a craving for an adrenaline rush.

Abused women are not hooked on a fight-or-flight-or-freeze high.

---

[71] Dworkin 1997 p19
[72] Jones 1980 p299

Restrained
A Female Retelling

Jeremy wasn't exactly a knight in shining armor, but you know, he seemed real. He wanted to date me. And my mom is diagnosable, you know? Whatever else she is, she's certifiable.

They've called her all kinds of things through the years – clinically depressed, manic depressive, then bipolar. And borderline. What is that? What's she on the border of? Maybe the paranoid schizophrenia the doc she never agreed with suggested....

And my mom had custody of my daughter! She's who fucked me up, but they figured they'd give *her* another chance!

I was looking for a good man. If I made a stable marriage, I might win her back.

So I thought I'd check him out. We met online. He looked cute enough. Had a house, deep in the Pines. So I went to see. A date. A chance to get to know someone new. What could it hurt?

Met him at a little diner in the small town nearest his place. He looked just like I thought. And he seemed sweet.

We agreed we'd date for a while, get to know each other better. So I started traveling back and forth whenever I could. The bus ride was long, so sometimes, he'd come my way. And one day, after we'd been dating for a few months, I went with him back to his place.

The problem wasn't the sex. By then, I was pretty hooked on him, so I was down with the idea of a getting closer. I had seen lots of his body already, you know, by text. We had been texting a while. And I figured I was ready.

I got in his car and watched as we traveled further and further back into the Pines. As we left the main roads, the tree cover got deeper and deeper. Soon there were no more houses and the pavement gave way to dirt. *'Wow! You really live in the sticks,"* I noted, like it was profound. He simply answered, *"Yeah,"* as the path veered deeper into a thicket. I noticed the bars on my cell phone disappeared. Finally, he stopped short at a structure, set in the side of a man-made mound, that passed for a house.

The front that bordered the driveway looked like the remains of an old passenger bus, single-decker, with large dark windows and a full windshield, but we entered a door next to it. He led me through a narrow, dark galley kitchen and up into the sunlit space of the front. There you could sit on a handful of bench seats, or on the driver's seat, still riveted to the floor, and gaze over the steering wheel and out the windshield to the squirrels frisking on the power lines that descended to the unused bus door.

We didn't stay long in the front though. He wanted to lead me back to the "bedroom." Back we went, back through the galley kitchen, and into the interior. He took a key and unlocked a door to a cavernous room with no source of natural light. The only windows were behind us, in the bus. Some light from the front reached the galley, but this other space was lit only by the light from a dim bulb in the ceiling and a floor lamp on the far wall. Also against that far wall, on the floor, rested a frameless box spring and mattress draped with a dark comforter. To the left side stood a low, dark dresser. On the right, stood an open toilet and next to it, a sink stuck out from the bedroom wall.

My heart sank a little. It didn't look like he had much to start a life together, if I wanted to get my kid from my mom, but I didn't let on. He was cheerful and playful, but a little strained. I thought, *He must be worried I'll judge him by his house,* so I tried my best to put him at ease. I would think about the possibilities of this house tomorrow, when I was home again. Maybe there was a way to fix it up. Samantha would need her own bedroom, and a tub. I hadn't seen a tub....

I looked around for a TV, to relief the tension, but there was none.

He took my hand and led me to the bed. I was good with that. The kissing was a little awkward, but we made our way through it, and after he came, I dosed off comfortably. It had been a long night, dodging my mother's anger, and now that the stress of the first encounter was behind us, I was suddenly a little fatigued.

When I woke, I was alone. I got up, gathered my clothes and headed to the door, looking for him. It was locked. The key slot was on my side, but no key. I pulled and jiggled. I pounded and called his name. After a few minutes, I saw the knob turn, and Jeremy pushed his way into the room, pushing me back ahead of him, a tray of food in his hand.

I started for the door, but as he let himself in, he had already spun the tumbler on the other side, pulling the door tight behind him.

"I would be living here now," he explained, softly. *"It was, what"* I *"wanted, anyway, what we had talked about."* He *"had decided"* he was *"good with keeping me."* He would *"bring me food once or twice a day, and visit"* me, *"so I wouldn't be lonely. If"* I *"tried to get away,"* he would *"have to discipline me, so I would know who was boss. But if"* I were *"good,"* he would *"be good as well."*

I told him, I needed *"to get back to my daughter."* I reminded him that my mom couldn't *"be trusted to be good to her all the time, all alone."* They needed *"the balance I added to the house, at least, until I could get my daughter out of there."*

He just laughed, low and distant. Mumbled something about giving *"me another baby to replace her."*

I started to think, *My cell phone is dead, but my friends will come looking.*

Then I thought, *No, I don't call most of them for weeks on end. I'm never on Facebook. And my mom, she'll barely even notice. If she does, it will only be to document my lack of responsibility for The Court.*

I attacked him, but it did no good. He laughed and acted like my best blows were mere swats to him.

Day by day, he brought me food.

Day by day, he collected his sexual due, shoving himself in, even though I fought him. And after that first time, he stopped using condoms, and of course, I had no more access to my pills.

Once or twice, I raced him for the door. Each time I did, he beat me 'til I passed out. He told me he had *"warned me he would show me who was boss."*

Each time he came and went, he was careful to re-lock the door behind him.

Once, I thought I heard a truck outside. I felt it more than heard it, some vibration that felt like a truck engine rattled the ground. I tried to call through the walls. No response.

I found a crayon in a drawer and kept a calendar of sorts. Each day, I made a small scratch, low on the wall, next to the mattress. And about three months in, my period didn't come.

One day, a few weeks later, I heard a loud scuffle through the wall. From the other side, someone shouted, thrust the door open, then danced into, and out of the opening, weapon drawn.

I was free.

My father finally thought my prolonged absence fishy, reported me missing, and did the leg work of tracking me down. He found and followed the trail on my laptop to the diner. The townspeople gave him the rest.

I was so glad to see my baby! Even though she clung to my mother's leg, saying, *"No want 'a, Momma. Want Nanna,"* I still wept with joy. I had been so sure I'd never see her, *or even daylight*, again.…

My stomach's much bigger now. By the time I was free, it was too late to choose whether or not to **keep *his*** baby. From prison he writes to say that *"when he gets out, when they realize that the kidnapping charges are trumped up and that I wanted to be with him all those months,"* he'll *"be back to exercise his parental rights as Daddy,"* and *"we can raise **our** boy together in the Pines."* Other days he writes to tell me how, *"he'll get out for good behavior"* and *"kill me for being the lying bitch who sent him up there."* He'll *"raise his son himself, with me planted six feet under their vegetable garden."* He says, I'll *"make good fertilizer."*

Mom tells me how she'll *"take this baby from me too."*

5. Pathologizing the Victim

Viewing the problem through the lens of individual psychology has caused society to miss the forest for the trees, and to view the effect as the cause. We have moved from the public recognition that there are political issues around the treatment of women in society and culture and toward the private psychologization of political issues as personal deficits.

But the issues between men and women are **not just personal**. They **play out on a grand scale, on the stage of human history.** And since they are not solidly rooted in biology, but **heavily influenced by cultural socialization**, we need to move back again to the recognition that **the personal *IS* political** – and that which happens to one woman happens, at some level, to all women (is heard, like a hate crime, in the hearts of all women who know that it could, by chance or intent, be them next time).

These issues are not just personal,

to be dealt with as private family
matters.

They are political as well,

with repercussions that reverberate
throughout

our lives and communities

in all sorts of meaningful and
disturbing ways.

Jackson Katz[73]

~~~

While it is problematic that women are socialized to view the world romantically, the problem of abuse does not really lie in the traditional female misdirection toward *marriage AS career* - for **abuse has not lessened with women's entrance into the market place**. (Neither was it less when white and middle-class women did not work outside the home.)

A woman's safety against assault by her partner does not increase with the acquisition of a salary, **nor does it increase if the woman defends herself by returning violence for violence.**

And abuse **does not necessarily end or decrease when the "relationship" ends**, not unless the abuser lets it end.

The problem is not that psychologically-hobbled women choose the "wrong" men.

It is instead that there are so very many men who are wrong.

---

[73] Katz 2006

6. The Root of the Problem – Ideology/Belief

The root of the problem lies in ideology – *how men are taught to think about women.*

> A study that analyzed how victims and offenders in marital homicide perceived their sex roles found that *men were more than ten times as likely as women to define their spouse as* **"an object** *of personal property"* and to treat her accordingly.[74]

Also, at the root of this problem of ideology is *the way men are taught to think about themselves.*

This social problem originates in the socialization of men.

~~~

Violence is not typically talked about

as a gender issue,

but the fact is that **one gender,**

men,

perpetrate approximately **90% of the violence.**

Jackson Katz[75]

~~~

Some lay it to the charge of nature, even to testosterone-induced aggression. But the *nature* shoe does not fit comfortably. If women are less violent by *nature*, does that mean that women are morally superior?

No. Women are simply human too, and often, quite flawed.

---

[74] Jones 1980 p298, emphasis mine
[75] Katz 2000

If women are less violent, is it by nurture or by socialization?

The anthropological record on gender roles indicates that enactments of passivity and aggression are not writ in unalterable hormones.[76]

Rather, gender roles differed in many premodern societies: with some structured much like the West, in that men were the leaders and the aggressors and women were the followers and passive; and others in opposition to the West where women were the leaders and the aggressors and men were the followers and passive; and others still, where both genders were aggressive or where both genders were passive. Thus, male violence is not genetic – it is not unalterable *testosterone poisoning.*[77]

The ideology of male supremacy – the rule of the male - has been implicated as the root of all sexual oppression. It is also distinctly implicated in the oppression of woman battering.

> Wife-beating is commonplace and ordinary because men believe they have rights over women that women dispute. The control men want of women, the domination men require over women, is expressed in this terrible brutality . . . . Four million women in the United States, one every fifteen seconds . . . .[78]

In their work, *Woman Abuse on Campus*, DeKeseredy and Schwartz, lay the blame for male-on-female violence squarely on the shoulders of patriarchal ideology. They find that the abusive man (like a parent that believes s/he must control hir child at all times) believes that he must control "his" woman, even with his fists. He believes that he must be the head of "his" home, the "king of his castle" – or he will look bad "as a man."

---

[76] Coltrane 2005; Sanday 1991; Burke 1996; Fausto-Sterling 1992, 2000
[77] ibid
[78] Dworkin 1997 p43; one every 15 seconds for battery CDC 2008; one every 45 seconds for rape Kilpatrick et a. 1992

In the internalization of that ideology, such men find a mandate for abuse.

Male-on-female violence does not spring so much from the psychological warp of the individual man, as from adherence to the ideology of male dominance which - yielding privilege - demands that privilege be maintained:

> a substantial number of male actions, values, and beliefs are microsocial expressions of broader patriarchal forces. Simply put, this means that the problem is not one in which individual men simply all happen to suffer from the same psychopathy, or weak ego, or whatever. Rather, they all live in the same society, and the single individual man is partially a reflection of the values and beliefs that are expressed by the broader society . . . . These broader forces are patriarchal.[79]

Raised in the same cultures (and religions) as "their" men, **many women internalize male-dominance and cooperate with the prevailing, unequal, gender ideologies.**

> [This worldview] provides a political and social rationale for itself. Both men and women come to believe that it is "natural" and "right" that women be in inferior positions. Men *feel completely supported in excluding* women, and up to a point, women feel that their exclusion is correct . . . .[80]

> To someone (male or female) who believes completely in the ideology of patriarchy, the entire concept of equal rights or women's liberation is a pretty difficult topic, sounding

---

[79] DeKeseredy & Scwartz 1998 pp94-95
[80] DeKeseredy & Schwartz 1998 pp95-97, emphasis mine

not only wrong but unnatural – literally, it goes against nature.... [81]

Family patriarchy refers to male control in domestic or intimate settings . . . . [It supports the abuse of women who violate the ideals of male power and control . . . in intimate relationships.] [82]

Relevant themes of this ideology are **an insistence on women's obedience, respect, loyalty, dependency, sexual access, and sexual fidelity** . . . . When these beliefs are **correlated with** whether the men . . . engage . . . in **physical, social or sexual abuse**, *the results . . . demonstrate that* **men who espouse patriarchal beliefs and attitudes are more likely to engage** *in* sexual, physical, and psychological **abuse** . . . .

American men who sexually assault their . . . [female] partners tend to hold sexist or traditional beliefs.[83]

Even as there is a demonstrable connection between rape myths and rape, there is a demonstrable connection between patriarchal myths and abuse.

Because of these ideologies, "the hardest part of any program for batterers" **is "convincing them that** *they* **ha[ve] done something wrong."**[84]

Many men harbor the sense that it is **their duty** (as proper men) **to keep** "their" houses in order and **"their" women in line.**

DeKeseredy & Schwartz found that, **for men with these ideologies**, "the more serious the dating relationship, the more

---

[81] ibid
[82] ibid
[83] ibid
[84] Jones 1980 p308, emphasis mine

likely men are to physically and sexually abuse their girlfriends or dating partners."[85]

Modern Western society is sprung out of an imperialist patriarchy. Its view of women developed in the midst of an all-encompassing ideology of ownership that included human slavery – Hebrew, Greek, Roman, Medieval, Colonial, Antebellum (North and South) – and more.

This ideology of ownership included one's wife (and children), as well as the ownership of one's indentured or enslaved servants.

We still speak in these terms.

Many men still acknowledge their desire to "acquire," not an equal companion, but a wife (and children) the way they acquire a car.

This disparity is demonstrated in the way we refer to marriage, in our very linguistics.

A man "takes" a wife. We unite them *man and wife* (not *man and woman*, or *wife and husband*).

A woman does not, commonly, *take a husband.*   We never unite them *woman and husband.*

He walks in from the front of the sanctuary or ceremonial setting, fully-grown and under his own escort.

She is – still – escorted in – like a child – by her closest father-figure (in recent times, sometimes, now, also with a mother/mother-figure),[86] and is *still **given away**.* She is walked up the aisle wearing white gauzy "gift-wrap," (historically) her

[85] DeKeseredy & Schwartz 1998 pp115-116
[86] A recent addition to our traditions, not undoing the historicity of the import of the father-figure to this moment

face veiled, and presented by a father-figure to a man who walked himself in from the side. Her husband (figuratively and/or literally) asks for, and is figuratively – and literally – given "her hand."

She neither asks for, nor receives, his.

She changes last name, introductory designation (and for some formal occasions, even her first name) at marriage (from Miss Jane *Woman* to Mrs. John *Man*), while his last, first, and introductory designations remain the same from cradle to grave (Mr. John *Man*).

And at their reception, the new unit is introduced ("for the first time anywhere") to friends, family, and guests as *Mr. and Mrs. Man.*[87]

And although she will do the physical work of carrying and giving birth to children (and historically, the bulk of the tending and parenting), they will commonly be given **only** his last name, on the idea that "the family unit" should share a single name – *his.*

It is *his* name that "should be" carried down through the generations so it does not die out.

And she worries, if she were to keep her own name that she would not have the same last name as her children. This, of course, should be accomplished by the mechanism of all of them wearing *his* name. (Even as she ignores the potentiality of not bearing the same name as her children through the mechanism of divorce, remarriage, and resuming maiden name or taking on the names of new husbands.)

We never introduce them as *Mrs. and Mr. Jane Woman, or Ms. and Mr. Jane Woman.*

---

[87] Stannard 1977

And we continue (again) to designate a woman's marital status in her introductory designation — the Miss and Mrs. custom — utilizing with less frequency, the martially undefined Ms.

Young women today still read books about how to get, and keep, a man, or magazines about how to please him sexually. Such literature is not generally produced for, or purchased by, men.

Many women still subscribe to and support the teachings of male dominant religions. The pastor often still preaches a wedding sermon including the scripture, *Wives, submit yourselves unto your own husbands . . . . The husband is the head of the wife, even as Christ is the head of the church . . . . As the church is subject unto Christ, so let the wives be to their own husbands in everything.*[88]

From the cultural trappings attached to wedding ceremonies, to the recognition that (more frequently) mothers cook and do laundry after a hard day at the office while (more often) fathers watch television,[89] to the storylines in books, television, and movies, little boys are continually fed the message that they are superior to females — served and pursued by females — and that one day, no matter how base or how vile, each one will have an individual woman/servant/lover of his own to attend to his domestic and sexual needs.[90]

Wife is still more *job description* than term of endearment, and the *job* of a wife is *to take care of a man* and *his* children. Women, often, still accept nearly one hundred percent of childcare responsibility,[91] and frequently give up income, independence, and career advancement for a prolonged season in order to stay home and raise "his" children, all the while imagining that the inclination to do so is a purely voluntary choice, free of sociological forces.

---

[88] Ephesians 5:22-24
[89] Working mothers still average 336 hours more (unpaid) household care work per year than working fathers (Hochschild & Machung 2012 p266); Louis 2007
[90] Mill 1986/1869
[91] 82% of the time, see Hochschild 2012

Meanwhile, every message society sends in a lifetime, increases (or is meant to increase) the male sense of privilege, and to increase female acquiescence to the purported necessity of relationship subservience.

This sense of male ownership is implicated in abuse.

> Battering husbands . . . are usually described by their wives as *extremely possessive* people. Usually they force their wives to stop working or going to school. They are cool or rude to family and friends, gradually cutting their wives off from social contacts. Some keep the car keys; some permanently sabotage their wives' cars. Others make sure their wives never have enough cash to go out. Some won't let their wives use the telephone . . . . Some lock their wives in; others follow them when they leave the house. Some make their wives literal prisoners."[92]

Patriarchal demand for control of individual women in intimate relationships is also transmitted through male-to-male social contacts. DeKeseredy and Schwartz write,

> [M]en who receive pro-abuse male peer support are more likely to adhere to the ideology of family patriarchy . . . . [P]artners [who] reject or fail to live up to the ideals of familial patriarchy . . . are regarded as appropriate targets of abuse by some male friends. They tell their friends to sexually, physically, and psychologically mistreat dating partners who challenge their patriarchal authority and/or who refuse to provide them with sexual gratification . . . .[93]

Media violence against women is another contributing factor in male supremacy. The very existence of films with violence against women, or violent pornography showcasing the sexual exploitation and oppression of women, contributes to the overall denigration of women, and increases the sense of male

---

[92] Jones 1980 p298, emphasis mine
[93] 1998 pp98-99

privilege. In it, sexist privilege is acted out, violence is sexualized, and the subjugation and pain of a supposed "inferior" are eroticized.

"[M]en learn to sexually objectify women through their exposure to pornographic media."[94]

It is remarkably incongruous that this encouragement to the physical oppression of women is not only marketable, but highly profitable, in a time and place where consciousness blessedly forbids the same kinds of encouragement to violence against other people groups, and even species.

> [T]here are many types of films that cannot be found . . . mostly because they do not exist. Rather than outright censorship, North Americans have managed to express their outright disgust and dismay at even the slightest hint of harm to animals in motion pictures . . . . [T]here are virtually no movies that show animals burned, dismembered, stabbed or shot to death, electrocuted, beaten or kicked, or raped. *We save these images for stories about women . . . .* Similarly, there are no movies available showing approvingly the mass execution of Jews, gypsies, and the mentally ill by the German Nazis in World War II. There are no proslavery pictures showing approvingly how whites needed to beat, starve, and torture African slaves to get them to behave "properly." Why is this the case? Essentially, it is because people in North America have shown a very high intolerance for pictures of this nature . . . . *Why is it that we have very firm reactions against seeing a sheep raped and then burned to death but find it appropriate, or at least a free speech issue, to allow films approvingly showing women being beaten, raped, and then burned to death?* . . . We are not arguing here for censorship . . . . We are, however, arguing that *in a better society, it would be*

---

[94] DeKeresedy & Schwartz 1998 p109; Katz 2000

considered morally reprehensible to show or attend certain types of films, just as it is now for non-documentary films about animal torture, proslavery violence, or Nazi killings.[95]

As Ann Jones remarks, "open violence against women, urged on by pornographic propaganda, is the last weapon, as it was the first, of male supremacy."[96]

~~~

The Only Present

N. D. Rosechild

It was the only present I got

for my 21st year.

You said I was a "woman of the world."

You thought I could handle it.

Crossing every cultural taboo,

you incested me.

It was your right,

in your own polluted mind.

But you wore more than one face.

At twenty-one you were my godfather, great-grand uncle, blood

at twelve you were my best friend's uncle

at seventeen, my friend's former boyfriend,

---

[95] (DeKeresedy & Schwartz 1998 pp146-147, emphasis mine
[96] 1980 p308

released to me with her blessing,

At thirteen, fourteen, fifteen, sixteen,

eighteen, nineteen, twenty

You were the boys who asked me for dates

the aging, married men hitting on jail bait

the face that made my pulse race across a
crowded room

the slime that made my skin crawl when you
sleezed up next to me

You were all men –

one man at a time –

And all men in one –

godfather, uncle, brother, stranger, friend.

Above all, you were consistent

from the cat calls on the road,

to the pickup lines in bars,

to the chase around the office desk,

to the wrestling in the cars,

to the husband with violent fantasies

beneath the sheets,

You let me know that I was good

for one thing,

and one thing alone.

You were the same perpetrator

   lurking behind every different face –

Never looking to love.

Never giving respect.

Only looking to take –

   that which might have been won

If you'd ever bothered with the heart.

~~~

Uncle Charlie
A Memoir

Charlie was blood to me. He was my paternal great-grandmother's brother. My dad had known him all his life. When my father was born, he was the age of a grandparent to him. And when I first met him, I was swathed in a little white gown, bonnet, and bootie set; and trundled into his sister's, my great-grandparents' parish church, The Ascension of Our Lord, in the archdiocese of Philadelphia, at Westmoreland and F Streets. My twin and I were recent releases from the hospital nursery, where we'd each been kept incubating until we'd attained the requisite weight of five pounds (four weeks for me and six for him). Charlie and his wife of forty years, Margaret, had agreed to stand up for us. As part of the ceremony, they swore before all assembled, their church, and the hosts of Heaven, that if my parents predeceased them, they would raise us for God in the rites of our Holy Mother, the Church.

I didn't see him often, but my parents would sometimes take my siblings and me to visit them, and my grandmother took me for an entire week the summer I turned twelve, and again, the summer I turned fourteen. I remember sitting on their enclosed front porch, listening to the three of them talk as people in the neighborhood passed by on the street out front. I remember Breyer's peach ice cream, and the sudden rush of spicy bubbles when they let the cap off a new bottle of Canada Dry ginger ale and poured me a glass, as they settled down to their evening shots of Crown Royal on the rocks. And I remember the cards they sent. Every Christmas and birthday, without fail, five dollars would arrive in the mail, which I would then dutifully turn over to my father (against my will) to be deposited in "my" savings account, that had his name on it, in trust for my 25th birthday. And when, in the same summer, my older brother and I got our drivers' licenses, one of our first big adventures was to brave the forbidding stretches of the Pennsylvania Turnpike, and the Schuylkill Expressway, between our home in Willow Grove and their home in Clifton Heights.

I didn't know them well, but I treasured the thought of them – my own godparents – separate from my sisters and brothers – my Aunt Margaret and Uncle Charlie – sweet old people who seemed just as ancient when I was newborn as they seemed unchanged when I was seventeen. God-fearing folk, who went to church regularly, and served as icons of the person I was expected to become.

Sometime after I left home, I got word that Aunt Margaret was changing. She was becoming "senile," and so my parents were taking her, and Uncle Charlie, in. They rearranged the bedrooms and gave my younger sisters' room to Uncle Charlie and Aunt Peg – the altered version of my icon, Aunt Margaret.

As he always had, Uncle Charlie went to mass every day, and he convinced my parents to join the Blue army – a Catholic dedication to praying the rosary daily for the salvation of the world. And other things happened.

I heard how Aunt Peg came running down the stairs and out onto the front lawn – naked (a psychic scar I'm sure my then-adolescent brothers still bear to this day) – because "that man" (her husband) wouldn't "leave her alone." And I heard how she made "tomato soup" with the ketchup.

And then, she died.

I wept at her funeral, overwhelmed with the hope she had gone someplace good, someplace better than here.

Weeks passed, and one day while I was visiting, Uncle Charlie asked me to come upstairs for a minute. He had something for me.

When I got to the doorway of their second floor room, he went over to their dresser and brought back Aunt Margaret's engagement ring. It had a raised rectangular platinum platform, with two filigree platinum hearts on each of the long sides, and two diamonds on top. *We didn't want to bury it with her,* he said, *and I know she'd want you to have it.* Tears filled my eyes.

I left deeply moved and blessed to have been thought of – to have had my love for her recognized in so significant a way.

A few weeks later, I was visiting my parents again, and Uncle Charlie did the same thing. He asked me to come upstairs for a minute, indicating that he had something for me. I knew he was clearing out her things, and I went with the expectation that he had discovered another of my godmother's possessions that he thought she would want me to have. When we reached the doorway of the room, suddenly, Charlie spun on his heel and planted his right hand firmly on my left breast and his mouth tightly on mine.

I knocked him off, and turned and ran down the stairs, out of the house, and to my car.

In a flood of tears, I drove to my best friend, Regina's, house.

I remember crying so hard I was having trouble seeing. I remember almost swerving into an occupied lane to the right of me, and ducking back into the left, realizing I hadn't even seen the other car.

Regina listened patiently as I unburdened my heart to her, encouraging me to tell my parents. I remember saying, *I can't tell. They won't believe me.*

He was the pillar of the church, the devotee of Mary, a member of the Blue Army, a daily communicant.

I remember, *I can't tell,* being followed with the thought, *I have to tell. I have younger sisters in that house.*

For the next few weeks, over and over in my head, I repeated those conflicting mantras – torn between the urgency to tell, and the surety that telling would protect no one, because I would not be believed.

About three weeks after Charlie molested me, my parents went away on vacation, leaving the oldest siblings, still living home, to watch the youngest.

The phone rang. On the other end, one of my younger sisters sobbed out my name, followed simply by the words, *Uncle Charlie . . . .*

I started for my car. A friend and roommate, there when the call came, seeing my condition, stepped in, took my keys and drove me. We picked up my sister and took her back to the safety of our home. There, we talked. We listened to her. We encouraged her. We fed her M&M's. We reconfirmed her worth. We assured her she had done nothing wrong.

She had been sitting on the couch. Charlie sat down next to her, which was not, at all, unusual. Suddenly, he leaned over and kissed her as he simultaneously tried to slip his hand beneath her shirt.

She, also, had broken away, and immediately, called.

When our parents got back, before we could get there, the siblings who had been babysitting described to them how I had swept in and spirited my sister away. As we entered the house, our parents sent her upstairs, to interrogate me. *How dared I have taken her away without their knowledge or permission?*

I began to explain what Charlie had done.

In unison, both parents and one brother, leapt to their feet as though stung, loudly exclaiming, *She's lying! You're lying!*

That attack was followed by Dad, pounding his fist on the table, demanding, *What did **you** tell her about sex, that she was able to make up this lie?*

My younger sister was the model of veracity. She had never been spanked, not because our parents didn't believe in spanking, but because at the first hint of adult (or older sibling) displeasure, she would hop up and comply.

Nothing about her deserved even the hint of a suggestion that she would lie. She may even, at least at that age, have been constitutionally incapable of lying.

And nothing about her accusation revealed any actual knowledge of sex.

From a purely physical perspective, what Charlie had done was minimal. He had not gotten far. She had gotten out of it. She had gotten away.

Charlie was called in for questioning. Looking me, defiantly, in the eyes, he stood and denied touching her.

Then, finally, I told what he had done to me just weeks before.

That he did not deny.

Instead, he justified.

In front of me, he responded, *But she lives on her own. She's a woman of the world!*

In that instant, he finished the betrayal he had begun by touching me, and for me, his humanity evaporated.

He showed me that, to him, his years as my godfather did not matter. His vow in the church, before God, with me – an infant in his arms – did not matter.

Neither did it matter to him that I was blood.

The 62 year difference in our ages – 83 to 21 – did not matter.

All that mattered was that I was female, and female in a way he felt made me questionable.

I had *left home*.

I *must* be *a whore, a slut*.

I must be indiscriminately sleeping with men.

Why else would I leave home?

I must be *promiscuous*.

I must be, "***that kind*** *of girl*."

Since I was, in his imagination, *dishonorable*, he had *the right* to take what I had not even conceived it possible to desire – or to give.

Unknown to us, at that moment, one of our younger brothers, Shawn, listened from the other side of the pocket door that separated living room from family room.

He heard our sister called a liar.

He heard Charlie deny what he had done to her and be believed.

He heard Charlie justify what he had done to me, and heard that no one, no parent, no sibling, raised a word of objection on my behalf.

He heard our parents stand with Charlie. For him, it confirmed that he had been right *NOT* to tell, not to speak out against his own abuser.

In the aftermath, our parents did not make Charlie move.

For the next year, he continued to live on, in our parents' home, unsupervised, with no protective measures taken to insure the safety of any child.

Each night, at the dinner table, refusing to be afraid, my younger sister bravely forced herself to continue to occupy her assigned seat – which had, all along, been right next to his.

And each night, during dinner, underneath the table, Uncle Charlie slipped her a five dollar bill.

Also each night, just after dinner, my sister would wait until our mother was busy washing dishes. Then she would march into the kitchen and poise, hand extended over the trash, until our mother turned around to see who was there. Then, in plain sight, she would drop the $5 bill into the trash.

Our mother never once asked, *Where did you get that money?* Or the obvious, *Why are you throwing money away?*

About a year later, of his own choice, Charlie decided to move out and move in with some relatives of Aunt Margaret's.

A short time later, of old age, he died.

I did not attend the funeral.

My younger sister had no choice.

Neither did my brother Shawn who listened that night from behind the door.

Until the day each of our parents died, whenever Charlie's name came up (often in the midst of a "funny" story about Aunt Peg's senility), one or both of them would look at my sister or me and say, *Well, you know, Charlie had diabetes, and the research shows diabetes can make you do all sorts of things.*

To which I invariably responded, *Diabetes can make you tired. Diabetes can make you cranky. Diabetes can make you confused. Diabetes can even make you comatose. But diabetes can never make you find a flat-chested prepubescent girl an attractive or appropriate sexual object. Diabetes cannot make you a pedophile. Neither can it make you commit incest.*

Shawn could not escape his perpetrator.

His was not an old man.

He was not able to knock him off or get away.

For him, the abuse began about the age of 5. The night he listened outside the living room door, he was 10. Confirmed in his intuition not to tell, for many more years the abuse continued on relentlessly, affecting every area of his life, even his grades. Teachers accused him of not paying attention or of daydreaming in class. In regard to schoolwork, they assumed he was lazy. In reality, he was unable to concentrate, out of the daily necessity of planning, scheming, searching for ways to keep out of the path of the abuser he knew was waiting.

Along the way, he learned to disassociate. Eventually, he developed traumatic amnesia, repressing the memories of the abuse, and the abuser (common psychological adaptations that allow the personality of the child to survive until they get old enough for the abuse to stop and it becomes safe to begin to process, what are finally, memories).

At 33, an incident in the life of one of his children brought the repressed memories flooding back. After that, Shawn only managed about an hour's sleep, long night after long night. He would wake, night terrors filling him with the reactions that attend the victims of childhood sexual abuse (the symptoms of post-traumatic stress (PTSD) and generalized panic disorder (GPD)).

He remembered how, when he was young enough to still take his bath with two younger brothers, he had gotten in trouble with our mother for marking himself up with a permanent marker. The older boy had drawn a bulls-eye around his genitals.

He remembered being raped orally, anally – behind the garage, in the basement, around the neighborhood.

He remembered this neighborhood boy – the best friend of a brother who was between us in age – tying a rope to his penis and leading him around as if it were a leash, yanking it painfully backward or sideways if Shawn in any way displeased him.

As the memories tormented him, he sought help. He found an online group for male survivors, and a therapist experienced at working with issues of sexual assault, and began the work of recovery.

At 36, he had surgery to correct the damage the rope leash had done to his penis.

Shawn is still working through the years of sexual terror. (Even now, at 49, the night terrors wake him several times a week. Recently, in the midst of a nightmare, he attacked his partner in his sleep . . . .)

As part of the process of his recovery, with the support of his therapist, he pondered the idea of approaching our parents and sharing his experiences. Finally, alone with Mom in her kitchen, he ventured to share his childhood experiences.

The first words from our mother's mouth were, *Why didn't you stop him?*

Later, at a diner, he told Dad. In response, Dad, dubiously, as though questioning whether or not the former 5-year-old Shawn had been a willing participant, paused, then drew out the words, 'He . . . *forced* . . . you?????? as a question.

Nadine Rosechild Sullivan, Ph.D., Rev.

SEXUAL ASSAULT OF CHILDREN

1. Statistics & Long-Term Effects

While all statistics on interpersonal and sexual violence are under-reported and under-prosecuted, and those against children particularly so, the statistics on the rape and molestation of children in this country must also be based on calculations made from reported cases and then extrapolated from there to our best educated estimate.

Our best estimates are that approximately 1 in 3 girls (1/4th of girls before age 14) and 1 in 6 boys are sexually assaulted (either molested or raped) before puberty.

It is certain that these figures are more likely to be an underestimation than an overestimation.

Also, almost all (90%) of adolescents, and 65-75% of adults, who barter or sell sex are victims of prior sexual assault or incest.[1]

Violence against children, sexual (and non-sexual), leaves children (and the adults they become) with a host of long-term, catastrophic, generally psychological, and sometimes physical effects, including:

- increased aggression
- lowered self-esteem
- emotional confusion
- anxiety and mood disorders
- antisocial behavior
- disrupted attachment
- posttraumatic stress disorder
- eating disorders
- sleep disorders
- dissociative identity disorder
- addictions

---

[1] RVA 2008

- sexual dysfunction
- and sometimes, sociopathy.[2]

These traumatic effects are made all the more long-term and catastrophic when the victims cannot protect themselves from ongoing physical contact with the perpetrator – when the violation just does not stop.

If it is a one-time event, the adolescent, or even the child, survivor may be able to work hir own way through the stages of grief over the trauma, eventually, find hirself[3] on solid footing again – emotionally.[4]

If, however, the perpetrator is an entrenched part of the child's life (a parent, guardian, caregiver, grandparent, uncle, aunt, older sibling, older cousin, neighbor, teacher, school personnel, coach, pastor, youth pastor, children's pastor. . .), the perpetrator has (or has the potential for) repeated access.

This ongoing lack of safety and control, the child's inability to escape physically, leaves only the possibility of escaping mentally (disassociating), which may lead, ultimately, to the child repressing the memories.

For the individual who CANNOT escape hir abuser, repression and denial are valuable survival tools.

However, the unconscious has a way of demanding that we process trauma. It demands that we categorize and make sense of our experience, even to the point of bringing it back in the night hours (or in any moment when our conscious control wanders, as in meditation or daydreaming) as internal visions (nightmares) of being chased or of the monster in the closet.

Or the unconscious may bring memories or feelings from the trauma back at the most inopportune time (like when we are

---

[2] Feuereisen & Pincus 2005; Chu & Bowman 2003; Ainscough & Toon 2000; Hunter 1990; Herman 1997; Marshall 2002; Greven 1990
[3] A gender-neutral pronoun, inclusive of both women and men
[4] This process could, of course, be vastly helped by a trustworthy and educated therapist.

participating voluntarily in desired, consensual, sexual encounters) and taint the experience of the present with the unprocessed burden of the past.

There is no way to sufficiently give voice to the depths of despair plumbed or the intensity of torment felt by those who struggle each day with the remnants of someone else's misplaced lust and sadism.[5]

2. The Pedophile Perpetrator

While women do commit assaults, sometimes against adults and sometimes against children, **whether the victim is female or male**, statistically, **the overwhelming majority of sexual perpetrators against children (between 85 and 95%)** are males[6] who **identify as heterosexual in their adult-to-adult relationships and attractions**.

Simply, males are more socialized to violence in our culture (and in most present-day cultures) than are women, and sexual assault is primarily an act of violence and control, not of love or passion.[7]

The fact is that **the sexual proclivities of pedophiles do not equate to their adult-to-adult sexual orientation**,[8] and, statistically, adult males who identify as gay are *less likely* than adult males who identify as heterosexuals to be pedophiles.[9]

Adult-to-adult sexual orientation – who a person is attracted to among adults – has no bearing on whether or not one has fantasies of, or will act to violate, children sexually.

---

[5] I say sadism, because I believe that any perpetrator of average intelligence must be aware that their victims are being traumatized, and thus, presses forward to meet their own needs despite the horror/shock/frozenness on the face of their victim/s.

[6] Katz 2000

[7] ibid

[8] Clark 2006; Murray 2000

[9] Stevenson 2000; Clark 2006; Murray 2000

Neither is the biological sex of a child victim an indicator of the adult-to-adult sexual orientation of those who assault them – and therefore, the sex of the victim should not be used as shorthand, or as a label, for the adult-to-adult sexual orientation of assailants.

Molesting/raping little girls does not indicate that a male perpetrator is heterosexual in his adult-to-adult sexual/affectional orientation.

And molesting/raping little boys does not indicate that a male perpetrator is homosexual in his adult-to-adult sexual/affectional orientation.

Logically, who one likes to harm is not an indicator of who one loves (as harm is not love at all).

Instead, being a sexual assailant against defenseless children is an indication of profound difficulty in the perpetrator's sense of self that likely leads to difficulties in adult-to-adult interactions and relationships. Being a sexual assailant is an indication that something is broken in the violator's capacity to love – to develop healthy consensual adult attachments – as perpetration is about power and dominance, and indicates an inability to feel empathy for the pain and vulnerability of one's victim.

Therefore, violating a child is certainly *not* an enactment of adult sexual orientation itself – straight or gay.

In fact, it is not "the gender of the child" that is important as an indicator of whom a particular perpetrator will seek to harm. Instead, researchers have found that "*age, immaturity, lack of power, [and] vulnerability*" are primary indicators of whom is likely to become a victim.[10]

It is the helplessness of the child against the assault – the sadistic violation of innocence – that is the sexual turn-on – not specifically the gender of the child.

---

[10] Clark 2006, emphasis mine; see also: Murray 2000

And since most children are (by age and physical size alone) vulnerable, it is the likelihood of the child's silence, the lack of repercussions, and the opportunity – or *ease of access* – that play out as key in determining who will be targeted.

Both ease of access and powerlessness play a stronger role in perpetrators' choices than does the gender of their victims.

~~~

The frequencies with which men molest boys as opposed to girls does not reflect motive as much as it does opportunity.

In our culture, adult men have much more unsupervised access to boys than they do to girls.

The surprise then is not that there are so many reports of men molesting boys,

[but] rather that girls [still] outnumber boys as victims by a factor of two.

The frequency of same-sex versus opposite-sex molestations [may reflect the] differential access of adult men to boys and girls, rather than the sexual orientations of the molesters.

Stephen Clark[11]

~~~

Statistically, it has not been/is not "***gay*** priests" who perpetrate/d against little boys.

And, difficult (and unrealistic) as celibacy may be as a discipline, it is not celibacy[12] itself that drives priests to assault

---

[11] Clark 2006; Murray 2000
[12] Sanday 1991

children. (A non-pedophile, having a difficult time keeping a vow of celibacy, would seek out an adult partner – there are any number of options that spring to mind – not commit an act of emotional/physical/sexual violence against a child.)

The problem in the Catholic church has not been males who are gay (defined as attracted adult-to-adult to other grown males) – who somehow couldn't tell the difference between a prepubescent child and a man.

The problem in the Catholic church, and in our society as a whole, has been pedophiles (defined here as individuals with a broken conscience, because they have been damaged in some way that blinds them to (or causes them to get off on) the terror of children who are sexually traumatized, who (while generally identifying as straight and often being heterosexually-married) fantasize about – and give themselves permission to act out against – children (a defenseless population with neither the cognitive development required to give consent nor the physical size and prowess necessary to enforce a "no").

And the further problem in the Catholic church is the same one we have had in society at large – turning away from the pain and the truth of children and defending and/or justifying the adult who perpetrated – sweeping it all under the carpet in the hopes it will just go away. Society-wide, we have moved "Uncle Charlie" around, the same way the Catholic church has moved pedophile priests from parish to parish.

So, while it is likely that same-sex spaces (the priesthood, the convent, the military, etc.) attract proportionally-higher numbers of same-sex attracted people (gay men or lesbians) than do mixed-sex spaces, overwhelmingly, it is not priests who identify as same-sex attracted in their adult-to-adult interactions who have been the main perpetrators against prepubescent boys in Catholic church settings. It is pedophiles – those who perpetrate against children who have not reached puberty.

The use of boys by pedophile priests has, however, been high because, "historically, priests have had much greater unsupervised access to young boys than to young girls. Until fairly recently, girls did not serve [the altar like] altar "boys" and priests also ran boys-only youth groups."[13]

~~~

It's not just women who will benefit if men's lives are transformed. In fact, while **men commit a shameful level of violence against women in our society (24%),** statistically speaking, **the major victims of men's violence are other males.**

There are millions of male trauma survivors walking around today – men who were bullied as adolescents or abused physically or sexually as children. Thousands more men and boys are murdered or assaulted every year – **usually by other men.**

So men have a stake in dealing with these problems, and not just those of us who've been victims, but also, those men who are violent or who've taken on the Tough Guise. They do so, also, **at the expense of their emotional and relational lives.**"

Jackson Katz[14]

~~~

13 Clark 2006
14 Katz 2000

3. Body Betrayal & a Sense of Internal Psychological Complicity

Issues of significance for children who are raped or molested include not being believed – as for the sister in *Uncle Charlie* – or being expected to be invulnerable[15] – as for the brother in the same retelling.

Further issues include the adaptive survival response of disassociation, especially when perpetration is not a one-time event, but an ongoing, inescapable fact of life, followed by the repression (instead of the processing) of the memories.

Also, children who are sexually assaulted are being prematurely sexualized and may become confused if their bodies begin to respond to sexual touch, especially as they approach puberty.

Body betrayal is the pleasurable physical response of the child's nerve endings to being touched, sometimes leading to erection, lubrication, perhaps even physical orgasm.[16] Genital nerve endings are specialized and even when the mind or emotions are screaming or in shock,[17] the nerve endings themselves respond to touch – deepening a child's sense of complicity.

BUT **BODY BETRAYAL IS NEVER CONSENT.**

---

[15] In this case, invulnerability equals the expectation that the child be able to resist the interaction even when the perpetrator is markedly different in body size and strength

[16] It can be particularly damaging and confusing when it is during body betrayal that a victim first experiences the physiological response of orgasm.

[17] As former talk show host, Oprah Winfrey, has pointed out, many times, in her on-air discussions of her childhood experiences with assault.

Body betrayal is not an indication that the child wants the abuse.

It is, instead, a physiologic response – not a psychological or emotional response – to physical stimulation.

In working with clients who have suffered abuse in their childhoods (physical, emotional, verbal, and/or sexual), it has become clear that, even as tiny infants, we may internalize a sense of complicity when we are harmed.

It complicates our relationship with our own sexuality, to have first learned sexual excitement or orgasm through (or later connected them to) abuse.

I have had occasion to guide clients, in a deeply relaxed meditative state, back into their sense of self in childhood, and it appears that no matter what age we are, we have a sense of self as an active agent. When I have regressed survivors of childhood trauma back to the time of traumatization, they report feeling like they should have been able to stop the violence.

One exercise is to regress the survivor back to a time when they were very little and to have them imagine their adult self comforting and consoling their child self. I have had clients tell me, in that space, that they cannot pick up or hug or comfort the child self *"because that child is bad."* In the space of memory, they hold the sense that even a child as young as infancy – only months old – should have been able to stop hirself from being violated. They will report things like, *"I didn't say "No.""* And I will ask, *"How old were you?"* And they will report ages like, *"Two-years-old"* or *"So young I couldn't stand up yet in my crib."* And I will ask, *"How could you have stopped it?"* And they will exclaim, *"I still should have tried."*

These clients reveal a truth about human consciousness. No matter what age I am, I feel – at core – essentially the same. I feel now, essentially the same as I did at 35 or 15 or 5. And hence, at least retrospectively, I attach to my child self the same sense of agency that I have now – that I should have been able to be good enough to stop my parent from beating me or resistant enough to stop the perpetrator from sexually violating me – and this, despite the concrete fact that it is impossible for a child to resist a determined older/stronger/manipulative perpetrator.

My sister and I were able to physically resist Uncle Charlie, in large measure, because of the frailty of his age.

Most perpetrators are younger and more physically fit.

Many perpetrators groom their victims, seeking to build a bond of emotional attachment or sympathy or "specialness" that conditions the child to the abuse before it happens.

In *Uncle Charlie*, the little sister's life was full. She was not the lonely child on the edge of the herd who could be induced to cooperation based on a need for attention.

And Uncle Charlie did not have the persona to pull off being threatening. Many perpetrators threaten harm to a child's self – or other family members or loved ones – and thus, induce compliance, because there is something in their eyes or demeanor that convinces the child that this assailant will, indeed, harm them (beyond the assault) or their loved ones if they don't acquiesce.

Adults and adolescents who assault children use a range of techniques to gain access and insure silence. Uncle Charlie relied on the element of surprise, and while the little sister was empowered by the older sister's support, the older sister was still silent too long. The neighborhood boy induced compliance in the little brother because he was believably sadistic.

Moving from victim to survivor is a process, the core of which is coming to affirm one's own position in the interaction/s. In general, it requires recovering and processing the memories. And specifically, the path to healing includes coming to the recognition that – at least in those initial interactions – it was not the child who committed the assault – it

144

was not the child who set out to hurt another – and thus, the (now grown) child is not the one who should be ashamed about that/those interactions.

Along with body betrayal, and the internalization of a sense of complicity (based on a range of circumstances, like "not saying no" or not "fighting back") another area of confusion for many children who are prematurely sexualized is that, by the time they approach adolescence (if not earlier), they may begin to seek out sexual contact – even from a former perpetrator.

Just at the point when they can (and feel they "should") physically stop the perpetrator, some children may begin to initiate sexual contact.

This, also, is not consent.

It is the aftermath of their abuse.

In such a moment, their adolescent hormones are beginning to kick in and their bodies are getting old enough to experience age-appropriate desire, but their minds have come to slot this activity into categories that may lead them to seek out more of that which they have already known.

Nevertheless, victims can become survivors.

Although doing so requires the work of confronting and processing the pain, with a sympathetic therapist educated in the empowerment of survivors, it is very possible to work through the past, rebuild one's sense of self, come to understand that (at least initially) you were not the assailant, and finally, truly become someone who has come out on the other end – survived – and reclaimed hir own essence.

Watched
A Male Retelling

My dad left his magazines around. I was good with that! Well, not really "around." More like hidden in the back of his closet, but they did just stand there, under his dress slacks and sport coats, like a little, leaning, mini Tower of Pisa. It was great to sneak in there and scan them, either by myself or with Jeff, the neighbor next door. Whenever both of my parents went to work, and my sister locked herself in her room to talk on the phone *in private*, Jeff would come over, and we would go through the stack in the closet, and then, through my parents' night tables and dresser drawers.

Like detectives on a case, we would look for grown-up things.

We found one of those pink flesh-colored, hard plastic, ribbed-bottomed, "back" massagers you could buy in the drugstore, the kind that took 2 C batteries and had a picture of a flowing-haired woman on the box holding the pointed top to her left shoulder muscle. But we had no idea what you did with it, in part, because the picture misled us.

In the same drawer, I saw my first condom.

Again, for a little while, we drew a blank, though the shape kind of gave us an idea.

But we knew what we wanted to do with those pictures. When the stack got tall enough, we would each slip one magazine out. (I hid mine under my mattress, but my mom found it when she made the bed, and yelled at my father so long, he left for the bar and didn't come home 'til after dinner.)

We discovered masturbation.

We didn't really say much about it, but if one of us slept over the other's house, we would pull out the hidden magazine, look awhile, and then both pretend to go to sleep. In a few minutes, I could hear Jeff making breathing noises on the mat on the floor where he slept, and his sleeping bag started moving.

I looked up to my dad.

We weren't what you'd call close. He worked a lot, and when he was around, he sort of just huffed and puffed and ate.

He had trouble breathing, and he never said much more to me than, "Hey, Man. How ya doing?" But having him live there was important.

I was not like other kids who'd lost their dad.

And I figured anything he did was something I should do too. I thought it was heroic, how hard he worked, even when he clearly didn't feel good, and I wanted to know all he knew about those pictures, and the adult stuff in the night tables, and women.

He swung shifts and days.

Sometimes, if his day off from work fell on a weekend, he would take me out with him – just us two guys. (Twice, he even took me to the shore by himself. He got in trouble with my mom for my sunburn that day.) But always, we'd end up at a bar part way across town where everyone seemed to know him, and he bought a round of beers for a couple of buddies and a woman or two. Afterward, he'd tell me, "Don't tell Mommy about the broads," and it would be our own little secret.

As I got to be about twelve or thirteen, a couple of times, when Mom was working and my sister was out with her friends, he would suggest that I see if Jeff were around and invite him over. If Jeff could come over, he'd watch us play ball, then suggest we take a shower – to cool off.

One time, when we went to take the shower, quietly, Dad just let himself into the bathroom. (We never locked doors in our house, so I didn't think much about it.) He said he had to take a dump, and our house only had one bathroom.

147

But the shower door was glass, and except for the steam, it was clear. I glanced over at him sitting there. Like the water from the shower head, I was swept with the oddest sensation, deep in my stomach. He was fondling his own erection.

I distracted Jeff and pretended not to notice until Dad moaned a couple of times and left.

I stopped going with him on weekends after that.

After that, I just got too busy with other stuff.

~~~

Showing Off

A Female Retelling

I don't really think of my parents as abusers.

In my family it seemed like everyone was just . . . relaxed . . . .

No one was concerned with modesty.

Whatever you had, everyone saw it. And whatever you had, someone was likely to reach out and grab it. They just pinched you on your ass or tweaked you on your tit as you walked by.

Overall, I wasn't sure there was anything wrong with that. It was all I knew. But pretty much, I just wanted to be left alone. I didn't like being grabbed, or seeing, or being seen.

The feeling was that your safety *was all on you.* You should know well enough to stay away, far away, especially from certain uncles. And on a bad day, maybe even from Aunt Rose. It was just on you.

No one really pinned you anywhere, but right in front of everyone, someone might just try to cop a feel.

It was irritating and humiliating and once in a while, it hurt when an uncle twisted a nipple.

And along with the general touchy-feely-ness, there was the overall nakedness.

I had two sisters, and even as we got older, our parents would just come out of the shower naked and stroll down the hall to their bedroom to get dressed.

I remember when we were really little, there was at least one time (I guess our mom wasn't home), when our dad just unzipped his drawers and started chasing us three girls around the room with his dingle hanging out. It was all limp, and everything. We were giggling. I remember how it flapped as he trotted behind us. I don't think he caught us, and I don't think anything more happened.

But there was also the time I thought he peed in front of us while he was sitting on the living room couch. I realized later, at about 16, that it wasn't pee. It dawned on me as I watched my boyfriend come, and it just kinda' turned my stomach.

You shouldn't have a memory of your dad's face and body like that, doing that, making those expressions, those noises. It fucks you up.

But my mom is what I wonder about now.

She used to sit on the toilet, with the bathroom door wide open. And she sat in such a way you could see it all. She sat leaning way far back, exposing herself, and then she'd call us by name, one by one. Those would be the times she'd choose to comb out our hair or approve our outfit for church.

She never touched us, but I know what she looks like down there.

I know what she looks like naked, her and my dad. And I know what he looks like coming.

And I know what she looks like, leaning back, legs open.

None of these images work to my advantage when I try to make love with my partner.

SEXUAL ASSAULT & HARASSMENT OF ADOLESCENTS

Rape does not stop, but the rates decrease for males with mid-to-late adolescence. Older teen boys often gain enough physical size and strength with puberty to resist the single assailant. Thus, for the perpetrator, ease of access to the male victim markedly diminishes.

Yet, males do continue to be raped, and not just in prisons. With 95% of violence being perpetrated by other males, [1] not just women, but, men also are at great risk of violence from other men.

Seventy-six percent of overall male violence is male-on-male,[2] and sometimes that violence is enacted sexually. Also, while this does not only occur to men who are perceived to be gay – or in some other way gender nonconforming – there is a significantly increased likelihood of males being raped if they are perceived to be gay or gender variant.[3]

Also, even as a male child can be sexually assaulted by an adult female perpetrator, so too can a male adolescent.

In teaching on rape in college human sexuality classes, I am often honored by my students with their own stories – either in class or on paper. I have heard more than one story of adolescent males being sexually assaulted.

Many readers may feel that a male cannot be raped by a female – even an underaged teen male and an older female. A

---

[1] Katz 2000

[2] ibid

[3] Males make up 10% of all rape victims (National Center for Victims of Crime 2011; RAINN 2006); "the most common type of male-to-male rape is the rape of a man who is perceived to be gay by a heterosexual man" (atvp.org 2012 (Jan16) [accessed])

common cultural response is that the adolescent male, assaulted by an older female, simply "got lucky."[4]

Yet, that is often not the way the adolescent male victim feels.

And it is not the way the same scenario, enacted against an underaged girl, is viewed.[5] Reverse the gender, and society has no doubt that the scenario was – at least statutory – rape.

And yet, young males may be left feeling just as violated, after the fact, as the early teen girl in the retelling, *My Best Friend's Uncle.*

The complication of male body betrayal, the fact of experiencing an erection in the midst of an uninvited and unwelcome violation, is never an indication that the victim's mind and heart is not screaming.

1. The Hebophile Perpetrator

So, yes, overall, the rates of sexual assault go down for males with the advance of puberty.

Not so for females.

In our youth-deifying[6] culture, as the bodies of adolescent girls become anatomically-mature, even though their minds are not yet in a stage of psychological development that would permit *fully-cognizant,* adult-to-adult, *consent,* they become the prime and common target of sexual solicitation by heterosexual *adult* men.

They also become a prime target of sexual harassment. Walking down the street – rural, urban, or suburban – takes on a new level of risk. Simply mention sexual harassment to a class of twenty-something, undergraduate females, and they all get the

---

[4] as when female teachers make the news for perpetrating against male students
[5] assaulted by an older boy or man
[6] and often, female-denigrating

shared experience of feeling unsafe on the street. Almost all have similar stories to tell – of walking past construction sites, of trying to catch a bus, of walking a short distance from home to school or work or to visit a friend – and being made to feel like an object on display for the sexual gratification of uninvited, often inappropriately older, males.

Hebophilia[7] – the sexual objectification and misuse of adolescents – is distinct from pedophilia in that the victim/object has developed an adult-like body. The perpetrator is not a pedophile, attracted to the undeveloped body of a child,[8] but he is a perpetrator nonetheless, because the object of his often-overt and demonstrated sexual attention is still adolescent – existing in that netherworld between childhood and adulthood in which the mind is not yet sufficiently developed (has not yet passed through sufficient psychological stages of development) to make a free choice to consent to sexual interaction with one who is already an adult.

Hebophilia is the common experience of underaged adolescent girls. Grown men – often middle-aged and married, often old enough to be their fathers or even grandfathers – violate the teen girl's sense of age propriety to make sexual suggestions, advances, or assaults – presumably attracted to the (youthful) womanliness of their developing bodies, forgetting that their minds and expectations are not yet grown – and perhaps in personal denial about the actual differences in their ages.

It is the experience of the older sister in *Uncle Charlie*. It is arguably the experience in *My Best Friend's Uncle*.

It is the experience, as well, in the following female memoirs and retellings: *Street Walking, Around the Desk, Shattered,* and *I'm Gonna Get What I Came For.*

---

[7] "pubescent but below the age of consent" (Clark 2006 pp13-16)
[8] Pedophilia is defined by the age of the victim – younger than puberty – therefore, physically and mentally a child.

It is so commonly experienced by teenage females (so commonly practiced by adult males who do not think of it as a form of pedophilia), that, for many girls who were protected until their teens, it forms the substructure of an increasing sense of not being safe in the world.

It is also the experience, along with rape, of the following male retellings, *Climbing on Top* and *Internet Predator.*

~~~

Street Walking
A Memoir

From the time we were eleven, Rita and I walked the street. We walked out of desperation. We walked out of boredom. We walked to the *Five and Dime.*

Young as we were, we should have been safe. Young as we were, we had no idea there was anyone in our world to hurt us.

There was nothing else to do, other than watch a little television or dance to the Motown playing on local pop radio. And much as we loved those two pastimes, they got old.

Oh, and we also told each other stories. We made up adventures in which we were female private eyes or secret agents, hunting down criminals and jet-setting around the globe.

So we walked the street. Every possible Saturday or summer afternoon, after our morning housecleaning chores were done to our mothers' satisfactions, we begged change from our mother's aprons and walked the mile to the W. T. Grant on York Road to share a plate of French fries.

It was exciting stuff, sharing French fries!

Maybe some of the high school boys lingering over by women's lingerie would notice us.

Or maybe we would troll the aisles for paperbacks or record albums.

Sometimes I longed (and looked) for a particular fountain pen or unique paper notepad, though generally (unless we had had a great haul from babysitting), there was little actual shopping we could do, and we had to content ourselves with the fries.

As we got a little older, we finagled ways to get just enough cash to split a pack of cigarettes (I took to stealthily lifting nickels from my father's dresser. He always noticed but was never sure who to blame.). And we would spend even more time on the street, so we could enjoy our illegal and parentally-unapproved activity.

And sometimes we had somewhere to go, like our weekly guitar lessons, or a trip to the store for cans of the liquid diet drink, Metrical, for my mother or an extra pound of provolone for Rita's.

Once, for the freedom of the time out of the house, we walked about 40 minutes from Rita's house in Warminster to my then-boyfriend Jay's house in Hatboro (a total of about 3 miles). But when we got there, he exclaimed, "What the fuck are you doing here?" and I broke up with him on the spot, which made the walk home much less exciting (if more animated and rapid) than the walk there.

But street walking was not safe.

Not even in our sheltered and upwardly-mobile suburb.

We didn't know it when we first undertook the activity, but we were developing.

Uninvited, our breasts were growing.

One day, they just got sore. And then they got achy. And then the nipples got painfully tender. And then our shirts got full, and we needed bras and didn't know how to get them – 'til the day my father walked me into that same W. T. Grant's, right past the 8th and 9th grade boys who hung by women's lingerie, and up to an open bin of brassieres – only to hold one up in front of me and ask, "Do you think this is the right size?"

Mercifully, I was saved by a perceptive, if frumpy and middle-aged, saleswoman who swooped in and spirited me away to a private dressing room – away from the tittering teenage boys – where she stripped me down and "fitted me" (still unbearable). Finally, she told my father, "Buy her this one," and sent us on our way.

Little by little, we were turning – physically – from girls into women, but our minds were not racing ahead.

Like our bodies, they were experiencing consistent gradual change.

Yet, suddenly men were everywhere, as if coming out of the proverbial woodwork. They began, at every turn, to treat us as though our bodies were fully adult – though in actuality, our bodies were quite new to us and we were quite new to our bodies.

But, like a calendar page had flipped, the sexual harassment began.

It began while walking to W. T. Grant's.

It began with the horns honking.

Initially, we were safe as I headed from my house on Henry to her house on Gibson, or as we made our way from her house on Gibson up Cypress to York Road. But we, demonstrably, were no longer safe walking on York Road.

Suddenly, it seemed that car after passing car blew its horn or called out words that blew away on the wind generated by the vehicles' forward motion.

At first, we didn't know what to make of it.

But then, one day as we strode along York Road, one of the cars blowing its horn turned sharply into a driveway in front of us, cutting off our path, and its driver began to get out, entreating us to get in.

We ran around his road block, and he backed out and sped off, but our sense of safety was shaken.

As it was for me, again, another day, on Cypress Road.

I was walking alone that day, when a driver, busily craning his neck to watch my derriere, drove up onto a neighbor's front yard, rutting the grass and barely missing the mailbox.

And then, I moved to the city, where walking past a construction site brought a cacophony of voices hollering obscenities, or men slowed their cars on Broad Street just enough for me to hear their shouted enticement, *Hey, Baby! Wanna' fuck?* To which I always wanted, but never got the chance, to respond, *Wanna' know my name FIRST?*

And years later, there was the effect of pregnancy and lactation, during which, even walking the inside of a store or restaurant became running the gauntlet of the male gaze.[9] Or the friends' husbands, who would hold conversation with me while talking to my chest and not my eyes – a situation I always longed to address by stating, *Those aren't my eyes. I'm up here.*

In general, I refrained.

I was trained to social decorum.

I was concerned for my already-mortified friend.

And then, there were the men in the workplace – the ones who chased me around the desk – the ones with the power to promote or to fire me – the ones who made me quit.

---

[9] Kaplan 1990

Inside or out, street walking was not safe in this female body, and too, too many older men couldn't tell a teen from a twenty – or didn't care to try.

Maybe they never knew how old, and consequently, grossly unattractive, they looked . . . to me . . . .

~~~

Around the Desk
A Memoir

The year was 1971. As is often the case, there was something of a recession on. I had determined I wanted to go to college. I knew one thing. I didn't want to use marriage as a means to a financial future. I wanted a relationship to be a relationship, not an economic arrangement.

In grade school, once a year the parish priest would visit the usually female-run classroom.

At Nativity of Our Lord, we were segregated by gender. We had separate play yards for males and females. In the classroom, the boys sat in front, arranged shortest to tallest (so they could all see the blackboard), and the females sat in the back, also shortest to tallest – so that the shortest girls sat just behind the tallest boys. No one cared if short girls could see the board.

When the Father made his annual visit, he invariably looked at a handful of representative boys and asked, "*What do you want to be when you grow up?*"

He never asked a single girl. (Neither did anyone else, even in the more personal world of my family.) Instead he looked at the girls, en masse, and declared, "*When you grow up, you'll be wives and mothers, unless, of course, you have a vocation [to the convent].*"

At the (then, all-girls) Archbishop Wood High School, we were encouraged to no more. We were all assigned our state requisite math, science, and history courses, and if we showed any love or aptitude for the hard sciences, we were encouraged along the college track. But the college track was relatively, statistically, underpopulated, with what seemed to be mostly the geekier girls from the National Honor Society.

The vast majority of us were tracked toward business, on the idea that we should be minimally-employable while we waited for Mr. Right.

In the business track, we all took typing.

Beyond that, our only choice was between stenography (Gregg Shorthand) and transcription (Dictaphone).

It is an unfair underestimation, but it often feels like the only thing I learned those four years was to type without looking at the paper or the keys, lest the wrath of the typing nun fall hard on my bare knuckles through the wood of her yardstick.

Thanks to Wood, I can still type with my eyes closed, though I was only ever fast or accurate enough for the typing pool. Not executive secretary material.

So I had grown up with the social expectation that – like my mother and grandmothers before me – some future man's financial coattail was the tail of the comet I should ride to sustenance for myself and my children and my security for old age.

I don't recall that I gave that expectation much thought, at least, until the end of high school.

Instead, I turned my grade school and high school attentions to inventive ways to get out of doing my homework, or to escaping the boredom of my mundane life through the adventures to be found in novels, or to writing love poetry – reams and reams of love poetry.

I was so devoted to homework avoidance, that by the end of high school, my GPA was an underwhelming 2.5 – indubitably unworthy of any form of scholarship.

Nevertheless, I had discovered feminist literature: the reclaimed histories of great women of the past and the tracts and manifestos of a new generation of feminist activists and theoreticians, and I had come to a critique of the marriage for money model.

Suddenly, belatedly, I wanted a career, and I wanted to go to college. So, I dutifully took my SAT's and, with anticipation, immersed myself in college catalogs and filled out my application forms.

My father was our family mailman. It was to him that we gave all outgoing letters and from him that we received such mail as came in. As I made my choices and finished my college applications, I gave them to him to mail, then went back to my reading on the living room couch. He rose, importantly, from his workstation at the dining room table and strode to the couch.

He cleared his throat in the way he always did before making an ex cathedra pronouncement from the papal chair of Cornelius.

No doubt, I looked up as he stood, towering over me.

With a pregnant pause between each sentence, he declared,

I'll mail these for you, but you need to know this.

Your brothers need my help. They'll have families to support someday.

But you're a girl. You'll get married and have children.

You needed your education until now, because you may become the mother of sons, but college, for a girl, would be a waste of my money. It would not be a sound investment.

I'll mail these for you, if you want me to, but you have to understand. You'll have to work to pay the tuition. You don't have the grades for a scholarship, and I make too much money for you to get financial aid.

Understand, I won't even lend you the money.

My protests about not wanting to marry for subsistence, about wanting a career, about needing a degree in literature or writing, fell into his grandmother's antique oriental carpet.

And so, he mailed my applications, and I set about trying to earn my own college tuition.

From the schools that accepted me, I chose between the two local (and more-affordable) state schools, so I could save money by living off campus – at home.

And I hit the pavement, job hunting with a vengeance, to earn my tuition for my freshman year at Penn State Ogontz.[10]

The want ads, like my grade school play yards and my high school itself, were also sex-segregated. Separate columns declared, *Help Wanted, Male* and *Help Wanted, Female.* And the pay differential was huge!

My brother, one year ahead of me and already at Temple University, had found a job moving furniture and driving a moving truck. He was able, easily, to afford his in-state tuition and more.

The jobs in the female column paid poorly.

With my skill set, after a few mediocre results on the typing tests, the best I found was waitressing, cleaning, or doing credit collections at a local tire store.

I took credit collections.

I averaged $25 a week.

---

[10] now Penn State *Abington*

At first, the owner scheduled me during normal business hours, and I gained a reputation for being very successful at collections. I was so understanding of customers' misfortunes – that they ended up wanting to pay me and, often, sent someone around with a partial payment or cut a check for the mail as soon as they got off the phone.

As the weeks passed, under the guise of needing me to take shorthand, the boss began to call for me to join him in his office. Soon I was listening to his stories about his wife, who apparently, because she was pregnant, no longer "gave him any."

And then, as the air filled with the impending sense that he was about to make his move, I found myself navigating around the desk in his cramped, oily-tire smelling office, to reposition myself in a safer location.

Deftly, I would turn the conversation back to the business letter at hand, then scoot out of his office and back to my more open cubicle to type the letter that had only been a ruse to command my presence in his office.

One day, when I arrived on schedule, the store was closed.

The boss, however, was there, and I was to go on and make my collection calls as usual. A short time later, he said he had a business meeting to attend, just a few towns up the road, and he would need a stenographer for the meeting. Despite my hesitation, I got into his car.

We drove about an hour, when he turned into a motel. He led the way to a conference room on site.

I recall, there was an actual meeting. And I did take shorthand.

I began to let my guard down.

As the meeting broke up, we left along the second floor outside walkway.

Suddenly, he stopped, inserted a key in a lock to his left, and gripping my arm, stepped inside a standard bedroom.

I guess I let myself be pulled inside. I remember being outside. I know I ended up inside. I'm not sure I took the steps forward. It's possible I was lightly dragged, but I was inside when the door closed behind him.

Working swiftly, he began to pull off his coat and tie and shirt. He should not have worked quickly.

I remember his face bore a striking resemblance to Paul Sorvino and his body to the height and girth of Danny DeVito.

I remember the protruding, round, white, calcium deposits that outlined the semi-circles just below each of his puffy lower lids, and the Robin Williams-like hairiness of his upper torso and back, with which I was suddenly – dramatically – confronted.

He was talking about his wife again, and starting to wrestle with my clothes.

I backed away.

So did he.

He lay across the bed, talking. He was talking about my job, about my plans for college, about my need for tuition money.

He undid his zipper. His penis sprang free, erect within its nest of hair.

I remember thinking, *I can't do this.*

I remember thinking, *I'm gonna' lose my job.*

I remember thinking, *I could never be a prostitute. I just can't.*

I was, still, all but a virgin.

I remember thinking, *I have a weak stomach. I can't sleep with someone who repulses me. I can't sleep with him for this job, for money.*

I remember thinking, *I'm seventeen. He's forty-five!*

I told him to take me home.

He got up and, in a desperate attempt to persuade me, pressed up against me, trying to get me, *at least*, to *give him a blow job*. I walked to the door. I guess I should be grateful he let me.

He zippered his pants, gathered his shirt and coat, and followed me out into the sunlight. Silently, he followed me down the walkway, down the concrete and steel stairs to the parking lot, back to his car. On the ride back to the tire store, two or three times, he grabbed my hand to put it on his crotch. I wrenched it back and pressed myself hard against the far door.

I didn't exactly quit. I never gave two weeks' notice. I never called out either. I just never went back.

I never transcribed the shorthand from that business meeting or typed the minutes.

At home, no one asked why I didn't go to the tire store anymore.

Later, when the tuition came due for my third trimester at Penn State Ogontz, I went to my parents' room, and stated simply, *Mom, Dad, I have to drop out of school.*

Dad was silent.

Mom answered, suddenly wistful, like a bird had sung in the distance through the open window, *As long as you go back someday.*

The next day, Dad came home with a new Cadillac.

Someday didn't come for 26 years.

~~~

Climbing on Top

A Male Retelling

As a kid, my older brother was my idol. My attachment wasn't hurt any by the beers he gave me when Mom wasn't home. I would take two, down them like someone was gonna hijack them, then head back to my room to play. I was a gamer. I played every possible waking moment.

I kicked ass at *Halo*.

One night, when I had gotten to be about 13, I was back in my room, feeling the beers from his stash, trying to kick ass and laughing at myself, when my door opened.

I glanced over and went back to playing.

It was my brother's friend, Kristin. She was 22 and kinda drunk herself.

I tossed over my shoulder that she *was in the wrong room* and kept playing. Suddenly, Kristin was pushing me back and climbing on top of me. Even with the beer on my breath, the beer and cigarettes on her breath weren't all that good.

I said, *Hey!* and started to push her off, 'til she pulled up her skirt. She had no panties on and started rubbing herself all over my crotch.

I was like, *Kristin, I don't want to do this. I don't like you like that.*

I actually had always thought that the first time should be something special with someone special. And there was someone I wanted it to be – someday. Someone I was talking to and working up the courage to kiss.

But Kristin started taunting me. *What kind of man was I? Maybe I was still just a little boy. What kind of man wouldn't take it when he could get it?*

And she kept stroking me, working on my zipper and teasing.

Between taunts, her beer mouth was all over me, and before I was sure how, her breasts were out and in my face.

My mind was turned off, but my body was responding, and I got confused.

I didn't know what to do. I wanted her to stop, but suddenly, I wanted her to keep going, and as she pulled my pants down and sat on my dick, it was over almost before I knew it.

I've had this vague sense of being robbed ever since.

That was my first time!

My first time didn't go down the way I wanted it to.

I never told the girl I liked.

I just kind of dropped her, and later, when I got another girlfriend and she wanted to do it, I pretended – to myself – that it was my first time.

I never really thought about it as rape, but I think, if I were a girl and she were a man – a man nine years older – the fact that I said, "No," would make everyone think that it was . . . .

SEXUAL ASSAULT OF ADULTS

It is widely acknowledged that sexual assault and rape are not about intimacy or sexual release, but about power and domination. Our statistics on rape and sexual assault fall far short of accuracy, because shame still shrouds the issue. As Geneva Overholser has said in the quote with which we began this text, *As long as rape is deemed unspeakable and is therefore not fully and honestly spoken of, the public outrage will be muted as well."*

In an effort to fully and honestly speak of rape, it is worth recognizing that these statistics – that all statistics on interpersonal assault, are unfortunately, just the tip of the iceberg and represent to us that the pain and repercussions of sexual and intimate violation – if reported in their true numbers, would be found to actually affect, at some level, most of us.

A high percentage of individuals, including those of all backgrounds – and of both sexes – are sexually assaulted at some time in their lives. Sexual assault runs the gamut from acts we call harassment and molestation to those we call rape.

An individual is sexually assaulted whenever their body (and thereby psyche) are violated by unwelcomed, personal (generally genital) touching.

Many individuals, female and male, are assaulted as children, and spend the rest of their lives dealing with the psychological aftermath of assault.

From adolescence on, even greater numbers of females experience a range of violations.

Women who are violated suffer physically, psychologically, emotionally, and spiritually.

Women and girls who are never violated, also suffer.

Much like the effect of hate crimes on targeted populations, the sexual assault of any woman impacts both the direct victim, and indirectly every female who hears of it, by spreading the fear that, if they get out of line (or off alone), this can happen to them too.

Males who are violated deal with the aftermath of victimization in a culture that demands that no man ever be vulnerable. Males who are not violated, but hear of the violation of other men (especially when that violation was based on the perception that the victim was gay or gender-nonconforming) are thereby warned of the necessity of being perceived as conforming to masculine gender norms.

In his book, *The Gift of Fear*, violence-prevention expert Gavin DeBecker notes that *men are afraid that women will laugh at them, while women are afraid that men will kill them.*[1] (Men also may – sometimes rightly – be afraid that other men will kill them too.)

The disrespect of women is demonstrated in male violence in all its forms: including rape, molestation, sexual harassment,[2] battery of wives and other intimate partners, and even in the homophobia that punishes gay men for perceived similarities to women.[3] This imprints the consciousness of every hearer with a running concern, just below constant awareness, about her (or his) own personal safety.

Essentially no woman in this rape-affirming culture walks to her car in the dark, or approaches an unfamiliar situation, without processing her own likelihood of physical safety.

Superiors in the business or academic world, who could be punitive if their advances were rebuffed, have no right to suggest or engage in sexual contact with those over whom they wield power, no matter their ages. And, like anyone else, colleagues with equal power in the workplace or academy, must be able to

---

[1] 1997

[2] Roughly 40% of all employed women report that they have been sexually harassed at some time on the job. (NOMAS 2012a)

[3] Pharr 1997

take no for an answer. Accusations, false or real, are not generally made against colleagues who stop when the answer is no.

It is never alright to press one's advantage and take sexual contact beyond the level of consent one's partner offers.

A partner has the right to agree to kiss, without giving consent to genital contact or intercourse.

A partner has the right to consent to genital contact that stops short of intercourse and to be respected at the boundary line that s/he sets.

Sex is not about conquest. It is about mutual sharing.

Any act which takes from another sexually what they were not happy to give is an act of sexual assault.

~~~

Did I Do Her Any Favor?

A Male Retelling

As an undergrad, I was an RA in a dorm.

I came home one day to find a line of guys down the hallway. Most of the guys on my floor were from a ball team. They were very important to the university, and they knew it.

They were all lined up, and as I got to the head of the line, it turned into one of the rooms.

Inside the room, a girl was being held down on a bed. She was naked, and one guy was banging her. There were a handful of disheveled guys, in various states of undress by the head of the bed and around the room, shouting him on.

169

Just then, he finished, and as he pulled out with a hoot of victory, I noticed there was blood coming from every opening, her mouth, between her legs.

The guy standing behind him already had his zipper down with his Johnson standing erect, dripping with anticipation, and ran over to shove it in.

I started shouting, grabbed the floor phone, and dialed for help.

The line started to break up, with guys veering off from the rear, and back out into the street. Some of the guys in the line weren't even students. I found out later, that in the midst of it all, some of the team members had gone out, calling to men from the neighborhood – guys just outside – inviting them in.

The girl broke free and ran down the hall for an open window. We were on the fourth floor and the windows weren't sealed. I chased her, grabbed her by the waist, and held on until the college cops arrived.

I never saw her again.

I don't know for sure how many of them raped her. It looked like maybe seven or eight of the guys in the room had already gotten off, before I broke it up.

What must her life be like, living all these years with those memories?

As far as I could tell, she wasn't drugged. She wasn't drunk. She was just a freshman sorority pledge, who happened into "a relationship" with one of the guys on my floor, who set her up to impress his brothers.

I never saw her again, but sometimes, I wake up in a cold sweat, because I didn't let her go out that window.

~ ~ ~

1. Date Rape

In the U.S., as many as 90% of all rapes and sexual assaults are never reported, and the majority of victims are women 15 to 25 years old.[4] Approximately one in four traditionally-aged college undergraduates are raped ("forced to submit to sexual intercourse against their will").[5]

The overwhelming majority of rapes in the United States, an estimated 80%, are what we classify as "date" or acquaintance rapes. And legally, the situation is considered to be muddied by the fact the victim knows the assailant. The legal system gets stuck on the "he said/she said" arguments made in acquaintance rape cases.[6] Stranger rapes, and rapes with weaponry or apparent bruising, are much easier to prove legally, and so, more often, go to prosecution.

Hughes & Sandler also note that, "One in every twelve men admitted to having forced a woman to have intercourse, or tried to force a woman to have intercourse through physical force or coercion; that is, admitted to raping or attempting to rape a woman."[7]

Virtually none of these men, however, identified themselves as rapists.

At the same time, "only 57% of the women *who had been raped* labeled their experience *as rape*. The other 43% had not even acknowledge to themselves that they had been raped."[8]

~~~

---

[4] Hughes & Sandler 1999
[5] Douglas & Collins 1997
[6] See Appendix A: Who May Prosecute
[7] ibid
[8] ibid

Shattered

A Memoir

I had been saving it, saving it for so long. I had been in love, and still I saved it. I had been in the heat of passion, and turned away, so as to save it. I had wanted it to mean something. I had been raised to believe that it should mean something – maybe not something permanent, but at least something.

But he took it. It didn't mean anything to him, but he took it anyway. Or maybe I'm wrong. Maybe it meant a lot to him. Maybe the ability to conquer another has the power to salve a damaged ego. In any case, he calculated my humiliation. He placed his need to subjugate above my need to be whole. And from where I lay, bloody and violated, his victory didn't seem nearly as important as my loss.

Ginny had introduced us. A classmate with whom I shared senior year homeroom and biology class, she and I had gone to his apartment together the week before. She had dated him first, but wasn't interested anymore. Yet she still counted him among her friends. And he was considered hot. With chiseled features reminiscent of Hollywood icons, he could have had any girl he wanted. He was twenty-five and on his own. We were seventeen and still bound to our parents' homes.

The backbeat of the music throbbed as I gathered myself to rise and dress. A voice from the stereo warned, "I'm the friendly stranger in the black sedan," but it was too late to heed its warning. I knew that now. He was the stranger they had warned me about. But I hadn't known that a day, or an hour, earlier. I hadn't known it when I really needed to know it – in time. Instead, listening to the sinister voice rasping out the words, I was stuck in one of those moments, like when the priceless vase lays shattered at your feet and you wish that you could rewind time and avoid knocking it over in the first place. But it was not glass that lay shattered.

He had picked me up that morning at my parent's house. Six-foot-five and sandy-haired, he was good-looking enough that my mother had failed to ask his age and had instead, moaned in my ear, "Marry him!"

We had gone to the art museum. A mammoth three stories of imposing Grecian architecture, its entrance stands at the top of a cardiac-challenge they pass off as a flight of steps. We had wandered its halls for hours.

I thought he liked me. I thought he saw something in the tilt of my chin or the glint of my eye. I thought he saw something in the way I laughed or in the intelligence of my face. I thought he saw something in my soul that made him want to spend time with me – want to get to know me. We ate at the vendor's carts that lined the pavement at the base of those now-famous stairs. We drove away, and toured the turns of the Schuylkill River on the drives that curve along either bank. We strolled under the trees by the river's edge, and watched as rowers dipped their oars into its less-than-clear stream. We went back to his place, the place to which I had been the week before, with Ginny.

I little noticed the click of the latch behind me. This was after all, the big city, and I thought that he locked the door to keep the criminal element out. It did not occur to me that he might be turning the latch and locking the criminal, and his victim, in. I glanced over my shoulder as he slid the key out of the deadbolt, but did not think twice when I saw how high up he put it.

He brought out cashews and cheese. He uncorked the wine. He set out a tray of brownies and turned on the music. It was male music, too hard for my taste. They talk of "chick flicks" – relationship, or romance, movies that make you cry. This was not "chick" music. It was certainly not music that would put a girl "in the mood." There was an erraticism to the rhythm and a screech to the guitar – and to the male vocal lead – that defined it, in the 70's, as the male music.

As girls do, I pretended to enjoy it, lest he like me less.

I did not tell him that I preferred more melody, more harmony.

We sat on a bed – a rude mattress and box spring combination with no legs to lift it off the floor. It was the only sitting surface in the room, except for the handful of throw pillows left where we had tossed them the week before. I parked my back against the wall.

I intended to remain upright or, at the most, to just casually recline.

I intended to talk.

I was involved in the business of getting to know a potential future partner.

Kissing was in my plans too, and we started to make out. I wanted to make out. I wanted to be found beautiful and attractive. I wanted to be desired. Arms finally around him, I found his chest unusually hard. He explained that he had injured his back at work, and a doctor had put him in a body cast to heal.

My mother's sentiment of the morning rang in my ears, "Marry him!" and in those moments I fantasized that this might really be the one who would make my romantic dreams come true.

But it was a first date.

Standing on the threshold of a time they later labeled the sexual revolution, I was no longer sure I agreed with my church that marriage was a prerequisite to intercourse – but I was decidedly sure that a steady, "meaningful" relationship was.

I intended to save *it* – my virginity.

I wanted my first time to be special, to be with someone special. I had turned down opportunities for intercourse before.

I had turned down early opportunities with Rob. I had been in love with him. Or, more accurately, I had been in love with the idea of being loved *by* him.

Rob hadn't been that cute. He had been a little too skinny and a little too geeky. But he had looked at me in a way that sent shivers down my spine, and I had fallen in love with love.

God! What was that look? He looked at me like I walked on water. That look made me walk on air.

But Rob had not lasted. About the time our relationship had grown to where I would have considered him special enough, he was gone. He came over one night and took his school ring back. His mother found my letters. I had written about my growing sexual curiosity, and I had theorized about the Church's theology of premarital abstinence. She demanded he stop seeing me. So, like the boy he was, instead of the man he would one day be, he had done what his mother said.

Devastated, it had taken me months to rise from the ashes.

The last time I saw Rob he had another girl on his arm. She was my height, my then-weight, had similar hair, and bore a similar name – Deana.

Then there had been Matt, the poet I met at my junior prom.

As the literary editor of my all-girl's high school paper, I slipped some of his poetry into that paper under an androgynous pseudonym and dreamt I had found a soul-mate.

We would slip away in his mother's station wagon, lay the backseat flat, and work each other into a frenzy through the intimacies then euphemistically-called petting.

But we hadn't done more. We may have, given a little more time, but before we got there, Matt went away.

He never had the courage to tell me why.

Maybe another girl came along. Maybe the distance he had to travel to see me grew to be too much.

I never knew. He just stopped calling.

If I called him, he'd talk like nothing was wrong, but he stopped calling back. He was gone, and I was just as glad to still be a virgin.

Both he, and Rob before him, had been willing to stop, willing to listen to how far I wanted to go, willing to take it slow, willing to not demand it all on a first date from a virtual stranger.

There had been other men who were not so nice – men who had pressed me, as if they had some sort of right. But I had always managed to wiggle free. I had developed early and developed large, and I learned the hard way that that was not a good thing.

Middle-aged, usually-married men poured out of their homes and workplaces, to pursue me.

After puberty, I could no longer simply walk down the street.

Each stroll was a new experience in harassment. Cat calls rang the air. I still remember one man who drove off the road and up onto a neighbor's lawn, ogling me.

It was the late 60's and early 70's, and the teenagers of the world were hitchhiking. It was a different, a naive, time. We hitchhiked by the thousands, sometimes across the country. Others hitchhiked across Europe, crashing at hostel to hostel along the way.

Too young to drive, and beyond the reach of dependable public transportation, I hitchhiked often to get to my best friend's house. It seemed a reasonable solution.

Trying to get to Regina's one day, a man from whom I had accepted a lift, turned off the main road and drove me into the woods of a county park. There, for my chastity's sake, I wrestled with him for more than an hour, both pushing and holding his hands away – talking all the while a hundred miles an hour, as if my life depended on it, fast and slick. Maybe it did. Finally, I convinced him to let me go. Even that time, I had gotten away with *it*.

I was raised in a carefully-guarded, artificially-asexual, universe manufactured by my church, my church-run school, my home, and the climate of the decades of my childhood.

Adults told me that sex was sacred. The nuns in school told me. The priests in their pulpit told me. My parents told me.

Sex was something with rules, something that was supposed to be special, something shared by two people in love, something intended for the long-term commitment of marriage.

That was their ideology. However, when it came to the biological details, no one would tell me anything at all.

When I was twelve, my mom did try to talk, once. Knowing that I had been shown a menstruation film in school, she took her courage in hand and dared to ask if there were anything more I wanted to know.

Ignoring her red face and obvious discomfort, I plied her with questions.

I needed to know.

I asked the burning one. *Mom*, I said, *I know about the egg. And I know about the sperm. What I don't understand is how the sperm gets to the egg?*

Her color deepened. She stammered. Sweat beaded the surface of her brow. Forcibly, she gathered enough saliva to allow her lips to slide back down over her teeth and then proceeded in a near whisper. But she did not enlighten me.

Instead of telling me the "facts of life," she horrified me with the tale of how *she* came to learn those facts.

She answered, "I didn't know that *until* my wedding night. And then, *your father* was kind enough and loving enough to explain it to me. I just hope that someday, *you'll have* a loving and gentle husband who will explain it to you."

I didn't know much. And because she left the task to a future hypothetical spouse, at the end of her talk I didn't know any more than I had at the start.

But I did know that her scenario sounded more than uncomfortable.

As we made out in the darkened room, the music kept on pounding; but increasingly, the pounding was in my head. I started to feel high on something other than his kisses. The world no longer seemed right. My heart began to pound in a rhythm discordant with the drums, and I became conscious of the blood coursing through my veins as the room began to spin.

I had not minded too much when his hand had slipped inside my shirt. But with the increasing noise in my head, his demands increased. He began to fumble with my skirt. I tried to resist him, but found I had lost my usual agility. He pinned me underneath his six-and-a-half foot mass, and wrestled my underwear down. I was talking again, a hundred miles an hour, but this one wasn't listening.

Desperately, I tried to talk him out of it, to convince him that I didn't want it, to convince him not to.

As his clothes came off, his plaster body cast rose up in front of my face. With it, his weight was crushing. It covered him from arm pits to pubic bone.

He wasn't light, like Rob.

He wasn't willing to be told no, like Matt.

He wasn't young and used to going so far and no further.

I thought about the click of the deadbolt and how high up he had put the key.

I thought about screaming, but knew no one could hear – not in this city apartment, not over the pounding of the music, not over the pounding in my head.

Unable to move beneath him, I began to beg. If he *could* not stop, there were other things we could do. In desperation, I offered him release in those other ways.

Immobilized, I still struggled to move, to find some way to slide sideways or to shift his weight and escape. As I continued to plead with him, he pressed his penis between my legs. Trapped motionless beneath him, I had become an object – two mounds to be kneaded and a masturbatory tool to be pushed into.

There is a moment frozen in time, the moment he pushed in. In that jagged millisecond, reflected in the selfish intensity of his cold and hardened eyes, I am erased. In that moment, my cry is muffled in the plaster banging my face and slicing my pubic bone with each thrust of his impenetrable weight. He writhed above me as I ceased to feel.

I disconnected from the bodies on the bed.

This would be my only first time.

No restoration could be made.

It didn't take long, but it is a moment that never ends.

He finished, rolled off, and lay back, panting. I noticed in the dimness that he was not handsome anymore. "Marry him!" drifted across my consciousness and mocked me with its irony.

He rose, slid his pants back up his legs, and buttoned them around his cast.

The sharp sound of his zipper closing echoed with finality. He had done what he intended to do. He swung the needle arm back over the album and placed it down again. "I'm the friendly stranger in the black sedan, won't you hop inside my car?" mantra-like, renewed its chant.

Something foreign and sticky oozed down my thighs and dripped from me onto the sheets. At his gruff, "Let's go!" I struggled to stand and fix my clothes.

In the ethereal luminescence of his black light, the sheets glowed with a color that I thought would be red in white light.

He retrieved his keys from their hiding place too high for my reach, the top of the bookcase near the door. Unbolting that door, he led the way into the hall, this time leaving it unlocked as we walked away. Wordlessly, we started the drive home.

I studied the flaking, vomit-green of the aging paint on Falls Bridge as we sat silent, stuck in traffic. I studied the ripple of the Schuylkill below, and the trees that snaked East River Drive. I focused on the darkening twilight of the lengthening evening, fighting for mental clarity.

I wondered if the blood would stain through my clothes, and show when I passed through the front door at home.

I wondered if my parents would see change written on my face.

I didn't feel like a girl who had become a woman.

I felt like a string of pearls torn from a neck – broken, scattered, disconnected.

I wanted to call my best friend, Regina. I wanted to curl up in her arms, fetal position, and be rocked until the world became right again.

I wanted my brain to clear and the noise to stop. I wanted to stop being conscious of the pounding of my pulse and the path my blood was taking, spurt by spurt, through the valves of my veins.

He dropped me off and sped away.

I climbed the stairs silently, pushing against the soreness between my thighs as I made my way up and into the house, and then up the two more flights to my room on the third floor. No one looked up. No one saw the blood. No one saw my face. No one noticed anything.

I retreated under my covers, knees to my chest. I wanted to hide in sleep, but the pounding of my pulse kept me from it. I felt dirty, oh so dirty, so I showered. I showered, and showered, and then showered again. I reached into the back of the bathroom closet, pulled out the Comet cleanser, and showered again.

Someone yelled up the steps about my water use.

I could still feel the press of his mouth upon mine. So, I took the Comet to the bathroom sink, and with its grit tried to remove the feel, but it would not come off. As the numbness of shock began to wear away, a cold rush of fear swept across my scalp and down my neck and back – pregnancy! I had forgotten that! What if I got pregnant? Who would I blame? I could never, never tell the truth. But I had no one else to finger, no one else who would believe it was his own, and keep my humiliation from becoming public.

I crawled back into bed, and pulled the covers tight. I could not wrap my mind around it. Images swirled in my head – my name and face plastered across the local newspaper, right next to the sporadic column I wrote about my high school. The two headlines wove together, my lack of character intertwined with my review of our Spring production of "A Midsummer's Night's Dream," or my report on the latest girls' basketball scores.

I saw myself being tried in the court, instead of him.

All those I'd ever kissed were called to testify – Matt admitting under oath to the frenzy I'd worked in him, Rob's mother reading the letters I'd written on the stand, the parade of middle-aged men I'd wrestled-off making claims to notches in their belt they hadn't acquired.

The pounding in my veins and the ongoing spinning of the room distracted me from my terrors again.

My little sister, whom I never ignored, began to grow concerned and carried tales of my state down the stairs to the caretakers below. Realizing, finally, that something was wrong, someone was sent to ask how I was.

Suspicious that I had been drugged (or perhaps, that I'd taken drugs willingly), my doctor-father instructed me to produce a urine sample (which would later confirm the presence of an undetermined narcotic).

Beyond requesting that sample, I received no further treatment.

I watched the sun set and rise again, still pounding.

No one called the police. No one took me to the hospital. No one questioned what else might have happened on that "date."

The next day, I told Regina. She held me as I cried. She wondered aloud why I had gone to such an isolated place. Yet, every car we ever got into with a boy or a man was potentially just as isolated. Still, it gave me some comfort to know that she knew, and believed that I hadn't wanted it.

One of her boyfriends, Fred, overheard a conversation between us, and corrected me. He let me know that it could not have been rape, because I had gone willingly to that apartment. *"What did you think was going to happen?"* he demanded. He informed me that *"girls who go off alone with boys, and don't expect "to deliver," are "cockteases" who deserve what they get"*.

Regina didn't dump him.

As the days passed, and my head cleared, the fear of pregnancy set in. Pregnancy would have shamed me before my entire world.

It was not a time when unwed women got pregnant. Those who did were forced to marry the man, or were shuttled off to convent schools where they carried their babies in secret and were pressured into giving them up, their indiscretion never revealed to neighbors, friends or extended families. And there was no choice to not carry a pregnancy to term. Even if I had, or could get, the money, abortion was illegal.

Rape went unacknowledged. It just "didn't happen."

This was before the time when a female police officer might attend the gynecological exam in the emergency room.

This was in the old days. Male cops took down the story. Male cops watched you spread your legs in the stirrups.

Women raped on street corners, at gun point, by strangers, didn't press charges.

How much less the girl who said yes to dinner and a museum!

And pregnancy by rape was beyond my imagination.

I developed a plan. I sought out the boy I'd been mercy dating, and gave him his long-withheld wish. I needed someone to blame if I were pregnant.

He thought he'd died and gone to heaven. I thought how much his sweating and grunting seemed just like the week before.

It was only later, after my period arrived, that it dawned on me, I had doubled my chances of pregnancy by intercourse with him. My only thought then was reducing the risk of the rape being discovered.

And every morning, my stomach wretched at first memory. With each dawn of consciousness, waves of impotent rage wracked me – physically. Every afternoon after school, defeated again into self-blame, I crawled back under the covers. Every night, hopelessly, I sobbed myself to sleep. To avoid consciousness, I slept as often and as long as I could. My period came, and went, and came again twice over; and still I retreated from life. Time crawled. Life went on, but I was not clean.

I can't remember his name. Maybe I've blocked it. It doesn't come back no matter how I dig. But I have never been to bed with a man since, that he has not been there.

Each and every time, I find myself trying to undo his damage, trying to pretend that this – and not that – is the first time.

Washing has not undone it.

Time has not either.

Love has not.

The men I have met since have not.

The innocence that saw intercourse in the light of love died that day, and has found no place of rebirth.

And yet, he has likely never thought of me, or that day, again.

By now, he may have done the same to a thousand others.

Graying, balding, paunching, middle-aged, married, divorced, and remarried, he most likely continues to "deflower" virgins and pursue jailbait.

Trapped by the trust with which I chose to go off alone with him in the first place, I bore what should have been his shame, in secret, for years – nearly failing to ever call it aloud by its real name.

But now, I have long since absolved myself of blame.

It was no more my fault, than it is the fault of the victim of a mugging that they walked to their car, or were out on the street, that day.

A criminal mind planned it.

Someone, unable to empathize with the feelings of another, took what he wanted, without concern for the cost to me.

But even knowing that, even absolving myself, has not undone it.

There is a moment, frozen in time, a jagged moment reflected in the calculating intensity of steeled and hardened eyes, in which my humanity is erased, my autonomy shattered.

~~~

2. Fear of False Accusations

Part of our tendency to deny and to disbelieve those who report (publicly to the criminal justice system or privately to family and friends) sexual assaults of all kinds is rooted in the fear of false accusation.

In no other crime is the victim so likely to be disbelieved.

But when violation and crime is of a sexual nature, often the first reaction, even a knee-jerk automatic reflexive reaction, is to disbelieve the one who has suffered assault.

Victims are regularly accused of lying. Insinuations are made, or the statement made outright, that the victim "must have wanted it" or s/he could not have been assaulted – that s/he could have/would have stopped it.

Many people, especially men, fear false accusations.

After all, *HOW would one clear one's name if a false accusation were made?*

And now that public consciousness has increased, now that victims have come forward and our culture has begun to duly criminalize inappropriate sexual perpetration, *how can one be sure that one won't be falsely accused, just by someone with a grudge?*

With an increase in workplace romances facilitated by women's move into the workplace side by side with men and a growing consciousness of the dynamics of power in that workplace, the workplace alone has become a contested center for sexuality.

The difference between the individual who wants to begin a relationship or suggest a sexual liaison, and the individual who is committing an act of inappropriate sexual perpetration against another, is actually relatively simple. The recognition and abidance by only a few rules is necessary.

1. Never approach or touch anyone who has not (or cannot) give full, clear consent.
2. Never approach or treat someone as a sexual object – or a sexual partner – if there is a power dynamic between you in which they are on the underside.
3. Never make your initial approach lewd or crude. Exhibit some class and tact when approaching someone who is appropriately positioned to you in status/power/age in the workplace.
4. Never persist with someone who has said no.

Never touch anyone who has not (or cannot) give full, clear consent.

To be legally, morally, and ethically able to give full, clear consent, an individual (any individual) must be above the legal limit for statutory rape. When you are a legal adult, NO CHILD OR ADOLESCENT, no one who is NOT a legal adult CAN give you legal consent. **It is never alright to initiate sexual contact with an individual too young (or too different in age or power from oneself) to be able to give consent. Children are not fit sexual partners for adolescents or adults.**

No one whose mental faculties are in any way reduced can give you legal consent. Factors that reduce the mental capacity to give consent may be obvious, like being born mentally challenged, developing dementia, or suffering catastrophic brain injury, or they may be legally murky, like being drunk or drugged.

Never approach someone as a sexual object – or a sexual partner – if there is a power dynamic between you in which they are on the underside.

Power dynamics matter.

If you are "in charge" in some way, then the individual you approach for sex may perceive hirself as unable to refuse. If you are someone's boss, there is a likelihood that your employee "needs" their employment for their living expenses and/or career goals, and therefore, may not *feel* "free" to tell you *no*. If you hold their job, or their promotion, or their evaluation, or their grade (etc.) in your hand – then you cannot/should not initiate sexual *or romantic* contact – because the power differential means you cannot be sure the object of your affection or desire does not feel – at some level – coerced. And coercion equals assault.

Never make your initial approach lewd or crude.

Exhibit some class and tact when approaching someone who is appropriately positioned to you in status/power/age in the workplace. The workplace is a sphere of economic activity and advancement. Respect for equally positioned coworkers includes respect for the way they, and your treatment of them, will be viewed by others.

Never persist with someone who has said *No*.

Stop when you are told *No*.

Men in our culture are taught to persist – to push for what they want, even when being told no. Cultural messages teach that a "real man" persists until he persuades the object of his desire to give consent. To complicate this further, there are fetish communities of individuals who enact staged scenarios in their sexual play that may include pretending to say no while meaning yes.

But the overwhelming reality in society at large is this – when you approach someone (whether directly for sex or for a date or companionship or friendship or relationship) and that person says *no* – you need to hear *no* as *no*.

No means *No*.

And at whatever point along a sexual trajectory your partner of choice says, *Stop*.

Stop means *Stop*.

It may well be that there is a point in sexual arousal where it is difficult, even impossible, to keep oneself from coming to climax, but it is NEVER IMPOSSIBLE to stop your interactions with that other individual.

A partner has the right to say, *Yes* to dinner or coffee, and nothing more.

A partner has the right to say, *Yes* to kissing, and nothing further.

A partner has the right to say *Yes*, to what we used to call heavy petting, to some non-genital foreplay, and then say, *Stop*.

A partner has the right to say *Yes*, to manual sex (fingers/hands), and nothing more.

A partner has a right to say *Yes*, to receiving oral sex, but not giving it – or to giving it but not receiving it – and then, nothing more.

A partner has a right to say *Yes*, to anal sex, and nothing more.

And where applicable, a partner has a right to say *Yes*, to vaginal sex (or anal sex), and then to say, *Pull out.*[9]

And no one has a right to continue when and where a partner has said *Stop*.

It's all about the legitimate consent.

~~~

Was It Rape?
A Female Memoir

Anonymous

Was it rape?

I can't truthfully say that I thought it was at the time.

---

[9] If you and your consensual partner have agreed you will withdraw as you approach climax [*NOT* a recommended safe or effective means of birth control], it is a violation to fail to do so, to maintain penetration so long that you lose control and ejaculate inside.

Only now, in retrospect, I ask myself, *Was it rape?*

With the advantage of the years between then and now, with the perspective of maturity and the benefit of education and experience, I think, perhaps, it was.

What I do know to be true, the fact is, I felt as though I had no control – no "say" as to whether or not it happened – not the first time or the 100th.

I pretended to assent, because I wanted, needed, the plastic illusion of intimacy it seemed to provide, but never quite accomplished.

But I felt humiliated every time – especially when interrupted by an innocent co-worker who I just knew, knew. I knew my face betrayed my guilt.

I allowed myself to be coerced. *Does the fact there was coercion make it rape?*

He was 20 years my senior. He had power, authority, over my life. It was certainly, by today's legal definition, sexual harassment.

I didn't turn him in. I didn't call the police.

Even though, when it started, I was only 19, I didn't tell my parents.

I didn't tell my husband.

He was someone I admired. At times, I even imagined I was in love with him.

Could it possibly still be rape?

Surely by the age of 24, when I left, I should have been able to answer that question.

Surely by now, at 60, I should be able to say.

Was it rape?

He had my job in his hands.

Why is it I felt I had betrayed myself?

I was not *"the type of girl"* who engaged in illicit affairs. That couldn't be me!

How could I have allowed myself to be removed from my own personhood, my own humanity, my autonomy, by my utter, deafening silence?

I never said, "Yes."

I did say, "No," when I wasn't saying nothing.

I allowed myself to be pushed up against the wall, rammed, kissed, ignored, fucked.

It felt like rape . . . mostly.

And sometimes, it felt like attention, sophistication, though I knew the pretense of equal enjoyment was just that – a pretense – a lie.

And so did he.

Sometimes, it felt like escape from the monotony of my life – like possibility for something better, more exciting, a flight from boredom, a respite from the occasional abuse forced on me by a husband who did not count me his equal – yet was keen to my sense of something to hide – of anything or anyone who played a role more central in my life than his.

Was it rape?

I've called it that for the last twenty or so years. I finally consider that rape may have been the truth of the matter.

But I'm often, still, not sure.

I know this . . . . *It never felt like love.*

I don't think he considered that it would change the course of my life.

Yet, it opened the door for others to do the same. It reframed my sense of self-esteem. It relegated physical intimacy to the land of less significance.   It   made   me   a   woman relieved when I miscarried and incapable of fidelity to a husband who disappoints.

Was it rape?

When you decide, please let me know.

~~~

3. Gang Rape via Date Rape Drugs

Unfortunately, it is not uncommon for women to have been gang raped, sometimes, while drugged.[10]

Having gone out with friends, having gone to a club or a bar or a party, one moment they are in control of their faculties, their own drink in their own hand, and the next, they are disheveled and stripped in the company of one or more strange men – with only nightmare flashes of pain, memory clips of violation, and the overwhelming fear of sexually transmitted infections (and, perhaps, of pregnancy) – to fill in the missing blocks of time.

And they face years of struggle ahead, as their minds seek to remember and process. Questions about what happened to their known companions; a sense of betrayal; not knowing who adulterated their beverage or how; rape kit data from a hospital with DNA for one or multiple unknown assailants; positive drug tests after the fact for drugs they did not willingly or knowingly

---

[10] Reeves Sanday 1990; Benedict 1998: Katz & Kilbourne 2004

take; and at the end, no one to prosecute – and not even (for the victim) the right to decide to whether or not to prosecute.[11]

Even when the assailant/s are known, there may be a lack of empathy or action on the part of (and even blame from) a patriarchally-based criminal justice system that views a woman's going to a club, or having a drink, *as if it were* consent to (one or many, known or unknown) sexual acts or partners.

~~~

Drugged

A Female Retelling

I had gone to the bar with a girlfriend. Not a best friend forever. Just a genuine acquaintance with whom I had some social history. We'd partied before. Sometimes with a crowd. Sometimes just the two of us in a crowd. I don't know that we had that much in common, that much to talk about, but it was nice having a friend for clubbing. Made me feel safer. And it helped with that awkwardness when you go someplace alone.

That night though, she found a guy she wanted to go home with, and I didn't.

I was looking for someone significant in my life. Not at the club. In the club, I just wanted to dance, have a drink or two, blow off some of the steam from the incredible pressure at work right then. We were always under the gun at that season of the year. It was kinda' rough.

---

[11] Whether or not the perpetrator/s are identified and/or caught, the decision to prosecute is in the hands of the prosecutor and the district attorney (and the care of the evidence and approach to the crime taken is often in the hands of local police). There is even less of a chance that a case will be prosecuted when a victim cannot recall hir assailant/s.

But I wasn't looking for a one night stand. First off, I wasn't into that anyway. I mean, I had to be in a relationship to have sex. It didn't feel right otherwise. You know?

But Amanda didn't care about that. I thought we were just out to get a margarita or two. I didn't realize she was hunting. Seems she just wanted to get laid. Or so she was saying, as drink plied her jumbled thoughts from her innermost recesses and caused them to spill forth across her ever-thickening tongue.

I had one. She had a second. Then a third. Then she danced off with Mike , or Mic, or Ernie, or whatever his name was.

I went looking for her a few songs later. I found her long enough for her to shout, above the music, in my ear that it was a good thing I'd driven, 'cause I could get myself home. Then she slurred something else, incomprehensible, and was gone.

I went back to our table to gather up my things. I collected my coat. Felt in my clutch for my keys. And took one last shot of the pomegranate-flavored delectable delight I was counting on for workplace stress relief, then headed for the door.

Suddenly, the sun was in my eyes. It beat through the window in rhythmic rays, and my head throbbed in response. I tried to lift it, but something about it was heavy and too, too large. I closed my eyes against the bright and the spinning. I felt around me for my clutch. I was sure I must have dropped it when my head hit the floor.

But it wasn't floor around me. My hand found sheets. I was in a bed?

And then, skin.

Steeling myself against the pain and the dizziness that bordered on nausea, I peeked through my eyelids. I was in a room. Not in the club. Not on a floor. But a bed. And by the strength of the sun, it was midday. And there was a man next to me. A man without clothes. And just beyond my feet, lay another one, curled up, fetal style.

Or maybe more like a cat, satisfied from the kill.

I felt my own sides – skin – and gingerly turned my head the other way.

I recognized my shirt next to a dark mass on the floor that I hoped was my skirt.

A wave of fear swept from my scalp to my feet.

I had the intense impression that I should move quietly and carefully.

With stealth, I extracted myself from the mattress. Some part of my mind registered the dark stain on the sheet where I had been and the blood streaked across my knee, but I kept going, trying not to breathe too sharply, trying to ignore the sharp stabbing in my ribs and the dull ache between my thighs.

I picked up the dark mass of cloth and the recognizable blouse and stepped between the creaks of the hardwood floor, quietly spreading the already-ajar door and creeping down the stairs and out the front door and into the nearest patch of trees before stopping to slip my print blouse over my open bra and pull my skirt up over my ripped pantyhose.

It was a neighborhood.

Tree-lined streets.

Cookie-cutter, vinyl-sided houses.

I had not looked for my shoes.

Damn! My shoes! I really like that pair! The soles were just the right thickness to make the heel comfortable, even though high, and they were leopard and went so well with so many outfits!

Each step was a challenge. The grass was rutted and prickly. The sidewalk, cold and uneven. I scurried along from bush to bush, sometimes ducking out between parked cars, sometimes back, seeking cover along a hedge-lined sidewalk.

Where was I? What was the last thing I remembered? I was at the club! I got my things. I headed toward my car. I had taken one more shot to let the week go, to brace myself for the week ahead.

Where was the main road? Any main road? Was I still in the same town? How did they transport me? Were there more than two? No clutch. No ID. No car keys or idea where my car was. My house keys were in my car, and the full wallet, but even if I could find it, no one would help me break into it without my ID, and I couldn't drive it anyway, without a key. No cell phone! Amanda left me alone. That bitch! None of this would have happened if she had stayed with me! Or would it have happened to both of us?

A woman driving by slowed, looked hard at me, then sped off. I didn't blame her. She had young kids in the car. I would have done the same. Then I thought, *What did I look like? Was I that scary? Too scary to be worthy of help?*

Damn, it's cold! I wished I had my coat!

I caught sight of a woman working on her holiday lights.

"Which way is the main road? How do I get out of here? Do you know where I can find a payphone?"

"About four blocks that way," she pointed, barely lifting her eyes from the tangled mass of outdoor tree lights she was working on.

I found the store, and the town name, and called my roommate. She had been too busy to go out the night before. Some homework assignment for her perpetual online degree. It took her forever to arrive.

Two hours I sat still, waiting on a milk crate behind the dumpster, parked on the side of the building, braving the cold rather than braving the stares I got when I bummed the money for the phone call.

All I wanted was a long hot bath – in chlorine.[12] I wanted to get the dirt off of me, out of me.

Sarcastically, my roommate said, *"Guess you had fun. You look a mess!"* Then, oblivious, went back to a discussion of the theory of random probability sampling on which she'd spent the last eighteen hours.

Briefly, just before I stepped into the tub, I thought of going to the hospital for a rape exam. But who would I finger? I had never seen the two men, passed out cold in that bed, before. I was so busy escaping, and fighting the fog in my brain, I forgot to note the house number or the street as I skittered away from their neighborhood.

I didn't feel well at all.

I needed the bath, needed to scrub my skin off. And the thought of nurses and doctors and police officers and statements, and testimony – if there would even be testimony – if they didn't just blame me because I'd been out clubbing and *must have been* drinking *too much* – was too overwhelming for my still off-kilter head to bear.

I filled the tub with bubble bath, then lowered myself into the water.

It wasn't enough.

I let the water out, then refilled it with Epsom salts.

It wasn't enough.

I let the water out, then refilled it with near-scalding water and added the chlorine I wanted so badly, then began to cry as

---

12 Do not try this. Chlorine is poisonous through the skin and through the vapors.

the heat and chlorine attacked the space that had been my vulva the night before.

I let the water out and got a hand mirror. My lips down there were dark. Blueish. They hadn't been that shade the last time I'd looked, which had been about five years before, but they were tender and visibly swollen, and I was pretty sure the blue meant they were bruised.

I soaped up and rinsed off three times, like a ritual. I made sure to wash where the blood had been on my thighs and on my knee. Then I found an old douche bag I'd bought once (before my GYN told me douching was bad for you), filled it with more vinegar than water, and washed myself out. Damn, it stung!

I remembered a prepackaged, medicated douche I'd seen on a drugstore shelf once, found a bottle of Betadine in the back of the linen closet, and douched again with straight Betadine.

I took the beach towel from last summer from the back of the shelf, wrapped myself in it, and crawled into bed, pulling the covers over my head.

I lay there three days.

Every so often, I made my way back to the bathroom and lowered myself carefully onto the toilet, wincing as the pee burned as it crossed my open wounds.

Then, one day, about two weeks later, I felt it, a nerve tingling that didn't tickle and that didn't stop, followed by a new soreness, then a different burning.

My GYN fussed at me for not coming in sooner. By the time I saw her, it felt like the sores were everywhere – inside and out. My vulva felt four times its normal size, like it hung down to my knees. I hadn't peed in days. The blisters were so bad inside my urethra, they had to catheterize me.

I burst out sobbing.

But I couldn't tell.

Not even her.

I let her think whatever she would – that I'd had unprotected sex out of sheer stupidity. After all, what could I say? Even I didn't know what had happened, or with how many.

She prescribed an antiviral and took a full screening for other STI's.

I came back negative on the rest, but anytime I try to reduce my dose of the antiviral, the tingling, then the blisters, come back.

I'll *have the risk of infecting others with herpes all* my *life*, she told me, *so* I *need to be more careful from now on – for* my *lovers' sake, if not for* my *own*.

She did think I'd been a slut – and a fool!

Now, if I find that special other, that *someone significant*, I will have to *come out* to him. I'll have to tell him that I'm dirty and can never get clean again. And if he still wants me, we can be careful.

But if we ever decide we want children, *will we have to run the risk of his catching it in order to get me pregnant?*

And what if I have an outbreak when I give birth?

My GYN said, I *have to redo the HIV test in six months. If* I'm *negative then*, I'll *have dodged a bullet*, she told me.

Can't say I feel like I dodged much of anything.

~~~

The Better Man

N. D. Rosechild

The sharp sound of your zipper closing

   signaled the end.

But it was only the beginning.

Your message driven home.

  I was without worth.

Used like a tissue, then discarded.

Not subject to love,

   but object to masturbate in.

Your level of concern,

   written between my thighs.

All the pretty words,

  All the promises,

     All the things you said to lure me there –

    to get me out with you –

    to get me off alone with you –

Lies.

I bore the shame.

It was my scarlet letter.

I kept the secret, your secret.

Didn't tell for years.

Knew I'd not be believed.

I Trusted You

Intuited the disdain

   telling would have brought.

Lost my voice.

Muffled the screams.

But still you're here,

   in other men

      other men's faces

      other men's actions

Products of a culture

   that says it's okay

To dominate

   to enforce submission.

That pain is sexual.

I am really nothing anyway -

   to you –

Not fully human.

Not worthy of concern.

Nothing to be honored –

   let in –

   given place –

Promoted.

Nadine Rosechild Sullivan, Ph.D., Rev.

The warp of you, the thread,

    runs the fabric of my days.

You were the better man.

The one fit to survive.

Victor in the contest.

And I the vanquished –

    still.

If I reclaim the voice,

    If I unmute the scream,

Is there any way to make you hear?

    To get into your head

'Til you see me

    human too?

'Til you see

    I think, feel, love, hurt, bleed?

In all your intimate violence,

    it's been I who was the better man.

Better men –

    don't always win.

~~~

I'm Gonna' Get What I Came For
A Female Retelling

My mom didn't like me on the Net, but she had to let me on the computer to do my homework.

We had an old desktop on dialup, and she kept it in the living room. I could only surf under her *supervision*. Every so often, she would come up behind me and look over my shoulder. Pretty quickly, I developed my technique for shrinking one window and popping up the other. I never surfed just one place. I had to be careful, 'cause she might check the bar at the bottom and find out what I had open. She gave me permission to chat, but only on a Christian site. There was a site I liked, a music site where kids discussed the best Christian and crossover artists.

I had a lot of time on my hands. Some of it I spent on school, and some of it I spent chatting with friends around the country, and around the globe, who shared my interest in music. And when she did check, other than getting in trouble for not doing my assignments, if I was on that site, she didn't look too deeply.

One day, I made a mistake though. I saved a chat log.

There was this guy who hung out on the board, Jeff. He said he was 35 and that was probably about right. I liked a lot of what he said about the artists. Then he started to focus in on me. I was complimented.

He asked me to meet him in a private room. He wanted me to send a picture file. After I did, he said great things about my looks. And he started to flirt.

I'd never really been flirted with before. I mean there was the guy in school who kind of acted interested. We'd kissed a couple of times, but then he'd backed off. I was never sure why.

But here was this new guy. He was a little old, and not great looking, but not too bad on the other hand. And we had great conversations. And he started making me feel really good about myself. My looks. My mind. My depth of spirituality. My insights into the power and passion of music.

I wanted to keep some of the things he was saying, so I downloaded the log and saved it to what I thought was a private file on the harddrive.

He started to talk about what he was looking for in a relationship. He was saying what a hard time he had finding what he was looking for and wondering why there was no one near him who had all the qualities he saw in me.

My mom found the log.

She went ballistic. She took the phone cord.

I came home, and she was sitting in the living room, in the dark, like a spider lies in wait, phone cord in her hand. There was nothing I could say, so I just ran upstairs yelling something about her messing around in my life, and slammed my bedroom door.

About a half hour later, she came up and gave me some long Christian lecture about waiting for marriage, and about men, and about his age and my age, and I just shut her out. I didn't worry too much about age.

What did she know anyway?

She was the one who was old.

She just couldn't understand.

Besides, I had no life. She was always afraid of what would happen if I were "running the streets," so I had to have someone to talk to.

Eventually, about two weeks later, after I agreed to be on my good behavior, she gave me the phone cord — at least when she was there to "monitor" me. She didn't know I picked one up at the store the day after she took it and got online sometimes when she wasn't home.

Someone on the chat room came up with the idea that all of those who could would get together. The East Coast group picked a location that was not too far from me, and my mom, feeling sorry for me I guess, agreed to drive me to meet them.

She didn't know Jeff got on the boards and said he would buy a plane ticket and that it would be great to meet all of us.

I forget why now, but that meeting of the chat group got cancelled. Since she didn't have to drive me, my mom said yes to a commitment to go out of town that weekend for her job.

Jeff said he couldn't get a refund for the plane ticket. My seventeenth birthday was just days before. Maybe he should come out, and we could meet.

By that time, we'd been chatting in the public room, and in private rooms, for close to three years.

He said he was *in love with me* but *would totally respect my feelings if the feelings weren't mutual. How 'bout he fly in, get a car from the airport,* and *meet me at a location not too far from my house?*

I thought, *Sure.* I mean, you really feel like you know someone after you exchange thoughts online for a while. We had talked about everything. And my mom didn't know it, but once I got a cell, we had talked by phone daily for about a year too. We just had to wait for the unlimited minutes after 9 pm, so his calls would show on her cell phone bill. Sometimes, we talked all night. Pretty much, it was like we'd been dating. It felt like a real, long-distance, relationship.

I began to look forward to the break in my boredom that meeting my online romance would provide.

That day, I couldn't wait for Mom to drive away. Once she was gone, I swore my little sister to secrecy under threat of great bodily harm and got dressed the best I could. Makeup. Perfume. My best outfit. Then I drove to meet him at the restaurant attached to the hotel he was staying in.

He was older than he looked in his pictures. A kind of sick feeling went through me when I first saw him, but I brushed it aside. It lasted just a second, so I figured it was just nerves.

He was great in the conversation. It was good to finally get to talk face-to-face. We gossiped about the people on the board, and talked about life – his life, his job, his church. He played music in their worship service each Sunday. He was substantial, upstanding. He was a Christian musician, just not famous, like the ones we discussed on the board. He was on a church worship team. He had a house. It was only a trailer, but he said a lot of people had those in Missouri, and he said he had it fixed up.

He was *looking for a wife*, wanted *kids*. But he said, he had to be *patient*. She had to be *the right girl*. He was being *celibate, waiting* for *the one God would bring him*.

His fiancé had *broken his heart*. He didn't understand why. And his mother had been *mean* too, a *real bitch*.... He felt like he *always gave the best* to women, but *some just couldn't be trusted*. He needed *a submissive one, like the Bible said. A pretty* one – like me....

The restaurant was closing around us. He said he was *having so much fun*, and had *waited so long*, he just *didn't want the night to end*, but since he wasn't *from around here*, he didn't *know where we could go. Did I know anyplace?*

I didn't.

The waitress began to give us evil stares. As a desperate afterthought, he suggested – hesitantly – that we go up to his room, *just to talk*.

That sick feeling flashed across my stomach again, quietly, for just a nanosecond, but I thought, *Why not? I really know him well. We've been friends for years now.*

I wanted to keep talking too.

We got upstairs, and the only place to sit was on the bed. I sat carefully on the edge, talking. He put some music on the TV. We tried to keep talking but, somehow, the conversation began to lag.

It was getting late, and I started to worry about my little sister, home alone. I knew I could count on her for a while, but if she got freaked, she just might call Mom, and she was likely to get freaked past eleven o'clock.

I said, *I better get going now. My mom won't be home 'til mid-afternoon tomorrow. Maybe I can come back for breakfast, and we can talk again before you leave?*

I started to get up.

He wasn't very cute, but I was hoping for a kiss goodnight. Or at least, I was willing for one. Without our having said so, it still felt like he had been my online boyfriend for a while, and I didn't want to be the kind of girl who would judge a guy by his looks, or not give a guy a chance.

As I started to rise, he kind of lunged from where he was sitting on the long side of the bed, and dragged me under him. He started to kiss me, and though it was awkward, I tried to kiss him back. I had nothing to compare this moment with, except the kisses of that one boy at school who flaked off on me.

After a few moments, I started to push him upward, gently, saying, *Okay, I'll see you tomorrow. Maybe about nine?*

But he was panting and staring and that funny feeling was back in my stomach, and suddenly he straddled my abdomen, pulled up my shirt and jerked up my bra, saying, *Now, I'm gonna get what I came for.*

207

In moments, his penis was in my face, then bumping my chest, then hitting my cheek again, bumping my teeth, and his hand was wrapped around it, working it like a sausage going into a grinder. I tried to push him off, but I was too surprised to think of hurting him.

He sprayed all over my breasts, groaned, and fell off to the side.

I lay there a moment, stunned. I didn't know what to do.

I started to get up. He made no move to stop me, content in his post-orgasmic flush.

I pulled my shirt down over my dislocated bra. I pulled my coat on overtop, picked up my purse from the floor where it had been beside my foot when I was sitting, and let the heavy door click shut behind me.

I did not run, as I did not feel pursued. I waited for the elevator, then shuffled slowly, heavily, toward my car. My phone rang as I drove away. It was him. I didn't answer.

At home, I pressed past my little sister, who fussed at me as I came through the door for leaving her alone so long after the dark.

I washed myself carefully in the shower, wanting to be sure the soap from my chest didn't run down my belly, changing washcloths when I went to wash the rest of me. For good measure, I poured a bottle of rubbing alcohol all over my chest, let it air dry, then washed again, before stepping out.

I took my clothes to the barbeque outback, lit the gas grill, and let them flame.

I moved back to my room. In the quiet, in the dark, after I told my little sister to shut up and go to her own room, tears swelled in the corners of my eyes.

He was supposed to be a Christian. He told me he cared about me. He had muttered about the long-term. I had tried to imagine that – a life with him in a Missouri trailer living out long-term love.

But this didn't feel like love.

I had the fleeting thought that perhaps I should be grateful to him for leaving me a virgin. Maybe even for leaving my pants on. But there was something in his attitude, something in his eyes.

I couldn't sleep. My stomach kept churning. I lost it in my trashcan, changed the bag, lay back down again.

Mom was right. Damn it!

I drifted off, fitfully, then woke back up with a start – seeing him looming over me, panting and sweating, feeling the clamminess of his penis against my cheek, reliving the way he pressed my breasts together to make a tunnel for himself just before he ejaculated.

I lay, staring at the ceiling. The purple mesh butterfly I got at the Academy of Natural Sciences swung lazily in the breeze of the fan I kept on every night of the year, the fan I couldn't sleep without, the fan that wasn't helping me now.

My phone kept ringing. I turned the ringer off. The number in the upper left hand corner of the window indicated 17 voicemails.

Mom's car turned in the driveway about dusk the next day. My sister had fed herself breakfast and lunch. I hadn't bothered to do the same. Mom wanted to take us to the local diner, talk about her trip, ask about our night.

I couldn't eat. She noticed something was wrong. I didn't mean to, but I blurted out that I had met one of the people from the Christian music site. Pretty soon, she had the whole story. Well, most of it. Enough of it.

Mom checked with her friend whose husband was a cop.

My birthday had put me over the limit for statutory rape. I had gone to his hotel room voluntarily. There was no penetration. I had washed off (and incinerated) his DNA. It would be *he said/she said* anyway. I didn't have a case.

I refused to talk to the rape crisis counselor my mom found. I didn't want to talk to anyone. I just wanted to make it go away.

He hadn't raped me, after all. Not by the legal definition.

All he had done was prove I was a fool to trust him and violate my innocence.

I told myself I was also a fool not to strike back physically. I was mad about that. I had been too startled to know what to do. I determined, if I ever faced that again, I would bite. I would hit. I would claw. I would do damage.

I trusted him.

I thought I knew him.

I thought he cared about me.

The emails he sent, before I blocked him, called me a whore. Told me I was *a heartbreaking bitch*, *like* the *fiancé* who broke off her engagement to him, *like his mom* who ran around on his dad.

He told me, I *knew I wanted it*, and I *had no right to cut him off like that* after we *had been so close*.

My mom said a 35-year-old had no business with a 17-year-old. That he was an internet perpetrator, that his chatting with me, and his phone calls, over the years had been him grooming me.

It all just made me feel more like a fool. Him. The law. The suggestion of counseling. My mom.

And dirty. It took the longest while for the scent of him to wash off my chest, out of my body memory.

I spent a lot of time the next few months hiding behind my hair.

It felt like I just needed everyone to stop looking at me.

And my head felt too heavy to hold fully erect. I wanted a veil, a gauze curtain to make me less visible to the world.

I took a self-defense course the next year. I wanted to be sure, if it happened again, I would fight and not freeze.

And I don't much trust Christians anymore.

It's not just him. It's the guys I met in *Christian Fellowship* too.

Anymore, can't say I put much truck in *brotherly* love....

~~~

When we can talk as openly about
rape,
as we can about other crimes,
we'll be able to start lifting the
burden of shame.
That burden will never disappear
until women [and men] can stand
there and say,
"This happened to me."

Geneva Overholser[13]

~~~

---

[13] Overholser 1992

Nadine Rosechild Sullivan, Ph.D., Rev.

They Call It Post-Traumatic

N. D. Rosechild

They call it post –

    traumatic

That I flash back again

    every time we make love

To rapes long ago

    And struggle to undo

Labor to purge

    old

with new

Would that it were post

But it is trauma wrought anew

Lying under you

memory and sensation

one

And this is that

    returned again

This socially-coded act

Your dominance writ in my

    submission

This thrusting lacking tenderness

Your pornographic eye

I Trusted You

This emptiness in heart

    for time you did not invest

    in me

Not the making of love

Not post-trauma

New

~~~

Nadine Rosechild Sullivan, Ph.D., Rev.

RAISING THE FUTURE

I am a survivor.

Some of the narratives included in this volume are my own. Some of those who have perpetrated against me have been male. With lesser frequency, some have also been female.

I undertook this work as a female with a long history of good interactions with both men, and women, who have overwhelmingly meant me well.

I have warm loving memories of my great-grandfather, grandfather, and father, all of whom respected the females in their lives – including my great-grandmother, my grandmother, my mother, and me; and warm loving memories of the women in my family tree, who also lived lives of respect and did no one intentional harm.

I have good memories of decades of interaction with seven living brothers (and four sisters), and I still mourn the loss of the brother who passed before his time, my twin.

I married and have many happy memories of the twenty-four years I spent with my husband, with whom, even though we are now divorced, I have an amicable, fraternal relationship, and with whom, I continue to co-parent our now-grown daughters.

I know the devastation of being the mother of a deeply-grieved son who passed at birth.

I have nephews I admire and respect.

And I am in love, head-over-heels and indubitably, with the two sweetest twin grandsons ever born into this earth.

On a less familial note, I have many male colleagues, students, and clients whom I also respect and admire.

There is no part of me that under-appreciates males.

As a human being, situated in a given place and time, and as a U.S. citizen in the early 21st century, I have a vested interest in the well-being of males in our society – in their freedom to revel in the best of human experience – in their ability to live with autonomy and dignity, or, as Jean Kilbourne says, to live *"authentic and freely chosen lives."*[1]

As a woman located in the same time and space, I have a vested interest in my own, and other women's ability to also live *"authentic and freely chosen lives."*

I began this work with the *social science fact* that we know, incontrovertibly that there have been times and places where human beings did NOT – neither male nor female – exalt violence; and where men and boys did not dominate, harm, rape, beat, or subjugate women or girls (or vice versa).

~~~

A…serious problem for men is that masculinity

is so often linked with violence,[2]

with brutality, with ruthlessness.[3]

And boys grow up in a world in which men are constantly

shown as perpetrators of violence, as brutal.

They grow up in a world in which they are encouraged to be

tough and insensitive . . . .

Jean Kilbourne[4]

~~~

---

[1] Kilbourne 2000, 2010
[2] Kilbourne 2010
[3] ibid
[4] Kilbourne 2000, 2010

That fact alone, that not all societies have been *"rape-prone"* – that some societies have even been *"rape-free"*[5] – indicates that, as I contend, **rape and partner violence do not spring from (only, or even primarily) the individual psychopathy of the individual rapist – but from the sociopathy of a culture as a whole.**

It also indicates that we do – and can – affect the ways in which our societies **DO gender.**[6]

One of the things I appreciate about having grown up in my household is having had the opportunity to watch my father model a *broader* range of masculinity than I often, presently, observe within families.

My father played sports in high school and college (football and basketball), and the Turkey Bowl in the side yard every Thanksgiving. If one of his children were interested in a sport, he encouraged them.

However, to quote one of my father's former patients, in real ways, my father was a "renaissance man," in that he emphasized (along with hard work and accomplishment) education, science, religion/philosophy, *and the arts.* Whenever a classic or educational movie came on, he insisted that all of his children stop whatever they were doing and come and watch and learn.

Along with our mother, he filled our lives with the sound of music. For us, he bought and played recordings of great pieces. From early-grade school on, along with our mother and himself, he had us in adult choir, and he paid for music lessons for all.

And he filled our home with books, installing built-in bookcases in every dining room and family room we owned, and filling the shelves with as wide a range of literature and educational materials as he could buy. And he induced us to use

---

[5] Sanday 1981
[6] West & Zimmerman 1987

them. If, in that house, you ever dared utter the words, "I'm bored," you were told to "go read."

Through the years, friends often commented on how, whenever anyone asked a question, my father would start the train to the bookshelves in pursuit of the answer – pulling off volume after volume (in ever deepening spirals) of the encyclopedia he had purchased when the first of us entered grade school – until nearly half the set had to be put back.

He took us to the theater and to the opera, often and regularly.

By the time his medical practice began to be truly established, he had joined (along with our mother and a changing assortment of their children) local productions of musical theater – and we were induced to learn the music and script too, even when we didn't have a part in the play, because he needed help rehearsing.

All of this modeled a cultured masculinity, which is not to say that my father was not a gendered man, or a man of his times, or a religious man with an ideology about the place of women.... But it is to say that he was not a narrow man, in terms of the interests he let himself (and his sons) pursue. He did not limit his masculinity to our mainstream model of violence and anger and broken communication skills.

If my brothers, as heirs of his masculinity, can do anything, it's talk. And sing . . . .

And appreciate the greats, and the greatness, of theater and literature and history and science....

~~~

And certainly boys get the message early on that

talking, communicating,

218

is seen as a weakness in men . . . .

The truth is, if you're a man who wants an intimate
relationship with a woman

– and most men do –

you better be the one she tells her deep dark secrets
to,

because it's impossible to have an intimate
relationship,

a successful one,

without being vulnerable,

without communicating.

Jean Kilbourne[7]

~~~

The question before us is, *How then should we bring up boys,
that we may reduce the ubiquity of violence, including violence against women
and girls, in our culture?*[8] (That question must also be asked,
globally, by those in other cultures about their own societies.)

Concurrently, we need to ask, *How should we bring up girls so
that they too, first, pursue authentic and freely-chosen lives for themselves,
and second, desire broadly cultured and authentic partners?*

From the cultural trappings attached to wedding
ceremonies, to the ideology that (primarily) mothers cook and

---

[7] Kilbourne 2000, 2010
[8] Jones 1980 p5

do laundry after a hard day at the office while fathers watch television,[9] to the storylines in books, television, and movies, males - alas – are still, continually, fed the message that they are superior to females – served and pursued by females – and that one day, no matter how base or how vile, each male may expect to have a female as individual woman/servant/lover of his own *to attend to* his domestic and sexual **needs**.[10] And these males are raised, in our society, in our day and time, to be violent – or at least, to exalt and admire violence. As masculinity scholars point out, violence has become normative masculinity.[11]

This is unacceptable. It is the source of great harm, great pain – unnecessary harm and unnecessary pain.

In both the first and second wave of women's work for fairness and equity, activists set about responding to the problems of partner violence. Women *"have spent…[almost a century and a half] exposing wife abuse with insistence and accuracy,[12] [and decades] organizing shelters[13] and escape routes and changing law enforcement practices so that, increasingly, [woman]-beating is recognized as a violent crime."*[14]

However, there has been no serious change in the central problem - male (and often female) *belief* in **male privilege** (or male right of rule).   .

Today's youth achieve majority in an era in which media, and the youth subculture, promote a highly sexist standard of distinctly different ("complementary") sexual roles.

---

[9] Hochschild & Machung 2012; Louis 2007

[10] Mill 1986/1869

[11] Katz 2000; Coltrane 2005; Connell 1995; Messner 2004; Reeves Sanday 1981

[12] The first wave of women's activism addressed partner violence through its connection with substance (alcohol) abuse, forming the Temperance Movement, in the belief that prohibition would reduce woman battering. There remains a direct connection between partner battery and alcohol.

[13] The shelter movement began in 1971, in London, with Erin Pizzey; see also Jones 1980 pp282-283

[14] Dworkin 1997 p43

While young women expect to work for pay (the traditional male sex role), and more and more young men expect them to work (and to benefit by their incomes),[15] the same young women, by and large, still carry a larger share of the burden of housework and childcare (the traditional female sex role)[16] – sometimes prompting a nostalgia for oppressions-gone-by.

Yet, returning to a life limited by the cloister (and the financial dependence and servitude) of the home, is not actually the balance that would rectify this inequality and make life (home and work life) more fulfilling.

Three-quarters of women with children under age eighteen now work for pay outside the home, as do two-thirds of women with children under age three (73% work full time). Yet, among heterosexual married couples, the male partner factually carries the burden of housework, childrearing, and day care responsibility less than the female partner.[17] "Full-time working moms with preschool kids put in [at least] an extra . . . five to seven hours [a week], or an extra two weeks a year of twenty-four-hour days" doing childcare and housework. .[18] Because of this ongoing, *unequal* distribution of *necessary domestic "care work,"* between procreative partners, young women still stunt their career advancement, making career decisions based on their perception of juggling a given career with childcare.

Also, there is ongoing backlash, leading to ongoing gender role confusion. Through the power of mass (television) evangelism, the conservative movement has more adherents now than before the 1980s. This movement, with its spill-over ideology from the Religious Right, calls for female submission,

---

[15] The need for dual income couples is also driven by economics. See Graff 1999

[16] Some, more highly paid women, "hand-down" their childcare and housework to low-income migrant women working as maids and nannies (Hochschild 2010 p269); See also Ehrenreicht & Hochschild 2002

[17] Hochschild 2012; Louis 2007

[18] Hochschild 2012 p266

an end to female access to contraception,[19] and a return to "God-ordained" "complementary" gender roles. Either through internalization of its ideology or through a nostalgia for a supposed past in which times were simpler and women "knew their place,"[20] some men still express gender role expectations for their wives in terms as regressive as those expounded before the changes of the 1970s (and some women express those same role expectations as well, for themselves and for their men).

Even as racism is passed down from generation to generation by ideology - by belief systems that espouse the "superiority" of the one over the "inferiority" of the other - **so the patriarchal demand for male supremacy in intimate relations is passed down, passed on, and passed over by an ideology** - *by a belief*.[21]

In order to oppress or harm another, one must see them as essentially different.

If you see yourself, or your group, as the prototype for human (as the "right" religion, ethnicity, race, gender, etc.), and *The Other* as *qualitatively different* than you, then by extension, that other must be *less than* you (or yours).[22] This is the foundation of the ability to oppress or to do harm, this emphasizing of difference over similarity, and it has shaped the history of imperialism and conquest for centuries.

It has also shaped the history of gender relations in Western culture for millennia.

It is ideological.

Men who believe in their own supremacy do *not* see women *as being as fully human* as they are themselves – and hence, have

---

[19] To all means of controlling reproduction – to all forms of contraception – not to abortion alone
[20] Coontz 2000
[21] Sexism
[22] Kilbourne 2000, 2010

few pangs of conscience for treating differently those whom they perceive to be quite different. Yet, "different but equal" can be no more equal than "separate but equal."

When you know that I am essentially the same — that I (*as The Other*) feel like you (*as The Prototypical Human*) feel, think like you think, and will hurt like you would hurt (that your action [because I, too, am fully human] will affect me as it would affect you), you will stop yourself from doing me intentional or callous harm.

To be rid of woman battering and sexual assault, more than shelters are necessary (though shelters are helpful). More than laws are necessary. More than good treatment at the hands of criminal justice systems is necessary. It is necessary to have more than police who arrest, prosecutors who prosecute, and judges who exercise equal justice.

What is needed is a new way of thinking — in family life, in media, in entertainment, in religion, in *parenting* - in every segment and strata of society.

Little boys need to be raised *experientially learning the equality of their sisters*.

Little girls need to share privilege in equal measure with little boys.

Individuals of all sexes and genders need to be given all the tools and encouragement needed to help them develop their full human potential. They need to grow up loved and directed and protected from all forms of abuse.

All sexes and genders need to learn and share the full set of responsibilities, including household chores.

One cannot *honestly* love that which one does not respect and consider to be, truly, fully equal to oneself.

Once they believe in the human rights and the equality of the women they have sex with, men will not use their fists in a free expression of temper that aims to enforce obedience or acquiescence, because they will no longer desire the acquiescence or the subservience of the (recognizably) fully-human women they claim to love.

~~~

[We are] trapped in **very rigid roles** and in very **crippling definitions of femininity and masculinity**.

In general, **human qualities**,[23] qualities **that we all share, that we all need**,[24]

are divided up, polarized, and labeled "masculine" and "feminine,"

and then the "feminine" is consistently devalued....[25]

Which causes women to devalue ourselves and each other[26]
and
men to devalue, not only women, but also
all those qualities that get labeled "feminine" by the culture

(and by that, I mean qualities like **compassion, cooperation, nurturance, empathy,**[27] **intuition,**[28] **sensitivity**).

We may give lip service to these qualities, but in fact

they have very low priority in our society, and
we all lose, and we lose very badly when we're told that

---

[23] Kilbourne 2000
[24] Kilbourne 2010
[25] Kilbourne 2000
[26] Kilbourne 2010
[27] Kilbourne 2000
[28] Kilbourne 2010

one gender can have only one set of human qualities and one gender, only the other.[29]

And men are still very rigidly socialized to **repress** these **human qualities** in themselves

at enormous cost to all of us.[30]

We obviously **end up** *being half or less of what we otherwise might be.*

And certainly, **this dehumanizes all of us**, men as well as women.

Jean Kilbourne[31]

~~~

At this writing, my twin grandsons still display a full range of human emotions. It is quite evident that – despite being born *un*ambiguously male – they experience (and express)[32] emotions like joy and excitement and delight and curiosity and sadness (yes, and anger). And along with the human qualities designated as "masculine," they also possess those human qualities Kilbourne notes are disparaged as "feminine" – compassion, cooperation, nurturance, empathy, intuition, and sensitivity.[33]

Were they, in future, to feel (and acquiesce to) the social constraint to "repress these human qualities in themselves," it would not only be at the *"cost"* of their *De Dé*'s (grandmother's) broken heart. It would be at the cost of their own detriment. They, themselves, would *"end up being half or less of what"*[34] they already so obviously are – full human beings with an inborn ability to experience the range of human emotional

---

[29] Kilbourne 2000
[30] Kilbourne 2010
[31] Kilbourne 2000, 2010, emphasis mine
[32] They spin. They squeal. They skip. They dance. They investigate. They touch. They cry. They sob.
[33] With each other, with other children, with their parents, with me.
[34] ibid

connectedness – with this world and with those other human beings in it.

It is imperative that we – you and I – find the way to raise boy *and* girl children to walk in the fullness of their human capacities for all things. Boys – in their human capability for emotional connection, empathy, expression, and interdependence; and girls – in their human capacity for excitement, action, exploration, adventure, courage, and independence. In order to hold onto, grow into, and express the fullness of our humanity, we all – all genders – need to be affirmed to that fullness.

We have a society in which social and economic resources are stratified by gender, race, class, sexual orientation, ablebodiedness, and more.

This social stratification is unjust. It is unfair.

All must be educated to know that the one who benefits from the enrichment of social privilege did not earn it, and the one who suffers from the immiseration of social disprivilege did not deserve it.[35] As they grow, children need to be taught about the power structure, about their individual location in that power structure, and about ways to improve, update, and change that power structure. The one born to privilege must be actively taught NOT TO BE PREJUDICED or discriminatory, lest "he" think it is to his credit that things come more easily to him – or that different things come to him – and he must be encouraged to work toward making a difference.

Insuring the equal distribution of resources and power should be the province of all in a *democracy*.

Even so, boys need to be taught (through example, experience, conversation, text, and film) that Daddy is not *better than* (or even particularly all that *different from*) Mommy, that maleness is not *better than* femaleness, and that – as a matter of

---

[35] Feagin 2001

biological and social **fact** (except reproductively), females and males are not even all that different (*that the statistical distributions of abilities, interests, physical strength, height, intelligence, and qualities (erroneously) labeled "male" or "female" overlap*) – that we have more in common across gender than we often do within gender.

Boys need to grow up in homes where they *see* women being respected and where they *see women respecting themselves*.

Instead of being taught to see women as physically and intellectually frail beings who *need* male help for subsistence, boys need to be taught to see women as full, equal human beings with an inborn right to fair and equal treatment – and to fully equal opportunity. They need to grow up in homes where they see women being independent – not taking abuse (also, not dishing it out) – but respecting themselves enough to stand on their own two feet and to give – and demand – fair and equitable treatment in return – women who will not stay where they are not respected.

We must change ourselves, and then the society around us. Where we cannot change the society, we must counter the cultural and media messages that demean girls and reify rigid gender roles.

We must make sure that boys, growing up, know and understand the basic humanity and similarity, across gender, of girls; and that girls know and understand the basic humanity and similarity, across gender, of boys – *and their own basic humanity and similarity with boys*.

And culture-wide, we must get over our internalized homophobia – our society-wide fear of all things *"gay"* or *"different"* or *"queer"* or *"trans"* or *"intersex."*

This fear is a form of sexism,[36] in that, more than being concerned with the gender of one's romantic/affectional/sexual partners, it is about the social policing of gender role

---

[36] Pharr 1997

presentation – and at its core, about any breakdown of the sex/gender line.

It challenges the female-bodied person who presents as "masculine," because she has no right to power, and disparages the male-bodied person who presents as "feminine" or "effeminate," because he has power, and has no right to give power up – to prefer the presentation that is less respected, the traits (erroneously gendered and) labeled "feminine." Privileged males must not give up or modify their privilege by appearing "feminine" or "weak. And disprivileged females must not press into power by appearing "masculine" or "strong." And, in our culture, those who are transgender in mind and identity, or intersex in body, simply may not exist, because they challenge the biology behind the rigid, binary, divide of gender role presentation.

We must nurture the full breadth of the humanity of our children, including the softness, gentleness, joy, artistic urges, [37] and ability to nurture[38] of males and the daring, engagement, creativity, and desire to explore in girls.

Whether straight or bi or gay, or somewhere else along the continuum, sexual orientation[39] *IS TO BE CELEBRATED.* In her coming out episode, the character Ellen (played by Ellen

---

[37] All things we currently socially-construct as "not manly," because they are not limited to a masculine identity that is in opposition to all things viewed as "feminine."

[38] Practiced through early childhood play with dolls shaped like human babies that have human baby needs that must be attended to by a "parent" figure. Most boys grow up to be, biologically, fathers. Like the other sex, they, too, should get to practice future parenthood in their own childhoods.

[39] Sexual orientation is inborn. Or at the very least, in whatever measure sexual orientation is socialized, almost all of the socialization is *intended to cause one to conform* to a *normative gender presentation* (to be standardly male or female) and to make one *straight*. No man has ever been made gay because he was allowed, as a baby or toddler, to pretend to nurture another human baby by playing with a doll, or because he was allowed to express his creative urge to draw or study music. If you think you know of such a case, it wasn't the doll, or the crayon, or the piano. The fact that there was a doll in the hands of a toddler who grew up to be a gay man is mere coincidence. There is no correlation. And the doll/crayon/instrument is definitively NOT causative of same-sex orientation or gender presentation diversity.

DeGeneres) pointed out, *"You never see a cake that says, "Good for you! You're gay!"*[40]

That needs to change – culture-wide. The oppressed must always take the helm of their own liberation. No group gives up privilege to the group that is disempowered, except the disempowered group empowers itself – and then persistently and vocally demands equality.

In order to give boys the homes, the families, the broad upbringings that will allow each of them to become fully all that they have the potential to be – in order to make this generational shift in how men see, and treat, women – the women of this (and each) generation must shift how they see themselves, and how they allow themselves to be treated.

Women must again be educated to come to consciousness.

As stated in 1848, in the *Declaration of Sentiments*, ratified and passed as the first Women's Rights convention in Seneca Falls, New York:

> *Resolved: Women ought to be enlightened...*
> *that they may no longer publish their degradation*
> *by declaring themselves satisfied*
> *with their present position,*
> *nor their ignorance,*
> *by asserting that they have all the rights they want."*
>
> *Elizabeth Cady Stanton*[41]

Women today, like the women of prior generations, must demand the change they need.

We must demand mutually respectful relationships, with a truly equitable division of labor within each relationship.

---

[40] DeGeneres 1997
[41] Resolution. Declaration of Sentiments. Seneca Falls, NY, 1848

When we work for pay outside the home, we must demand that our partners share the burden of domestic and childcare work.

When we choose to work, without pay, within the home, and raise children and tend house, we must demand that such care work be seen *as work* and refuse to be financially abused in either marriage or divorce, *because we see and know that such work has financial value.*

And we must protect our children from abuse, wherever that abuse may come from.[42] And if they experience the misfortune of being attacked, we need to *hear* them and get them the help they need to move from victim to survivor.

And, women themselves must demand sexual autonomy.

I teach college. The sexual double standard is in full force, with boys/men having social permission to explore their (hetero)sexuality, and girls/women still (often viciously) being "slut bashed"[43] if they have "casual" sex outside of a "relationship," and/or have more than 2 to 4 sexual partners before settling into the conformity of long-term monogamy.

Males in the college classroom [44]still discuss the madonna/whore dichotomy with vigor, and often, in full agreement that there are "different kinds" of girls – good girls and bad girls, the kind you use and the kind you take home to your mother/family.

Girls/women are not yet socially entitled to the same kinds or quantity of sexual activity, or number of partners and degree of exploration, to which boys/men are socially entitled.

---

[42] We should be vigilant, but calm enough to hear our gut – our intuition. (De Becker 2000)

[43] Personal classroom observation; see also Tanenbaum 2000

[44] At least in the Northeastern United States in 2012

The sexual double standard plays heavily in today's gender divide – in general disrespect, in present-day rape myths, and in physical relationship violence (gendered assault).

Until the sexual freedom and autonomy of girls/women is viewed in the same way as the sexual freedom and autonomy of boys/men, we cannot raise the public outrage for rape or woman battering – because, in the minds of society, some women are the "type" of women who are "asking for" and "deserve" these horrific disrespects.

The sexual double standard also affects the kinds of men women choose to reward with their attentions.

Because they feel unsafe, women still (often) demand a man who can "protect" them and "make the decisions" – the "big, strong man" to whom she is not a physical equal, but who can make her feel safe from other men (*until or unless* he becomes her assailant). And, with the help of the media messages of pop culture, many women still look for a macho male – a man who is enacting the *tough guy pose*[45] – a pretense about the violence and lack of communication that all-too-often becomes the long-term reality of male-female relationships.

Our sexual tastes or proclivities[46] (especially within normative heterosexuality)[47] are, in good measure, social constructions that we receive from the culture around us and then internalize.[48]

Through every media and social outlet, women have been sold on, have been marketed the image of, the *big strong protective male*, and our programmed desires for that image both undercut our own independence and autonomy and place us in harm's

---

[45] Katz 2000

[46] Not the same as our romantic/affectional *orientation*.

[47] Gay people have not, historically, been sold by media on the wonders **of being** gay. Straight people are, and have been historically, sold by the media (and other sociocultural and religious groups) on **how to be** straight.

[48] Seidman 2009

way with a man who has internalized his right of rule. Jackson Katz makes this point,

> **Girls and women** are ***not responsible***
> for men's violence,
> [but] they too **have an important role to play**,
> because the Tough Guise is attractive to men
> in part,
>
> because they see many girls and women validating it.
>
> Girls and women have to show that they're **looking for more** in men than bad boy posturing, and in particular [that] **they value men who reject the Tough Guise**.
>
> Jackson Katz[49]

Women need to, again, rise up and declare themselves equally, fully human and worthy of all rights and fair treatment – with-in and with-out relationships.

And, in the midst of our gratitude, as U.S.-based first world women, that we do not (from our culture) suffer **all** *of the same kinds of abuse* as our sisters in other parts of the world, we need to **come out of denial about the kinds and quantities of abuses we do suffer – often, simply because we are female – and stop blessing ourselves and genuflecting.**

In the U.S., we are not immune. Even as overseas, girls and women suffer gender abuse, assault, and discrimination *here* **– because they are girls and women.**

---

[49] Katz 2000

One of the problems with sustaining women's activism has been the fact that – rather than being ghettoized together, in community with one another – women are, by and large, segregated from each other (from a majority of the other members of our subordinate group) by our placement within families.[50] Each of us, straight, or lesbian, or bi, or gender queer, or trans, is in relationship with members of the dominant group – with fathers, and grandfathers, and brothers, and sons, and grandsons, and uncles, and nephews, and male in-laws – and that segregation from women's collectivities into mixed gender family structures creates qualitatively different problems for women's organizing into activist groups and movements than are experienced by other subordinate groups.

This is further complicated by cultural and religious memberships and identities that divide us from each other – that mitigate our sisterhood as a whole.

Nevertheless, we must again **come to see our common cause.**

This time, our fight is not so much about our place in the spheres of education and employment (though we do not yet have *full* equality there either), but about our place in interpersonal relationships – in those very private, familial and social relations with the males we love. We need to demand that we be treated with full fairness, respect, and equality ***within* our relationships.**[51]

As Kilbourne has argued,

The changes have to be profound and global.

We need to get involved in whatever way moves us,

to change … [the] attitudes that run so deep in our culture,

---

[50] Mill 1986/1869
[51] We also, still and always, need the right to effective contraception.

and that affect each one of us so deeply –

whether we're conscious of it or not.

It can be frightening to speak out, to stand up in this way,

but as more and more people – men and women –

find the courage to do this,

the environment will change.

…Because **what's at stake** for **all of us** …

is **our ability to have authentic and freely chosen lives.**

Nothing less.

Jean Kilbourne[52]

I will finish with two more thoughts. Of his journalistic work for the safety and liberation of women worldwide, Nicolas Kristof,[53] has said,

I'm just outraged

by the atrocities that I see.

One way to fight warlords and rapists is with
U.N. peacekeepers and large guns.

**Another way to fight them is with small
notebooks and pens.**
That's what I do.

Nicholas Kristof[54]

---

[52] Kilbourne 2000, 2010
[53] co-author with Sheryl WuDunn, of *Half the Sky*

And with this notebook, this electronic pen, I remind us once more of these words,

We are [all] caught in **an inescapable network of mutuality**,

tied in **a single garment of destiny**.

Whatever affects one directly,

affects all indirectly.

Rev Dr. Martin Luther King, Jr.[55]

And of these:

As long as rape is deemed unspeakable,

and is therefore not fully and honestly spoken of,

the public outrage will be muted as well.

Geneva Overholser[56]

Let us unmute the outrage.

Whatever affects one of us, affects us all.

---

[54] Kristof 2010
[55] Rev. Dr. Martin Luther King, Jr.
[56] Overholser 1992

Nadine Rosechild Sullivan, Ph.D., Rev.

APPENDIX A –
RAPE
&
THE CRIMINAL JUSTICE SYSTEM

1. Women and Children as Property

Our rape laws come down to us with a history. They were codified as a way to deal with the violation by one man of another man's (virginal/ or chaste) property.[1]

The response of the Criminal Justice System has its foundation in the British Common Law of Coverture, under which women were the legal property (and wards) of their nearest male relatives (generally fathers or husbands). In that women-as-property ideology, only the violation of the vagina (of a daughter's virginity or a wife's chastity), and not the violation of the woman's person as a whole – mattered to the legal definition of rape. The actual illegality of rape lay in this violation of another man's rights; not in the harming a fellow human being. Rape of a virgin lessened her marriageability (her *sale* value/her purchase price). Rape of a wife lessened her *status* as the chaste possession of a single male owner.

Antiquated as this ideology sounds today, rape victims are still viewed through this lens of male ownership.

Society still treats rape/sexual assault in the light of a perceived male right (or an evolutionary urgency) to sexual prowess – and to persistence against female resistance. Male right of sexual access is legally counter-balanced with the rights of other men to protection of their own *property*.

The rape of males has had no legal consequences,[2] which is why, in part, the victimization of male children has had so little consequence, in that rape of male children has not been seen as a damage to an adult man's property or a damage to the child/adolescent male's ability to own property in adulthood.

---

[1] Brownmiller 1975
[2] See upcoming section entitled, "Rape: Limited Definition"

Therefore, in contradistinction to the experience for assaulted males, it has not, historically, been viewed as a legally-important loss.

It is – still – a woman's responsibility to keep herself *safe*, which usually translates as, keeping herself *at home*. Women are responsible to circumscribe, to limit, the places they go and the people with whom they associate. A woman, even a girl child, is responsible to *know better than* to be alone with – or to trust – the acquaintance that suddenly turns into her perpetrator. It is her naiveté for trusting, for failing to suspect every male, which is seen as the problem, not the assailant's aggression. (In cultures that practice "honor killing," even the young female rape victim (6 years old) will be killed if she is raped – because she is considered to have reached an age of accountability *for keeping herself* safe and blamed because *she must have put herself* in jeopardy. The perpetrator is unlikely to even be tried.)

In reported rape, Western society still puts the victim on trial – both in the public sentiment and in the courts. Rape is discounted, covered over, under-reported, and under-prosecuted. Help for the victim is meager and slow, and after the fact, her *character* is still put on trial. And the protection of the rights of the perpetrator and his reputation continue to have primacy.

The second wave of women's activism made some improvement in societal attitudes toward the victim in the administration of emergency treatment after a rape. Women began to provide crisis intervention for each other through telephone hotlines, information, and empathy, and to provide in-person support during emergency room examinations and police interviews. Along with domestic abuse shelters, women themselves developed domestic violence and rape hotlines, women's centers, and rape crisis centers. Many remain to this day.

The women's rights spotlight on rape raised national consciousness about the impact on the victim, and set the stage for some legal change. Today, the court system is *supposed* to have moved away from the open and unashamed practice of (unofficially) prosecuting the victim, instead of the assailant.

There have been two legal shifts in response to women's activism. Each has met with limited success.

Rape Shield laws were put into place to prohibit the defense from cross-examining the plaintiff about her prior sexual conduct.[3] Yet:

> Despite legal changes that give victims more rights, some detectives noted that things don't always happen the way the law intend[s] . . . police personnel use the same defenses as the general public to distance themselves from rape. If women [in the system or on juries] believe that only certain kinds of women get raped, they can feel less vulnerable [through doing denial]. If men can place part of the blame on the survivor, they can partially deny that their own gender could do something so abhorrent.[4]

And the attorneys who defend accused rapists can no longer flagrantly discredit the victim by openly rehearsing her sexual history, as if whether or not a woman can be violated is based on *her chastity* or conformity to religious/social *morals*.

Also, the victim can no longer be polygraphed or forced to undergo a psychological evaluation to see if she is given to lying or delusions. Nevertheless,

> matters of her character and mental state can [still] be addressed in a court of law more covertly . . . . [The defense can still] bring up her poor judgment . . . [including] the way she was dressed . . . [the location/s to which she went and] . . . whether [or not] she was using alcohol or drugs.[5]

Since the late 1970s, the courts have also begun to recognize that a woman *in a relationship* (married/partnered) has an ongoing right to refuse consent to sexual interactions – even if that relationship is long-term or legally enacted (as in marriage). The courts have

---

3 O'Gorman Hughes & Sandler 1987
4 Madigan & Gamble 1991 p81
5 Madigan & Gamble 1991 p105

begun to recognize that **violation of** an intimate partner's ***refusal*** by a current (*or former*) spouse/partner) *IS* rape.

Yet, when it comes to partner rape, even today, a subtle form of persecution of the victim still remains.

> Jurors are often biased by the archaic notion of "claim of rights." This notion is based on the belief that *if* a woman has consented to sex in the past, [**then**] *the man has a continuing right to sexual satisfaction.* Medieval property rights pertaining to the entitlement of usage [of a wife] at any time and [any] place are still alive and well. This is particularly true in cases of spousal rape. The closer the relationship between victim and rapist, ***the more force must be exhibited*** [for the incident to be viewed as rape or assault].[6]

2. Who May Prosecute

Many victims are surprised to find out that it is not they who get to decide whether or not to press charges. Instead, it is the criminal justice system – not the victim – which decides which cases go to court and which do not.

Early in the process, it's the response of police officers[7] themselves that may prejudice an outcome.

Later, if the report makes it that far, it is not the victim, but the prosecutor who has the discretionary power to decide whether or not to prosecute a perpetrator. The prosecutor determines if the case will go before the district attorney. At this juncture, individual level prejudice, on the part of the prosecutor, can be a factor.

Beyond that, the determination of which cases are "founded" enough to warrant the effort and expense of the pursuit, arrest, and trial of a perpetrator – or are dismissed out of

---

[6] Madigan & Gamble 1991 p77, emphasis mine
[7] These include the sexism, racism, classism, heterosexism, and transphobia of individual police officers, whose attitudes often mirror the attitudes toward victims of society itself.

hand – is based on whether or not a case appears likely to be winnable in court.[8]

Despite the fact that date rape accounts for the highest proportion of rapes (in 75% to 80% of rapes, the assailant knows, or is known to, the victim before the assault),[9] prosecutors rarely pursue date rape cases. Attorneys in general (including prosecutors and district attorneys) resist taking cases they feel they can't win.[10] In date rape, the victim's mere acquaintance with the assailant renders her motives for *crying rape* suspect in the minds of many litigators, judges, and jurors.

> Women . . . are punished by the system whether they fight back or don't fight back. But if they almost lose their life or sustain serious injuries, they have a strong[er] case . . . . The district attorney we interviewed unanimously stated that the burden of proof lay with [the victim] – not [with] the defense [the alleged perpetrator] .
> . . . In rape cases, it is very difficult to get a guilty verdict . . . *because of the bias with which we view rape in our society.* When an attorney decides to file charges . . . he or she must consider how a *not-guilty* verdict would affect his or her career. A female prosecutor said, "There is tremendous pressure on us to win every case.". . . District attorneys refuse a case if they don't think it's convincing. Our egos and reputations are at [stake]. We like to win.[11]

The acquaintance rapist is, generally, met with a presumption of his truthfulness, and the case is viewed as *her word against his*, making it difficult for her to prove that the sex was forced. The insinuation that she *led him on* is enough to discredit her. The case is also prejudiced by the police ideology of a *victim-precipitated* rape,[12] one in which she *led him on*, or may be perceived as having initially *wanted him* (as in displaying some

---

[8] SATF 2008
[9] ibid
[10] For the sake of their careers
[11] Madigan & Gamble 1991 p95, emphasis mine
[12] Madigan & Gamble 1992 p75

degree of trust of a male, otherwise known as naiveté, by acts like accepting a drink or taking an offered ride home).

For the case to be viewed as legally valid, rape victims are held responsible to have *known better* than to take *any* male at face value, and to have demonstrated a high "level of resistance,"[13] such as evidence of physical injury.

Yet, the acquaintance rapist is less likely (than the stranger rapist) to use a weapon. Rather than weaponry, acquaintance rape generally relies on *grooming the victim to establish trust*, then *use of the element of surprise*. It may also involve physically overpowering the victim, but often, at close range and in a way that may not necessitate the use of fists or other weapons. In acquaintance rape, 70% of the time, no visible bruises or injuries are apparent, and 84% of the time, the assault is carried out without a knife or firearm.[14]

Yet, sexual assault is not, of necessity, less emotionally traumatic when there are no visible physical bruises. The emotional damage of being violated in such a personal way, the sense of helplessness, the probability of post-traumatic repercussions, is overwhelming – whether or not the body also has to (or even can) fully mend.

In the case of rape, "many people still believe the notion of "death before dishonor." In that thinking, only a woman willing to risk her life will be believed.[15]

Yet, *"**no other violent crime** requires **ANY** level of victim resistance."*[16]

> **In robbery**, victims are **not expected to fight back**. In fact, law enforcement agencies **recommend** that victims surrender their property **without a struggle**.[17]

---

[13] Madigan & Gamble 1991 p76
[14] SATF 2008
[15] Madigan & Gamble 1991 p76, emphasis mine
[16] ibid
[17] ibid

3. The Second Rape

The treatment of victims by the criminal justice system is often spoken of as the second rape.

The victim "is exposed to three specific aspects of [further] victimization by the judicial proceedings: delays, the public setting, [and] the treatment of the victim *as if [s/he] were the offender.*"[18]

> Statistics bear out the terror of [this] second rape . . . . Only one out of ten rapes is reported to the police . . . . Only two out of one hundred rapists are ever punished for the crime they have committed. Ninety-eight percent of all rapists go free.[19]

A Philadelphia Inquirer article demonstrated how police discretion can go awry. When the Philadelphia Police Department reviewed its sexual-assault cases, detectives "identified more than 300 rapes [in 5 years time] that were written off by investigators in the Special Victims Unit." The Department also "identified more than 2,000 cases that were improperly classified and shelved," and when they were reinvestigated, "all . . . were found to involve serious crimes."[20]

From the rape victim's perspective, hospital and medical treatment also leave much to be desired. The victim's freedom to choose whether or not to report is taken from hir by the act of seeking medical aid, and the evidence collection procedures inflict as many psychological wounds as the physical wounds they should help heal. "Medical personnel . . . are only one link in a chain of command that abides by society's myths and treatment of rape, and they can cause grave harm . . . ."[21]

The actual medical procedure is traumatic.

---

[18] Madigan & Gamble 1991 p99, emphasis mine
[19] Madigan & Gamble 1991 p7
[20] McCoy & Fazlollah 2000 pA1 & A14
[21] Madigan & Gamble 1991 p90

Depending on the extent and severity of her physical injuries and how crowded the waiting room is, she may have to wait an uncomfortably long time . . . . The [victim] is often not informed about what will be done procedurally . . . . The standard rape exam collects two types of evidence – physical . . . and the woman's medical history – both of which are extremely intrusive. A third type

. . . concerns details of the . . . assault . . . . Specimens of physical evidence are collected. Medical personnel scrutinize and probe the survivor's entire body, including her scalp and fingernails. Her outer body is examined for trauma to collect hairs . . . semen, and blood. A urine sample is requested for a baseline pregnancy test. During the gynecological part of the exam, medical personnel . . . take a swab of the cervical canal . . . . The physician also examines anal skin and inspects for anal penetration . . . . Photographs [may be] taken . . . . They [question the victim about] . . . pregnancy . . . type of contraception . . . voluntary intercourse . . . [for] four days prior to the assault . . . the date, time, and location [of the assault] . . . [and hir] previous use of alcohol or drugs, *an item of concern to the police* . . . .[22]

Juries tend to reflect the attitudes of society at large,[23] and juries "tend to be prejudiced against the prosecution [the state with the victim as its witness] in rape cases."[24] They will go to great lengths to be lenient with defendants [accused assailants] if there is any suggestion of contributory behavior on the part of the [victim], including hitchhiking, dating, and talking with men at parties."[25]

The entire process of reporting and prosecuting a rape exacts a tremendous price from the victim. It is a price

---

[22] Madigan & Gamble 1991 pp85-86
[23] Madigan & Gamble 1991 p75
[24] Estrich 1987
[25] Madigan & Gamble 1991 p75

which most women have only a hazy awareness of in advance. Yet, because of the victim's sense of violation, s/he can bear little additional trauma, and that awareness contributes to the underreporting which is common in cases of sexual assault.

> Usually the first place the [victim] must appear in the legal arena is at the arraignment or preliminary hearing. There, a judge determines whether there is sufficient evidence to bind the suspect, who has just been arrested, over for trial. The [victim], *who is now . . . a witness for the state . . .* may be called upon to testify. [S/he] can be cross-examined by the counsel for the suspect, who is now . . . the defendant . . . . If the judge finds sufficient evidence, or probable cause, the case is scheduled for trial in a higher court. The defendant is either jailed or released on bail (based on whether or not he has a record for felonies). If the case is not bound over for trial, it is dismissed . . . . Sometimes it is a shock for the [victim] to realize that [hir] attacker will be sitting in front of [hir] at the hearing . . . . The arraignment . . . can occur very soon after the initial report. *The [assailant] is entitled* to hear everyone's testimony, so as to rebut it later. The [victim] is a witness and *is allowed in the courtroom only while she is testifying . . . . [It is] not [the victim's] trial . . . . The attacker's rights [are] the ones being protected.*[26]

Most rape cases, if they come to trial, are eventually settled through plea bargaining. The decision to plea bargain is frequently made without the woman.

> The [victim] often . . . views [plea bargaining] as a betrayal . . . . One [prosecutor] reported, "Plea bargaining is not really the victim's choice . . . . We can override her.". . . Plea bargaining is *based on political and economic reasons and has little to do with the survivor.* A case can be plea-bargained

---

[26] Madigan & Gamble, 1991 p97, emphasis mine

any time, *even after the trial has begun.*[27]

cases do make it all the way through the trial

ag plea bargained, it becomes apparent that most judges are males who may identify with the male fear of false accusation and may also have internalized the culture's rape mythologies. Evidence of this is seen in the fact that in this country, stranger rapists who have impregnated their victims during their assaults, have, after their release from prison, sometimes been granted paternal rights of visitation and/or custody of the children created by their act of rape. An expression of misogyny, more than an act of sex, most rapists, caught and uncaught, remain repeat offenders; and society continues to blame their victims.

4. Rape: Limited Definition

At present (2012), there is an attempt to update and broaden the legal definition of rape. Since the 1920s (and until the time of this writing), the FBI has only accepted into its counts reports of sexual assault that meet a very narrow definition of rape – forced, male-on-female, penile-vaginal penetration. Typically, police departments have followed suit, *unfounding* cases that do not meet, or are more broad than, the FBI criterion of forced, male-on-female, penile-vaginal penetration.[28]

However, a definition of rape that most Americans today would see as more reasonable, would be a definition that includes – along with forced penile vaginal penetration – forced oral or anal" penetration, and a definition that would allow for the inclusion of the experience of male victims (and victims of all ages).

By these broader, more socially-valid definitions, it is likely that as many as "1.5 million [females] and 834,700 [males] experience sexual violation, annually, in the United States."[29]

---

[27] Madigan & Gamble 1991 p99, emphasis mine
[28] Savage 2012; SATF 2008
[29] Tjaden and Thoennes 1998, 2, 5

5. Unfounding

Unfounding (case closure or clearance) is a means by which law enforcement officials remove a case from their investigative to-do list.[30]

Unfounding is not based on evidence that a rape or assault did not occur, or on a perpetrator being found innocent after investigation, but is **based, instead, on the narrowness of the FBI definition**.

Even though unfounded by the system, "**over 92% of rape reports are**" **true**, "not false." Only 2-8% of reported rapes are found to be false accusations."[31]

Police departments routinely "unfound" reports of *forced* vaginal penetration by an object, oral and anal penetration by a penis or an object, and of *forced* male-on-male, female-on-female, or female-on-male sexual contact.

Also likely to be "unfounded" are reports of forced penile-vaginal penetration when the victim is known to the assailant prior to the assault (acquaintance and date rape), where there is no report of a weapon used, or when there are no bruises or injuries indicative of a physical beating (the lack of which may be perceived as a lack of victim resistance).

The FBI criterion may also be used to unfound cases in which the victim has been drugged or is otherwise incapacitated and, therefore, *unable* to give consent (as when the victim is mentally-challenged, very drunk, or even unconscious), is underage (and therefore, by state standards and by psychological standards, unable to give knowledgeable consent), or in which the perpetrator and victim had a prior relationship.[32]

---

[30] SATF 2008

[31] FBI 1995

[32] Gross 2009; A formerly-consenting partner (ex) always has/*should have* the free-will and legal right to withdraw present or future consent. Even a current legal spouse has no ethical right to forcibly *take* sexual contact from a presently non-consenting partner.

All of these factors mean that our collection of statistics on rape and sexual assault are severely undercounted, and in no way reflect the real frequencies of their occurrence.[33]

However, **legal unfounding renders the assault, and its effects, no less real**.

The unfounding of a rape or assault report by legal authorities does not by any means indicate that any particular allegation was untrue or was proven false through investigation.[34]

6. Recantation

As with unfounding, when a victim recants, recantation is not evidence that a report of rape/assault was false. The Oregon Attorney General's Sexual Assault Task Force found that:

> Recantation is most often used by victims to disengage the criminal justice, or other systems, because they no longer wish to participate. Victims may not realize the toll that a criminal investigation and trial will take on them mentally, emotionally, physically, and financially. As a result they may want their involvement in the process to end. Moreover, since most cases of sexual assault are committed by someone known to the victim, pressure from the offender or concern for the offender's well being may also be a factor.[35]

Because we internalize the messages of our immediate and larger societies, victims may also recant, or may fail to report at all, because their experience does not line up with the socially-accepted image of what constitutes rape and sexual violence.

Rape by a stranger at gun or knife point is likely to be reported, but victims of acquaintance rape may be confused as

---

[33] ibid
[34] SATF 2008
[35] ibid

to whether what happened to them meets the definition of rape or sexual assault.

Victims who are physically injured during an assault may seek medical treatment for their injuries and, in doing so, report the rape. But messages to women (or children) about strangers, and about physical safety outside at night, do not convey the societal message that forced sexual contact by a college classmate you have known for a window of time is also rape. And, even when you clearly said no, or asked the assailant to stop, rape on a date carries with it all of the complications of the fact that you were 1) willing to spend time with, 2) willing to be alone with, and 3) willing to consider a romantic relationship with your assailant. It is often viewed as a "he said/she said" situation, in which a man can be falsely accused. Despite rape shield laws, in both the court of public opinion and actual court, the victim's character (and, often, dress) are still likely to be put on trial – a treatment (that along with medical and police treatment is) part of "the second rape."[36]

Victims, who are raped by acquaintances or on dates, may be confused about what even happened.

If alcohol or drugs were a part of the interaction, if the victim gave consent for some acts but not others (say kissing or petting, but not penetration), the victim may feel shame or embarrassment for having trusted the perpetrator enough to let hir guard down. S/he may, perhaps rightly, fear s/he will not be believed.[37]

Complications of these sorts, and the internalization of shame and embarrassment at such personal violation, may lead victims to recant – or never to report at all. Nevertheless, all the effects and aftermath – post-trauma – of sexual assault remain in place for the victim across the decades ahead.

---

[36] See section III (8), page 36 of this text; see also Madigan & Gamble 1991 p7
[37] SATF 2008

.

APPENDIX B –
WOMAN BATTERING
&
THE CRIMINAL JUSTICE SYSTEM

1. Response of the System

In largely unexamined ways, our laws still mirror the attitudes and traditions of male supremacy. And justice is mediated by human beings. At all levels, the actions of criminal justice workers are affected by both the law, as it was and as it is, and by personally held beliefs[1] about *the gendered place* of men and women in family and social life. Inadvertently, and across their lifetimes, the attitudes of male supremacy have been internalized by many of the human individuals who work within the criminal justice system. Attitudes of male supremacy/superiority and female subordination/inferiority are a part of the smog we all breathe.[2]

Through these *human* criminal justice workers, male supremacy continues to inform the response of our system to the regular, repeated, violent, and brutal assault of (those who are overwhelmingly) female by perpetrators (who are overwhelmingly) male.[3] That response mirrors society at large in its judgment of "the abused woman" victim, and its complicity, blind-eye, and often justification of the male who perpetrates the violence against her.

---

[1] Internalized ideologies
[2] Tatum 2003
[3] Generally heterosexual women's male "intimate" partners. This is not to deny that males may be assaulted by their male intimate partners in same-sex relationships, or by other men, especially if the male victim is perceived to be, in any way, gender nonconforming. Neither is it to deny that males are sometimes (most often while still children or adolescents) assaulted by females, or to deny that females are sometimes assaulted by females (as children or in same-sex adolescent or adult relationships). Yet, the truth that domestic violence and sexual assault statistics paint is overwhelmingly a picture of male violence against females, at all ages: in childhood, in adolescence, and as adults.

When a woman is abused, her experience with those she turns to for help is impacted as much by cultural myths and attitudes as it is by the hard-won legal changes of women's social justice movements. It is not uncommon to have one law on the books, and another, unwritten social code acted out in an individual woman's experience of seeking help through the system. Violence is met with gendered expectations. Males are expected to be violent.

Women are expected to be non-violent, and when they enact violence in self-defense, female victims of male violence are held up to a standard of justice initially defined in the criminal code for male-on-male violence – a *standard of* **equal force** – that is generally unreasonable in a male-on-female altercation. Thus, women who kill their abusers are highly likely to serve much longer sentences than male abusers who kill their victims.

2   The Criminal Justice System

a.   Police

A woman who stands against an abusive male, ultimately stands alone. No matter her resources, family, or friends, no matter the statutes in place or the diligence of those who enforce them, no threatened woman can be sure that help will arrive before her assailant injures or kills her.

The system is ineffective. In largely unexamined ways, our laws still mirror the attitudes and traditions of male supremacy. And society cannot eliminate woman battering without renouncing these expectations.

Meanwhile, battered women are left on their own. Despite the changes in the law, police still provide little protection to the female victim of assault by a partner. In too many places, police still question women about an assault in the presence of their angry assailants (assailants who will soon have opportunity to strike again). Too often they still accept protestations that the "couple" was "merely" having a minor family squabble. Too often they still do not arrest, even when they are called to the same site routinely.

Almost always, if arrested, the assailant is out again within hours, whereupon, he immediately punishes "his woman" for whomever called the police.

> Even when the police officers perceive danger and remove the abusive partner for the night, they tend to do no immediate follow-up. Many a man returns the next day to thrash his partner for the night of incarceration. Judges pose a still greater problem, for they wield incredible power, and it is far harder to hold them to account. Judges commonly display rank sexism. They may find with the man, with little reason to do so. They often dole out token reprimands, accompanying these with . . . misogynous statements . . . . Where officers charge an abusive partner at the woman's behest and the woman changes her mind, her refusal to testify against her partner is itself treated as an offense.[4]

Many a woman escapes an abusive marriage, yet continues to live in fear that the assailant she has not seen for months or years may one day find her again.

When some women seek help to leave their "marriage," they find that, overall, people do not believe them, do not care, or are afraid to get involved in their defense. They may be forced to run, to hide.[5]

> I slept first on the floor of a friend's room . . . with her two dogs. Later, I slept where I could . . . . I slept in someone's kitchen . . . . In one emergency, when my husband had broken into

[4] Burstow 1992 p164
[5] Dworkin 1997 p21

> where I was living, had beaten me and
> threatened to kill me, I spent three weeks
> sleeping in a movie theater that was empty most
> of the time . . . . I lived in a state of terror.
> Every trip outside might mean death if he
> found me . . . . [T]he degradation had numbed
> me, disoriented me, changed me, lowered me,
> shamed me, broken me.[6]

This author writes, "Accounts of wife-beating have typically been met with incredulity and disdain, best expressed in the persistent question, *"Why doesn't she leave?"*[7] But after two decades of learning about battery, we now know that more battered women are killed after they leave than before."[8]

> What no one will face is this: *the problem is not with the woman; it is with the perpetrator.* She can change every weakness, transform every dependency. She can escape with the bravado of a Jesse James or the subtle skill of a Houdini. But *if the [perpetrator]* **is committed to** *violence* **and she is not,** *she* **cannot win** *her safety or her freedom.* The current legal system, victim advocates, counseling cannot keep her safe in the face of his aggression.[9]

When the criminal justice system responds to a domestic abuse call, "bias" may [still] be encoded in the interaction "as a matter of departmental policy." Police may still choose "not to arrest" an assailant. They may decide that, if the woman does not need stitches, there has been no abuse. [10] Also, instead of arresting the assailant, they may opt to "give the couple time to battle it out and cool off," leaving the woman in the midst of the abuse and with her abuser.[11] Or, "in contradistinction to other

---

[6] Dworkin 1997 pp18-19
[7] When I tell people I'm a psychologist specializing in gender-based violence, people always ask, when a man is beating his wife, *Why does she stay with him?*. . . They never ask…*Why would a man hit his wife?* **Men's violence is considered to be a given, and women's responses to that violence are seen as choices.** This **subtly makes women responsible for the violence.** (Kilmartin 2012)
[8] Dworkin 1997 p43, author's emphasis
[9] Dworkin, 1997 pp42-43, emphasis mine
[10] DeKeresey and Schwartz 1998 p17
[11] Jones 1980 pp311-312

types of assault, police trained in "crisis intervention" . . . may "steer the couple toward counseling" failing "to treat the assault" of a female intimate partner "with the same level of investigation" undertaken for other violent crimes.[12]

They may fail to determine the primary aggressor and arrest both parties or, even, the victim alone.

b. Rhetoric That Obscures

Society – still – does not take the beating of women seriously. Yet, "*the brutal reality* of many women's lives . . . [includes] *a web of long-term terror* through a barrage of ... abusive events" (emotional, mental, verbal, sexual, and physical).[13]

~~~

[The] very use of the term *domestic* violence

suggests that this is *tame* violence . . .

violence that is NOT to be taken very seriously.

Bonnie Burstow[14]

~~~

Calling the physical assault of a woman/partner "domestic violence" is euphemistic – making it sound tame (as in *domesticated*),[15] linguistically *making it seem more normal, and less brutal,* than it actually is.

---

[12] Jones 1980 p303
[13] DeKeseredy & Schwartz 1998 p17
[14] Burstow 1992 p164, emphasis mine
[15] Jones 1980 p283

As previously noted, "battered women's injuries are as [physically] serious as injuries suffered in 90% of violent felonies."[16]

a. The Male Standard of Justice

Women who are battered and take it – and women who are arrested for defending themselves against their batterers – both face a *male* standard of justice.

The first group is blamed for not getting, or staying, free.

The second group is blamed because the only path to freedom they could, in their estimation at the time, find, was homicide, and for a female, killing an assailant (especially a long-term assailant who started out as a romantic partner) is a definitive violation of gender norms.

The standard of justice is also classed and raced.

Working class women face a *rich* (or at least, *middle class) male* standard of justice.

Women of color face a *white male* standard of justice.

Working class women of color face a *rich* (or at least, *middle class) white male* standard of justice.

> The problem . . . for most battered women is that, at every step of the legal process, the prevailing standard of justice is male . . . . The body of law, made by men, for men, and amassed down through history on their behalf, codifies masculine bias and systematically discriminates against women by ignoring the woman's

---

[16] See above: "Battering" → 2. "Statistics" → section b. "Source of (Often Long-term) Physical, Emotional, & Mental Injury"

point of view [about interpersonal violence] . . . . [T]he law still is largely enforced, interpreted, and administered by men; so it still works in the interests of men as a group . . . . *[W]omen . . . are deprived at every step of equal protection* . . . . The discretion of law-enforcement officials is influenced by other considerations than sex. *Class is a factor, and race . . . . [I]f middle-class white women . . . are treated unfairly, poor women of color haven't a prayer. In fact, the success of the self-defense argument often rests not on the facts of the case, but on the color of the "criminal."* [17]

The male standard pertains at every level from the precinct to the Supreme Court. It is manifest in discriminatory laws, and in the discriminatory exercise of discretion by police, prosecutors, judges, and jurors alike. It makes criminal justice for women whimsical, punitive, divisive, and unjust. [18]

c. Judicial Discretion

Judicial discretion, a factor meant to make the law more humane, systematically works against women.

Often . . . male bias shows up at one stage or another of the legal process in the exercise of "discretion." That built-in flexibility which allows a judge or a prosecutor or a police officer to use "better judgment" is essential . . . to a legal system that tries to deal fairly with individual cases. But since discretion usually is exercised by men (or by women trained to the male standard), it is usually exercised for men, for the male standard. Judicial discretion . . . becomes a mask for the law's underlying systematic discrimination against women. The characteristic male slant of legal discretion tilts

---

[17] Jones 1980 pp310-311,316, emphasis mine
[18] ibid

every case of homicide committed by battered women.[19]

d. **Court Officials**

Court Officials may steer women away from criminal court and toward family and civil court.[20] Prosecutors may offer another level of systemic discrimination.

Historically, police and prosecutors have viewed battering as a family problem. The criminal justice system created a figurative "curtain of privacy" to shield husbands who beat their wives from public view, in the belief that the parties should be left to work out their "differences" privately. If outside intervention was appropriate, counseling was preferred over prosecution. [21]

Also, historically, "women who want[ed] to press charges . . . [were] actually [discouraged] from doing so. [Then and now] many women . . . have been killed by the men they have tried unsuccessfully to prosecute . . . .[22]

> It was only in the 1970's that the criminal justice system – at the prodding of battered women and their advocates – began to treat . . . [intimate partner] violence like other assaults . . . . Even though every state now defines domestic assault as a crime, each chief prosecutor has virtually absolute discretion in setting prosecution priorities and policies for his or her office. Furthermore, each

---

[19] Jones 1980 p311
[20] Jones 1980 p312
[21] MCAVA 2009
[22] Jones 1980, p312

prosecution staff member exercises discretion
in the handling of individual cases.[23]

e. <u>Judges</u>

Judges are as good, or as bad, for battered women as their own
biases allow. They can refuse to admit, or instruct jurors to
disregard, information that throws light on an abuser's history,
including the victims and witnesses' perceptions. A judge may be
concerned that the jury will be *unduly sympathetic to the defendant*
and therefore, may *exercise his discretion on the side of "law and
order.'*[24] In an intimate partner homicide trial,

> The victim's words [may] remain insignificant . .
> . *excluded from the trial . . . called "hearsay" and not
> admissible* in a legal system that has consistently
> protected or ignored the beating and sexual
> abuse of women by men, especially by
> husbands . . . The voice of the victim still has
> no social standing or legal significance. She still
> has no credibility such that each of us – and the
> law – is compelled to help her. We blame her, *as
> the batterer did. We ask why she stayed, though we, of
> course, were not prepared to stand between her and the
> batterer so that she could leave.* And if, after she is
> dead, we tell the police that we heard the
> accused murderer beat her in 1977, and saw her
> with black eyes . . . *we will not be allowed to testify.*[25]

f. <u>Female Jurors</u>

Women who have internalized a doctrine of male superiority
may not stand with battered women in the jury box, and women

---

[23] MCAVA 2009
[24] Jones 1980 pp313-314
[25] Dworkin 1997 pp45-46, emphasis mine

facing the intersecting oppressions of gender and race, or gender race and class may sometimes be conflicted about which side to take.

Centuries of racial abuse by a white power structure, the history of the false accusation of Black men used as the excuse for epidemic lynching nationwide,[26] a century of racial abuse by police departments, bumbling police work (intentional or otherwise) that destroys evidence, and the higher incidence of false arrests of men of color (because they *meet the description* of a given perpetrator), complicate the picture for women of color when the accused is also of color.

The O.J. Simpson trial was conducted within that historical framework, and also within the immediate framework of demonstrable incompetence on the part of the Los Angeles Police Department.

It is a fact that he was found not guilty.

It is also a documented fact that he had victimized his wife for over a decade and a half and that the *evidence* of his ongoing assaults, even after their separation and divorce, were deemed *not admissible* in court:

Five days before Nicole Brown Simpson was murdered...she called a battered women's shelter in terror that her ex-husband was going to kill her. The jury was not told this, because she [being dead] could not be cross-examined....

Most of the rest of the evidence of [his] beating and stalking [over a period of 17 years]...was also excluded.[27]

---

[26] Especially from the end of the Civil War through the 1930s and into the 1950s

[27] Dworkin 1997 pp47-48

In that acquittal, the overwhelming preponderance of evidence of battery - including his victim's diaries, photographs, 911 police call recordings, and numerous police interventions over seventeen years – was ignored, even by the women on the jury.

The judge, the jury, and the nation "looked right through" Nicole.[28] The [O.J.] jury, predominantly women, [did] not respond . . . to the wife abuse evidence . . . . One woman juror called the domestic abuse issue "a waste of time." Polls during the trial confirmed women overall were indifferent to the beatings Nicole Simpson endured.[29]

On the same day the police who beat Rodney G. King were acquitted in Simi Valley, a white husband who had raped, beaten, and tortured his wife, also white, was acquitted of marital rape in South Carolina. He had kept her tied to a bed for hours, her mouth gagged with adhesive tape. He videotaped a half hour of her ordeal, during which he cut her breasts with a knife. The jury, which saw the videotape, had eight women on it. Asked why they acquitted, they said **he** needed help. They *looked right through* the victim – *afraid to recognize any part of themselves* [in her], shamed by her violation. There were no riots afterward. *The governing reality for women of all races is that there is no escape from male violence*, because it is inside and outside, intimate and predatory. While race-hate has been expressed through forced segregation, woman-hate is expressed through forced closeness,[30] which makes punishment swift, easy, and sure. *In private, women often empathize with one another, across race and class, because their experiences with men are so much the same. But in public, including on juries, women rarely dare.* For this reason, no matter how many women are battered – no matter how many football stadiums battered women could fill on any given day – each one is alone.[31]

---

[28] Dworkin 1997 p48
[29] ibid
[30] Mill 1986/1869
[31] Dworkin 1997 pp49-50, emphasis mine

g. **Women Who Kill**

In her book, *Women Who Kill*, Ann Jones notes that, for a "group that makes up more than half the population," women commit relatively "few crimes. However, "the same social and legal deprivations that compel some women to [analyze and work against unfair treatment for gender] push others to homicide."[32]

Some women defend themselves, or if not themselves, their children.

When no one else will keep them safe, homicide may be seen as "a last resort," and "it most often occurs when men simply will not quit."[33]

Deprived of liberty, continually battered, unable to seek or obtain help, convinced that escape is impossible, [the woman who kills] finds that "murder is often situational," enacted by battered women in self-defense, and that "given the same set of circumstances, any one of us might kill."[34]

Yet, because of sex role taboos about "lady-like" or appropriately "feminine" behavior, the same act that might be viewed as heroic, or at least justifiable, for a male (especially in a male-on-male altercation), will be judged as reprehensible for a female (in a male-on-female assault).

Unprotected by the system (police, prosecutors, juries, and judges), abandoned by the ineffectiveness or fears of neighbors, family and friends – if a woman's assailant (boyfriend/husband/ex) escalates the violence high enough, a woman may be faced with the choice of either causing a death or accepting her own. She may have little recourse to save her own life, or the lives of her children, other than homicide. When

---

[32] Jones 1980 p12
[33] Jones 1980 p298
[34] Jones 1980 p14

women kill their intimate partners, they are "seven times more likely than the men to be acting in self-defense."[35]

Those working with victims of interpersonal violence have learned that only the victim can ascertain the seriousness of the threat she is under. Only s/he has seen the look in her stalker/assailant's eyes when he threatens to kill, and only she can assess whether or not he actually means it. She is the best judge of the level of real risk she is under of becoming the victim of his act of homicide.

As with Nicole Simpson, who knew – and repeatedly warned those who loved her – that "someday her husband would kill her . . . and get away with it," women who are battered know their "abuser's capacity to inflict harm and evade consequences" better than any of the individuals (or the court system) that might judge them.[36]

h. The Male-on-Male Legal Standard of Self-Defense

Our courts have failed to extend the right of self-defense to women in terms that realistically matter within the majority of male-on-female assaults. The standard of equal force – encoded for male-on-male altercations – assumes equivalence of body size and strength and mandates that neither party escalate from one form of weapon to another.

Historically, the system, "has mostly consoled and protected batterers," not victims.[37] Yet,

> It's the batterer who has to be stopped . . . . A
> woman [should have] a right to her own bed,
> [to] a home she can't be thrown out of, and [a

---

[35] Jones 1980 p301
[36] Dworkin 1997 p48
[37] ibid

right] for her body not to be ransacked and broken into. She [should have] a right to safe refuge, to expect her family and friends to stop the batterer – by law or force – *before she's dead . . . . .* And ***a batterer's repeated assaults should lawfully be taken as intent to kill.***[38]

While "a batterer's repeated assaults *should* lawfully be taken as intent to kill," [39] they are not given that much serious consideration. On the contrary, no matter the man's size, or training in violence, or history of violence, women may only meet weapon for weapon: fist for fist, knife for knife, gun for gun. "Traditionally, deadly force in self-defense is supposed to be exerted [only] against comparable deadly force,"[40] and that comparability of deadly force was/is judged by a male standard.[41]

There is a distinction in male and female socialization that physically compounds the problem. Little boys are taught to be physically aggressive; little girls are taught to be demure.

Most boys, like it or not, receive athletic training, while women have been barred from sports programs until [relatively] recently, and they still are "channeled" away from contact sports. And for thousands of men the armed forces provide a kind of finishing school in violence. (Many battered women complain that their husbands learned in the service how to inflict great pain without leaving visible marks.) This difference in physical and psychological training, coupled with the usual differences in

---

[38] Dworkin 1997 p50

[39] ibid

[40] Jones 1980 p288

[41] This may, ultimately shift, because of the 1977, the Washington State Supreme Court Wanrow decision, that held that "the standard of a "reasonable man"…did not adequately represent a woman's perspective and consequently threatened to deny women equal protection under the law….making it possible to argue…that a woman who killed to save herself or her children from imminent danger of death or great bodily injury might be acting in a reasonable and justifiable manner."(Jones 1980 pp285-286)

size and strength between marriage partners, makes self-defense a different matter for women.[42]

Aggressiveness training, differential levels of physical exertion, the way heterosexual couples are socialized to pair up by size, and the differences in the kinds of violence each sex is most likely to use mean that,

> To a **small** woman **untrained in physical combat**, a man's fists and feet appear to be deadly weapons, *and **in fact they are** . . . . Most women killed by their husbands are not shot or stabbed but* **simply beaten and kicked to death**. The woman who counters her husband's fists with a gun [or other weapon] *may in fact be* **doing no more than meeting deadly force with deadly force.**[43]

---

[42] Jones 1980 p299
[43] Jones 1980 p300, emphasis mine

Nadine Rosechild Sullivan, Ph.D., Rev.

APPENDIX C –
RESOURCE LINKS
FOR
VICTIMS & SURVIVORS

Women Thrive Worldwide. –
   http://www.womenthrive.org/index.php?option=com_issu
   es&view=issue&id=5&Itemid=115

National Domestic Violence Hotline – 800-799-SAFE (7233) –
   www.thehotline.org

National Sexual Assault Hotline – Free, Confidential, 24/7 –
   800.656. HOPE (4673)

After Silence Online Support Group –
   http://www.aftersilence.org/index.php

The National Organization for Men Against Sexism –
   www.nomas.org

RAINN: Rape, Abuse & Incest National Network –2000 L Street
   NW, Ste 406, Washington, DC

http://www.rainn.org/get-information/types-of-sexual-
   assault/male-sexual-assault

Male Survivors - http://www.malesurvivor.org/

Male Survivors of Sexual Assault – Booklet –

http://cmhc.utexas.edu/booklets/maleassault/menassault.html

Men Against Rape -
 http://www.rapeis.org/activism/prevention/menagainstrap
 e.html

Gay Men's Domestic Violence Project – http://gmdvp.org/

Jewish Survivors of Sexual Violence Speak Out -
 http://jewishsurvivors.blogspot.com/

Survivors Network of those Abused by Priests -
 http://www.snapnetwork.org/

*(Christian) The Hope of Survivors: Support, Hope & Healing for Victims
 of Pastoral Sexual Abuse* –
 http://www.thehopeofsurvivors.com/

Philadelphia Local

Women Against Abuse – Philadelphia Domestic Violence Hotline:
 866-723-3014 http://www.womenagainstabuse.org/

Women in Transition - 215-751-1111
 http://www.helpwomen.org/wp/

Women Organized Against Rape – 215-985-3333 -
 http://www.woar.org/

REFERENCES

Abel, G. 1981 (Oct15). *The Evaluation and Treatment of Sexual Offenders and Their Victims.* Paper presented at St. Vincent Hospital and Medical Center, Portland, OR.

Acker, Joan. 1990. *Hierarchies, Jobs, Bodies: A Theory of Gendered Organizations.* Gender and Society 4(2):139-158.

Adams, David. 1989 (Jul/Aug). *Identifying the Assaultive Husband in Court: You Be the Judge.* Boston Bar Journal. In SWNI (Silent Witness National Initiative). 2006. "Statistics on Domestic Violence: A National Crisis." http://www.silentwitness.net/sub/violences.htm

Ahterton-Zeman, Ben. 2006 (Aug). *Manufacturing Consent - Is It Rape?* NOMAS (The National Organization for Men Against Sexism). http://www.nomas.org/node/150

Ainscough, Carolyn & Kay Toon. 2000. *Surviving Childhood Sexual Abuse: Practical Self-Help for Adults Who Were Sexually Abused as Children.* Cambridge, MA: Da Capo Press.

AMA.1995 (Nov6). *Report: Sexual Assault in America.* Chicago, IL: American Medical Association.

ATVP.org. 2012 (Jan16) [accessed]. *Male Victims: Ten to Eleven Percent of Rape Victims are Men.* http://www.atvp.org/Pages/Information_Pages/MaleVictims.html

Bales, Kevin. 2007. *Ending Slavery: How We Free Today's Slaves.* Berkeley: University of California Press.

Baum, Katrina, Shannan Catalano, Michael Rand, & Kristina Rose. 2009. *Stalking Victimization in the United States.* U.S. Department of Justice, Bureau of Justice Statistics. Available at http://www.ojp.usdoj.gov/bjs/pub/pdf/svus.pdf. In FWF (Futures Without Violence). 2012. *The Facts on Domestic, Dating, and Sexual Violence.* http://www.futureswithoutviolence.org/content/action_center/detail/754

Benedict, Jefferey R. 1998. *Athletes and Acquaintance Rape.* Thousand Oaks, CA: Sage Publications.

Bielby, William T. & James N. Baron. 1986. *Men and Women at Work: Sex Segregation and Statistical Discrimination.* The American Journal of Sociology 91(4):759-799.

Bishaw, Alemayehu & Jessica Semega. 2010. *Income, Earnings, and Poverty Data from the 2007 American Community Survey.* U.S. Census Bureau. U.S. Department of Commerce, Economics and Statistics Administration. http://www.census.gov/prod/2008pubs/acs-09.pdf

Black, Stephanie. (director.). 2001. *Life and Debt.* Film. PBS: Tuff Gong Pictures.

Blau, Francine D. 1998. *Trends in the Well-Being of American Women, 1970-1995.* Journal of Economic Literature XXXVI:112-165.

Blodget, Henry. 2005. *Chinese Sweatshops, Manhattan-Style: Why Your Clothes Are Made In China.* Slate/Washington Post. http://www.slate.com/articles/arts/go_east_young_man/2005/02/chinese_sweatshops_manhattanstyle.html

Boeringer, Scot B. 1996 (Jun). *Influences of Fraternity Membership, Athletics, and Male Living Arrangements on Sexual Aggression.* Violence Against Women 2(2):134-148.

BOJ (Bureau of Justice Statistics Crime Data Brief). 2003 (Feb). *Intimate Partner Violence, 1995-2001*. In National Domestic Violence Hotline. 2012 [accessed]. "Get Educated: Abuse in America, General Statistics." Austin, TX. http://www.thehotline.org/get-educated/abuse-in-america/

Bracha, MD, H. Stefan., & Tyler C. Ralston, MA, & Jennifer M. Matsukawa, M.A., et al. 2004. *Does "Fight or Flight" Need Updating?* The Academy of Psychosomatic Medicine. Psychosomatics 45:448-49., http://psy.psychiatryonline.org/cgi/content/full/45/5/448

Browne, Angela & Kirk R. Williams. 1989. *Exploring the Effect of Resource Availability and the Likelihood of Female-Perpetrated Homicide*. Law and Society Review 23(1):75–94.

Brownmiller, Susan. 1975. *Against Our Will: Men, Women and Rape*. New York: Simon & Schuster.

Brumberg, Joan Jacobs. 1995. *Fasting Girls: The Emerging Ideal of Slenderness in American Culture*. In Linda K. Kerber & Jane Sherron De Hart. "Women's America: Refocusing the Past, 4th ed." New York: Oxford University Press. pp374-382.

Burke, Phyllis. 1996. *Gender Shock: Exploding the Myths of Male & Female*. New York: Anchor, Doubleday.

Burstow, Bonnie.1992. *Radical Feminist Therapy: Working In the Context of Violence*. Newbury Park, CA: Sage Publications.

Campaign for the Advancement of Women. 2012 [Accessed]. *Fashion Crimes: Women and Sweatshop Labor*. http://www.mtholyoke.edu/~nshah/fashioncrimes/Sweatshops.html

Catalano, Shannan. 2007. *Intimate Partner Violence in the United States.* U.S. Department of Justice, Bureau of Justice Statistics. http://www.ojp.usdoj.gov/bjs/intimate/ipv.htm

CDC (Center for Disease Control and Prevention). 2008 (Feb). *Adverse Health Conditions and Health Risk Behaviors Associated with Intimate Partner Violence – United States, 2005. Morbidity and Mortality Weekly Report.* http://www.cdc.gov/mmwr/preview/mmwrhtml/mm5705a1.htm

Chu, James & Elizabeth S. Bowman. 2003. *Trauma and Sexuality: The Effects of Childhood Sexual, Physical, and Emotional Abuse on Sexual Identity and Behavior.* New York, London: Informa Healthcare.

CMHC. 2007/2000. *For Men Only: For Male Survivors of Sexual Assault (I Never Thought I Could Happen to Me).* Austin, TX: Counseling & Mental Health Center, University of Texas, Austin. http://cmhc.utexas.edu/booklets/maleassault/menassault.html

Coltrane, Scott. 2005. *Chapter 7: Gender, Culture, and Fatherhood.* In "Family Man: Fatherhood, Housework, and Gender Equity." NY: Oxford University Press.

Commonwealth Fund. 2009. *Health Concerns Across a Woman's Lifespan. The Commonwealth Fund 1998 Survey of Women's Health, 1999.* In DomesticViolence.org. "Common Myths and Why They Are Wrong." http://www.domesticviolence.org/common-myths/

Connell, Robert William (Raewyn). 1995. *Masculinities.* Berkeley: University of California.

Connell, Robert William (Raewyn). 1994/1987. *Gender and Power: Society, the Person, and Sexual Politics.* Stanford, CA: Stanford University Press.

Coontz, Stephanie. 2000. *The Way We Never Were: American Families and the Nostalgia Trap.* NY: Basic Books.

Courvant, D., & L. Cook-Daniels. 1998. *Transgender and Intersex Survivors of Domestic Violence: Defining Terms, Barriers and Responsibilities*. In the "National Coalition Against Domestic Violence Conference Manual." (POB 18749 Denver, CO 80218). Denver: National Coalition Against Domestic Violence.

Clark, Stephen J. 2006. *Gay Priests and Other Bogeymen*. Journal of Homosexuality 51(4):1-13.

Crooks, Robert & Karla Baur. 2002. *Our Sexuality* (8th Edition). Pacific Grove, CA: Wadsworth/ Thompson Learning.

Day, Jennifer Cheeseman & Jeffrey Rosenthal. 2011 (Sep30). *Detailed Occupations and Median Earnings: 2008*. U.S. Census Bureau. http://www.census.gov/hhes/www/ioindex/acs08_detailedoccupations.pdf

De Becker, Gavin. 2000. *Protecting the Gift: Keeping Children and Teenagers Safe (and Parents Sane)*. New York: Dell Books.

DeBecker, Gavin. 1997. *The Gift of Fear: Survival Signals That Protect Us From Violence*. New York: Little, Brown and Company.

DeGeneres, Ellen & Alex Herschlag (writer). 2006. [original air date 1997 (Apr30)]. *Ellen, Season 4, "The Puppy Episode,Pt2." Episode 23*. TV: American Broadcasting Corporation. (2006. DVD: A&E Home Video).

DeKeseredy, Walter S. & Martin D. Schwartz. 1998. *Woman Abuse on Campus: Results from the Canadian National Survey*. Thousand Oaks, CA: SAGE Publications.

deLaHunta, Elizabeth & Asher Tulsky. 1996 (Jun26). *Personal Exposure of Faculty and Medical Students to Family Violence*. JAMA (Journal of the

American Medical Association) 275(24):1903- 1906. In Feminist.com. 2012. "Anti-Violence Resource Guide: Facts About Violence: U.S. Statistics." http://www.feminist.com/antiviolence/facts.html

DHHS. 2009. *Women's Health USA 2009: Intimate Partner Violence.* Rockville, Maryland: U.S. Department of Health and Human Services, Health Resources and Services Administration, Maternal and Child Health Bureau. http://mchb.hrsa.gov/whusa09/hstat/hi/pages/226ipv.html

Dirie, Waris (with Cathleen Miller). 1998. *Desert Flower: The Extraordinary Journey of a Desert Nomad.* New York: HarperCollins.

Dirie, Waris (with Corinna Milborn). 2005. *Desert Children.* United Kingdom: Virago, Time Warner UK.

Dirie, Waris (with Jeanne d'haem). *Desert Dawn.* United Kingdom: Virago, Time Warner UK.

DOL. (U.S. Department of Labor, Women's Bureau). 2010. *20 Leading Occupations of Employed Women: Full-time Wage and Salary Workers.* Bureau of Labor Statistics, Annual Averages. http://www.dol.gov/wb/factsheets/20lead2010.htm

DOJ (U.S. Department of Justice). 2008. *National Crime Victimization Survey: Criminal Victimization, 2007.* Bureau of Justice Statistics. http://www.ojp.usdoj.gov/bjs/pub/pdf/cv07.pdf. In FWF "Futures Without Violence, The Facts on Domestic, Dating, and Sexual Violence." 2012. http://www.futureswithoutviolence.org/content/action_center/detail/754

DOJ (U.S. Department of Justice). 2005. *Family Violence Statistics: Including Statistics on Strangers and Acquaintances.* Bureau of Justice Statistics. http://www.ojp.usdoj.gov/bjs/pub/pdf/fvs.pdf.

DOJ (U.S. Department of Justice). 2001 (Jan26). *Nearly 3 Percent of College Women Experienced A Completed or Attempted Rape During the College Year, According to a New Justice Department Report.* Bureau of Justice Statistics. http://bjs.ojp.usdoj.gov/content/pub/press/svcw.pr; and http://bjs.ojp.usdoj.gov/index.cfm?ty=pbdetail&iid=581

Douglas, Kathy A., & Janet L. Collins. 1997 (Sep). *Results from the 1995 National College Health Risk Behavior Survey.* Journal of American College Health 46(2):55-67.

DreamofJoy-Free of Abuse. 2012 [accessed]. *#1 Killer of Black Women Age 15-45.* http://dreamofjoyfreeofabuse.blogspot.com/2008/08/1-killer-of-black-women-age-15-45.html

DV (DomesticViolence). 2009. *Who Are the Abusers?* DomesticViolence.org http://www.domesticviolence.org/who-are-the-abusers/

DVI (Domestic Violence Institute.org). 2012 [accessed]. *Fact Sheet: Intimate Partner Violence in the African American Community. Institute on Domestic Violence in the African American Community.* http://www.idvaac.org/forthepress/factsheets/FactSheet.IDVAAC_A APCFV-Community%20Insights.pdf

DVRC. 2012 (Feb9) [accessed]. *Domestic Violence Statistics.* http://www.dvrc-or.org/domestic/violence/resources/C61/

Dworkin, Andrea. 1997. *Life and Death.* New York: The Free Press, Simon & Schuster.

Ehrenreicht, Barbara & Arlie Russell Hochschild. 2002. *Global Woman: Nannies, Maids, and Sex Workers in the New Economy.* New York: Owl/Henry Holt.

275

Estrich, Susan. 1987. *Real Rape*. Cambridge, MA: Harvard University Press.

Eyler, A.E., & T. M. Witten. 1999. *Violence Within and Against the Transgender Community: Preliminary Survey Results*. "International Longitudinal Transsexual and Transgender Aging Research Project Technical Report 1-12. 12846." San Antonio, TX. http://www.int-trans.org.

Faludi, Susan. 2011. *Stiffed: The Betrayal of the American Man*. HarperCollins e-books.

Fausto-Sterling, Anne. 2000. *Sexing the Body: Gender Politics and the Construction of Sexuality*. New York: Basic Books.

Fausto-Sterling, Anne. 1992. *Myths of Gender: Biological Theories About Women and Men*, Revised Edition. New York: Basic Books.

FBI. 1995. *Uniform Crime Reports*. Washington, D.C.: Federal Bureau of Investigation, Department of Justice.

Feagin, Joe R. 2001. *Racist America: Roots, Current Realities, and Future Reparations*. New York: Routledge.

Feuereisen, Patti & Caroline Pincus. 2005. *Invisible Girls: the Truth About Sexual Abuse – A Book for Teen Girls, Young Women, and Everyone Who Cares About Them*. Berkeley, CA: Seal Press.

Fisher, Bonnie. 2004. *Measuring Rape Against Women: The Significance of Survey Questions*. NCJ 199705

Fisher, Bonnie & Francis Cullen, Michael Turner. 2001 (Jan 26). *Sexual Victimization of College Women*. U.S. Department of Justice, Bureau of Justice Statistics. (data from National College Women Sexual Victimization Study).
http://bjs.ojp.usdoj.gov/index.cfm?ty=pbdetail&iid=1150

FMF. 2012. *Feminists Against Sweatshops*. Feminist Majority Foundation
http://www.feminist.org/other/sweatshops/sweatfaq.html

FMF. (Feminist Majority Foundation). 2012. *Domestic Violence Facts*. Domestic Violence Information Center. Feminist Majority Foundation.
http://www.feminist.org/other/dv/dvfact.html#crime

FWF (Futures Without Violence). 2012. *The Facts on Domestic, Dating, and Sexual Violence*.
http://www.futureswithoutviolence.org/content/action_center/detail/754

Getz, David M. 2010 (Sep). *Men's and Women's Earnings for States and Metropolitan Statistical Areas: 2009*. U.S. Census Bureau. American Community Survey Briefs.
http://www.census.gov/prod/2010pubs/acsbr09-3.pdf

Graff, E.J. 1999. *What Is Marriage For?* Boston: Beacon Press.

Gilbert, Barbara J, Heesacker, Martin. & Linda J. Gannon. 1991. *Changing the Sexual Aggression-Supportive Attitudes of Men: A Psychoeducational Intervention*. Journal of Counseling Psychology 38(2): 197-203.

Goodwin, Jan. 2003/1994. *Price of Honor: Muslim Women Lift the Veil of Silence on the Islamic World*. New York: Plume, Penguin Putnam.

Greven, Philip. 1990. *Spare the Child: The Religious Roots of Punishment & the Psychological Impact of Physical Abuse.* New York: Alfred A. Knopf.

Hall, Gordon C. Nagayama. & Christy. Barongan. 1997. *Prevention of Sexual Aggression: Sociocultural Risk and Protective Factors.* American Psychologist 52:5-14.

Heise, Lori L. 1997. *Violence, Sexuality, and Women's Lives.* In Roger N. Lancaster & Micaela di Leonardo. (eds.). "The Gender Sexuality Reader: Culture, History, Political Economy: pp411-433." New York & London: Routledge.

Herman, Judith. 1997. *Trauma and Recovery: The Aftermath of Violence – from Domestic Abuse to Political Terror.* New York: Basic Books.

Higley, Dr. Brewster. 1876. *Home on the Range: Oh, Give Me a Home Where the Buffalo Roam.* Lyrics. http://en.wikipedia.org/wiki/Home_on_the_range

Hill, Melanie S. & Ann R. Fischer. 2001. *Does Entitlement Mediate the Link Between Masculinity and Rape-Related Variables?* Journal of Counseling Psychology 48:39-50.

Hirschel, David. 2009 (Jun). *Making Arrests in Domestic Violence Cases: What Police Should Know.* U.S. Department of Justice, Office of Justice Programs, National Institute of Justice. NCJ 225458. https://www.ncjrs.gov/pdffiles1/nij/225458.pdf

Hirschel, David & Eve Buzawa, April Pattavina, Don Faggiani, Melissa Reuland. 2007 (May). *Explaining the Prevalence, Context, and Consequences of Dual Arrest in Intimate Partner Cases.* U.S. Department of Justice, National Institute of Justice, ePub. http://www.nij.gov/publications/dv-dual-arrest-222679/welcome.htm

Hochschild, Arlie & Anne Machung. 2012. *The Second Shift: Working Families and the Revolution at Home.* NY: Penguin Books.

Hotline, The. 2012 [accessed]. *Get Educated.* "2006 Harris Poll." http://www.thehotline.org/get-educated/abuse-in-america/

Hughes, Jean O'Gorman & Bernice R. Sandler. 1999. *The Project on the Status and Education of Women of the Association of American Colleges.* In Nadine Sullivan. 2000 Mar20. "Students Take Back the Night." Richard Stockton College, Pomona, New Jersey: The Argo.

Human Rights Watch. 2000. *International Trafficking of Women and Children.* http://www.hrw.org/news/2000/02/21/international-trafficking-women-and-children

Human Rights Watch. 2011a. *How Come You Allow Little Girls to Get Married? Child Marriage in Yemen.* http://www.hrw.org/sites/default/files/reports/yemen1211ForUpload_0.pdf

Human Rights Watch. 2011b. *They Deceived Us at Every Step: Abuse of Cambodian Domestic Workers Migrating to Malaysia.* http://www.hrw.org/sites/default/files/reports/cambodia1111webwcover.pdf

Human Rights Watch. 2011c. *We'll Show You You're a Woman: Violence and Discrimination against Black Lesbians and Transgender Men in South Africa.* http://www.hrw.org/sites/default/files/reports/southafrica1211.pdf

Hunter, Mic. 1990. *Abused Boys: The Neglected Victims of Sexual Abuse.* MA: Lexington.

IBIS-PH (Indicator-Based Information System for Public Health). 2011. *Complete Indicator Profile of Domestic Violence Fatalities.* "Violence and Injury Prevention Program, Bureau of Health Promotion, Division of Disease Control and Prevention, Utah Department of Health." http://ibis.health.utah.gov/indicator/complete_profile/DomViolRelHom.html

Inbaraj, Sonny. 2004. *Fistula Makes Social Outcasts of Child Brides*. IPS - Inter Press Service News Agency - Health-Ethiopia. http://www.ipsnews.net/news.asp?idnews=22242

Jones, Ann. 1980. *Women Who Kill*. New York: Holt, Rinehart and Winston.

Jones, Arthur & Shirley Smith. 1998 (Sep29)/ Revised 2001 (12Apr). *Married Women Joining Work Force Spur 150 Percent Family Income Increase, Census Bureau Finds in 50-Year Review*. "Economics and Statistics Administration. Bureau of the Census." Washington DC: United States Department of Commerce News. http://www.census.gov/Press-Release/cb98-181.html

Kaplan, E. Ann. 1990. *Women and Film: Both Sides of the Camera*. New York: Routledge.

Karch, Debra, Linda Dahlberg, Nimesh Patel, Terry Davis, Josepah Logan, Holly Hill, & LaVonne Ortega. 2009 (Mar20). *Surveillance for Violent Deaths - National Violent Death Reporting System, 16 States, 2006*. Atlanta, GA: Centers for Disease Control and Prevention. Department of Health and Human Services, Morbidity and Mortality Weekly Report 58 (S S01):1-44, http://www.cdc.gov/mmwr/preview/mmwrhtml/ss5801a1.htm

Kassindja, Fauziya (with Layli Miller Bashir). 1998. *Do They Hear You When You Cry?* New York: Delacorte Press/Bantam Doubleday/Dell.

Katz, Jackson. 2006. *The Macho Paradox: Why Some Men Hurt Women and How All Men Can Help*. Naperville, IL: Sourcebooks, Inc.

Katz, Jackson & Jean Kilbourne. 2004. In Ronit Ridberg (ed.). *Spin the Bottle: Sex, Lies & Alcohol*. Film: Media Education Foundation.

Katz, Jackson. (director). 2000. In Sut Jhally (director). *Tough Guise: Violence, Media, and the Crisis in Masculinity.* DVD. Northampton, MA: Media Education Foundation.

Kilbourne, Jean. in Sut Jhally (director). 2010. *Killing Us Softly 4: Advertising's Image of Women.* DVD. Northampton, MA: Media Education Foundation. www.mediaed.org, www.jeankilbourne.com

Kilbourne, Jean. in Sut Jhally (director). 2000. *Killing Us Softly 3: Advertising's Image of Women.* DVD. Northampton, MA: Media Education Foundation. www.mediaed.org, www.jeankilbourne.com

Kilmartin, Christopher. 2012 [accessed]. *Men's Violence Against Women.* NOMAS (The National Organization for Men Against Sexism). http://www.nomas.org/node/90

Kilpatrick, D.G., C. Edmunds, & A. Seymour. 1992. *Rape in America: A Report to the Nation.* Charleston, SC: National Victim Center & the Crime Victims Research and Treatment Center, Medical University of South Carolina.

Kimmel, Michael S. 2002. *"Gender Symmetry" in Domestic Violence: A Substantive and Methodological Research Review.* Violence Against Women 8(11):1332-1363.

Kristof, Nicholas & Sheryl WuDunn. 2009. *Half the Sky: Turning Oppression into Opportunity for Women Worldwide.* New York: Alfred A. Knopf.

Kubler-Ross, Elisabeth & David Kessler. 2007. *On Grief and Grieving: Finding the Meaning of Grief Through the Five Stages of Loss.* New York: Scribner.

Lev , Arlene Istar & S. Sundance Lev. 1999. *Sexual Assault in the Transgender Communities*. Domestic Violence Newsletter 4(10), http://my.execpc.com/~dmmunson/Nov99_7.htm

Lita, Ana. 2008. *Obstetric Fistula: A Dire Consequence of Child Marriage*. International Humanist and Ethical Union- Appignani Center for Bioethics. http://www.iheu.org/trackback/2994

Lonsway, Kimberly A.. & Louise F. Fitzgerald. 1994. *Rape Myths*. Psychology of Women Quarterly 18(2):133-164.

Louis, Vincent. 2007. *Bounded Empowerment: An Empirical Assessment Of Competing Perspectives On Persistent Gender Inequality And Race Differences In Housework Sharing*. Ph.D. dissertation, Pennsylvania: Temple University.

Madigan, Lee & Nancy C. Gamble. 1991. *The Second Rape: Society's Continued Betrayal of the Victim*. New York: Lexington Books/Macmillan.

Malamuth , Neil M., Haber, Scott, & Seymour Feshback. 1980. *Testing Hypotheses Regarding Rape: Exposure to Sexual Violence, Sex Differences, and the Normality of Rapists*. Journal of Research in Personality 14:121-137.

Marshall, Michael. 2002. *Why Spanking Doesn't Work: Stopping This Bad Habit & Getting the Upper Hand on Effective Discipline*. Salt Lake City: Bonneville Books.

MCAVA (Minnesota Center Against Violence and Abuse). 2009. *Criminal Prosecution of Domestic Violence*. http://www.mincava.umn.edu/documents/bwjp/prosecutev/prosecut ev.html

McCoy, Craig R. & Mark Fazlollah. 2000 (Jun21). *Review Turns Up Hundreds of Rapes*. Philadelphia, Pennsylvania: The Philadelphia Inquirer. ppA1, A14.

Messner, Michael A. 2004. *Becoming 100% Straight.*. In L. Richardson, V. Taylor, & N. Whittier. "Feminist Frontiers, 6th ed." New York: McGraw Hill.

Mill, John Stuart. 1986/1869. *The Subjection of Women*. New York: Prometheus Books.

Moriarty, Susan. 2000 (Jan). *Fatal Distraction*. Social Alternatives 19(1): 35-37.

Muehlenhard, Charlene L. & Carie S. Rodgers. 1998. *Token Resistance to Sex: New Perspectives on an Old Stereotype*. Psychology of Women Quarterly 22:443-463.

Muhsen, Zana. (with Andrew Crofts). 1991. *A Story of Modern Day Slavery*. United Kingdom: Little, Brown & Co.

Nazer, Mende (with Damien Lewis). 2003. *Slave*. Cambridge, MA: Public Affairs, Perseus.

Murray, J. B. 2000. *Psychological Profile of Pedophiles and Child Molesters*. The Journal of Psychology 134(2):211-224.

NCADV. 2012 (Feb9) [accessed]. *Domestic Violence Facts*. http://www.ncadv.org/files/DomesticViolenceFactSheet(National).pdf

NCAVP (National Coalition of Anti-Violence Programs). 2008. *Lesbian, Gay, Bisexual, and Transgender Domestic Violence in the United States in 2007*. New York. http://avp.org/documents/2007NCAVPDVREPORT.pdf

NCVC (National Center for Victims of Crime). 2012 (Feb20) [accessed]. *HIV/AIDS Legislation*. Washington, D.C.: National Center for Victims of Crime. http://www.ncvc.org/ncvc/main.aspx?dbName=DocumentViewer& DocumentID=32468

NCVC (National Center for Victims of Crime). 2011. *Male Rape*. Washington, D.C.: National Center for Victims of Crime.

NCVC. (National Center for Victims of Crime.) 2011/2008. *Domestic Violence*. http://www.ncvc.org/ncvc/main.aspx?dbName=DocumentViewer& DocumentID=32347

NCVC&NCVRTC. 1992. *Rape in America: A Report to the Nation*. Arlington, VA: National Center for Victims of Crime and National Crime Victim Research and Treatment Center.

Newton, MA, C. J. 2001. *Domestic Violence: An Overview*. Find Counseling.com (formerly TherapistFinder.net) Mental Health Journal. http://www.findcounseling.com/journal/domestic-violence/domestic-violence-statistics.html

NoCirc.org. 2011 [accessed]. *Answers to Your Questions about Female Circumcision*. National Organization of Circumcision Information Resource Centers. NOCIRC Information Series: Female Circumcision. http://nocirc.org/publish/9pam.pdf

NOMAS. 2012a [accessed]. *Why Are Anti-Sexist Men Confronting Violence Against Women?* NOMAS (The National Organization for Men Against Sexism). http://www.nomas.org/node/165

NOMAS. 2012b [accessed]. *Not a Two-Way Streeet: Men Are NOT the Victims of What is Meant by Domestic Violence and Abuse*. NOMAS (The National Organization for Men Against Sexism). http://www.nomas.org/node/220

NOW. 2012 [accessed]. *Violence Against Women in the United States: Statistics.* http://www.now.org/issues/violence/stats.html

NWLC (National Women's Law Center). 2007. *The Wage Gap.* Information Please Database. Pearson Education Inc. http://www.infoplease.com/ipa/A0763170.html

O'Gorman Hughes, Jean and & Bernice R. Sandler. 1987. *Project on the Status and Education of Women.* The Association of American Colleges. http://www.cs.utk.edu~bartley-acuaint-acquaintRape.

Osofsky, J. 1999. *The Impact of Violence on Children.* "The Future of Children." Domestic Violence and Children 9(3):33-49. http://www.ojp.usdoj.gov/bjs/pub/ascii/ipv.txt In Newton, MA, C. J. 2001. "Domestic Violence: An Overview." Find Counseling.com (formerly TherapistFinder.net) Mental Health Journal. http://www.findcounseling.com/journal/domestic-violence/domestic-violence-statistics.html

Overholser, Geneva. 1992. (Iowa Editor/Journalist). In Harry Winer (director) & April Smith (author). *Taking Back My Life: The Nancy Ziegenmeyer Story.* Film. Tribune Media Services: Lifetime.

Padavic, Irene & Barbara Reskin. 1994. *Women and Men at Work.* Pine Forge Press.

Paulozzi, Leonard J., Linda Saltzman, Martie Thompson, & Patricia Holmgreen. 2001 (Oct12). *Surveillance for Homicide Among Intimate Partners - United States, 1981-1998.* Center for Disease Control Surveillance Summaries 50 (S S03):1-16, http://www.cdc.gov/mmwr/preview/mmwrhtml/ss5003a1.htm

Pharr, Suzanne. 1997. *Homophobia: A Weapon of Sexism.* Berkeley: Chardon Press.

Press, Julie & Eleanor Townsley. 1998. *Wives and Husbands' Housework Reporting: Gender, Class, and Social Desirability.* Gender & Society 12(2):188-218.

RAINN (Rape, Abuse & Incest National Network). 2009. *National Crime Victimization Survey Results 2006.* Washington, D.C. http://rainn.org/news-room/rainn-press/2006-National-Crime-Victimization-Survey-Results

Reed, S. 1979 (Apr24). *Interview.* In Jones, Ann. 1980. *Women Who Kill.* New York: Holt, Rinehart and Winston.

Reeves Sanday, Peggy. 1996. *A Woman Scorned: Acquaintance Rape on Trial.* New York: Doubleday.

Reeves Sanday, Peggy. 1996 (Jun). *Rape-Prone Versus Rape-Free Campus Cultures.* Violence Against Women 2(2):191-208.

Reeves Sanday, Peggy. 1990. *Fraternity Gang Rape: Sex, Brotherhood, and Privilege on Campus.* New York: NYU Press.

Reeves Sanday, Peggy. 1981. *The Socio-Cultural Context Of Rape: A Cross Cultural Study.* Journal of Social Issues 37(4):5-27.

Rennison, M. & W. Welchans. 2000 (May) [Revised 7/14/2000]. *Intimate Partner Violence.* U.S. Department of Justice, Office of Justice Programs, Bureau of Justice Statistics. NCJ 178247. http://www.ojp.usdoj.gov/bjs/pub/ascii/ipv.txt. In Newton, MA, C. J. 2001. "Domestic Violence: An Overview." Find Counseling.com (formerly TherapistFinder.net) Mental Health Journal. http://www.findcounseling.com/journal/domestic-violence/domestic-violence-statistics.html

Ringel, C. 1997 (Nov). *Criminal Victimization in 1996, Changes 1995-1996 with Trends 1993-1996. National Crime Victimization Survey.* Washington, DC: U.S. Department of Justice, Bureau of Justice Statistics.

RVA (Rape Victim Advocates). 2008. *Children & Sexual Violence: When the Victim is a Child.* Rape Victim Advocates. Chicago, IL. http://www.rapevictimadvocates.org/children.asp

Sadusky, Jane. 2010. *Wisconsin Domestic Violence Homicide Report.* Wisconsin Coalition Against Domestic Violence. http://www.wcadv.org/sites/default/files/resources/2010%20Wisconsin%20Domestic%20Violence%20Homicide%20Report.pdf

SATF (Oregon Attorney General's Sexual Assault Task Force). 2008 (Jan10). *False Allegations, Recantations, and Unfounding in the Context of Sexual Assault.* http://oregonsatf.org/wp-content/uploads/2011/02/Position-Paper-False-Alleg3.pdf

Savage, Charlie. 2012 (Jan 6). *U.S. to Expand Its Definition Of Rape In Statistics.* New York: New York Times. http://www.nytimes.com/2012/01/07/us/politics/federal-crime-statistics-to-expand-rape-definition.html?_r=1

Schwartz, Martin D. & Carol A. Nogrady. 1996 (Jun). *Fraternity Membership, Rape Myths, And Sexual Aggression On A College Campus.* Violence Against Women 2(2):148-163.

Scully, Diana. & Joseph Marolla. 1984. *Convicted Rapists' Vocabulary of Motives, Excuses, and Justifications.* Social Problems 31:530-544.

Seidman, Steven. 2009. *The Social Construction of Sexuality.* New York: W.W. Norton.

Simonson, Kelly. & Linda Mezydlo Subich. 1999. *Rape Perceptions as a Function of Gender-Role Traditionality and Victim-Perpetrator Association.* Sex Roles 40:617-633.

Souad (with Marie-Therese Cuny). 2003. *Burned Alive: A Victim of the Law of Men*. New York: Warner Books.

Stevenson, M. R. 2000. *Public Policy, Homosexuality, and the Sexual Coercion of Children*. Journal of Psychology & Human Sexuality 12(4):1-19.

Rosechild Sullivan, Nadine. 2012. *The Status of Women in the U.S. Before and After Second Wave Feminism*. Philadelphia: Lifting Consciousness Press. Kindle Single.

Stannard, Una. 1977. *Mrs. Man*. San Francisco: Germainbooks.

Straton, Ph.D., Jack C. 2008/ 2012 (Mar3) [accessed]. *The Myth of the "Battered Husband Syndrome."* NOMAS (The National Organization for Men Against Sexism). http://www.nomas.org/node/107

Sullivan, Nadine Rosechild. 2000 (Mar20). *Women Take Back the Night*. Pomona, NJ: The Argo, Richard Stockton College. p1.

Sutton, Joe. 2005 (Feb24). *Homicide One of Leading Causes of Injury-Related Death Among Pregnant Women, New Mothers, CDC Study Says*. Medical News Today. http://www.medicalnewstoday.com/releases/20316.php

SWNI (Silent Witness National Initiative). 2006. *Statistics on Domestic Violence: A National Crisis*.
http://www.silentwitness.net/sub/violences.htm

Tanenbaum, Leora. 2000. *Slut! Growing Up Female With a Bad Reputation*. New York: Perennial Harper Collins.

Tarrant, David. 2005 (Feb 23). *Homicide the No. 1 Cause of Death for Pregnant Women*. http://www.freerepublic.com/focus/f-news/1349613/posts

Tatum, Beverly Daniel. 2003/1997. *Why Are All the Black Kids Sitting Together in the Cafeteria? And Other Conversations About Race: A Psychologist Explains the Development of Racial Identity*. New York: Basic Books.

Tjaden, P. & N. Thoennes. 1998. *Prevalence, Incidence, and Consequences of Violence Against Women: Findings From the National Violence Against Women Survey*. (Research in Brief). Washington, DC: U.S. Department of Justice, National Institute of Justice.

UN. 2012 (Mar12) [accessed]. *Violence Against Women: The Situation*. United Nations Secretary-General's Campaign to Unite to End Violence Against Women. http://endviolence.un.org/situation.shtml

UN. 2008. *Fact Sheet: United Nations Secretary-General's Campaign to Unite to End Violence Against Women*. United Nations Department of Public Information DPI/2498. (Data Sources: "United Nations Secretary-General's In-Depth Study on Violence Against Women 2006." UNIFEM (United Nations Fund for Women); UNFPA (United Nations Population Fund).) http://www.un.org/en/women/endviolence/pdf/VAW.pdf

UNICEF. 2011. *Child Trafficking*. http://www.unicef.org/protection/57929_58005.html

van Wormer, Katherine. 2009 (Jan/Feb). *Reducing the Risk of Domestic Homicide*. Social Work Today 9(1):18., http://www.socialworktoday.com/archive/011909p18.shtml

Varia, Nisha. 2011 (Jun29). *Human Rights Watch: The Hidden Victims of Human Trafficking*. The Huffington Post. http://www.hrw.org/news/2011/06/29/hidden-victims-human-trafficking

VPC (Violence Policy Center). 2006 (Apr). *American Roulette: Murder-Suicide in the United States*. In National Domestic Violence Hotline. 2012 [accessed]. "Get Educated: Abuse in America: General Statistics." Austin, TX. http://www.thehotline.org/get-educated/abuse-in-america/

Walker, Alice. 1992. *Possessing the Secret of Joy*. Orlando: Harcourt Brace Jovanovich.

West, Candace & Don H. Zimmerman. 1987. *Doing Gender*. Gender and Society 1(2):125-151.

Williams, Christine L. 1995. *Still a Man's World: Men Who Do "Women's Work."* Berkeley: University of California Press.

WOCPN (Women of Color Policy Network). 2011 (Apr). *Wage Disparities and Women of Color, Policy Brief*. New York: NYU Wagner. http://wagner.nyu.edu/wocpn/publications/files/Pay_Equity_Policy_Brief.pdf

Women and Global Human Rights. 2012 [accessed]. *Women and Sweatshops*. http://www.webster.edu/~woolflm/sweatshops.html

Wright, Jennie. 2008. *Back to Life! Your Personal Guidebook to Grief Recovery*. Wood River Junction, RI: Create Space.

U.S. Congress. 1990 (Jun18). *Hearing on Victims of Rape*. House Select Committee on Children, Youth and Families.

Young, Gayle. 1995. *"Bride Burning" Alive and Well in India: Police Say Every Two Hours a Woman is Killed Over Dowry*. CNN World News. http://www.cnn.com/WORLD/9508/india/burning_brides/

Zinn, Howard. 2004. In Deb Ellis and Denis Mueller (directors). *You Can't Be Neutral on a Moving Train*. Film: Tribune Media Services. [Viewed on The Sundance Channel 2006 (Jul24)].

MORE ABOUT THE AUTHOR

Dr. Sullivan's Public Speaking Topics include:

- What Do Gay People Really Want and Why? Lesbian, Gay, Bisexual, Transgender, Queer-identified, & Intersex People in the Family, School, Congregation & Workplace

- Which Bathroom Can S/he Use? The Differences Between Sex, Gender & Affectional/Sexual Orientation (and Why It Matters to You)

- Someone You Know Is LGBTQI (lesbian, gay, bisexual, transgender, queer-identified, intersex)

- Reconciling Spiritual and Sexual Identities

- Respect Between Genders ~ in the Workplace & Beyond

- Healing from Gendered (Sexual & Domestic) Assault

- Stress Reduction & Forward Motion: Self-Guided Positive Visualization & Affirmations for Personal Productivity & Creativity

- Using the Power of Positive Thought to Manifest the Life & Career You Desire

Other Public Speaking Topics:

Human Sexuality, Relationships, Marriage & Family, Gender in America, Gendered Dimensions of Globalization, Ethnicity and the Immigrant Experience, The History and Significance of Race in America, Equality/Inequality, Contemporary Social Issues, Minority Groups

Other Publications:

- *Gay 101: The Real Gay Agenda, What Gay (LGBTQI) People Really Want and Why (Forthcoming)*

- *Turn Your Life Around! Expand Your Use of 'The Secret' & Manifest Intentionally in EVERY Area of Your Life.* (2011). Philadelphia: Lifting Consciousness Press.

- *Pathways into Social Movement Activism, Altruism and Self-Interest: The LGBT and Marriage Movement in New Jersey.* (2011). Ph.D. Dissertation. Philadelphia. Temple University.

- *Intrinsically Disordered or Gay by God? How Gay People Reconcile Their Sexuality and Their Spirituality.* (2004). Candidacy Research Paper. Philadelphia. Temple University. (Presented: ASA Convention, Philadelphia, Pennsylvania; Society for the Anthropology of Religion Conference, Vancouver, BC, 2005)

Education:

Nadine Rosechild Sullivan, Ph.D. completed her doctorate in sociology, with concentrations in race and ethnicity and gender and sexuality, and a graduate certificate in Women's Studies. She is a member of the Golden Key International Honor Society. She completed a bachelor of arts in anthropology and another in sociology, with undergraduate minors in African American studies, women's studies, and writing, graduating summa cum laude, with program distinction and Alpha Kappa Delta. She also completed a certificate in Bible from Faith Oasis Bible Institute, won an award for her translation work in New Testament Greek, and was initially ordained Pentecostal but has studied world religions and has come to identify as interfaith.

Contact Dr. Sullivan at:
www.nadinerosechildsullivan.com
www.rosechild.org

When asked with the question,
"Is this one of those books that
bashes men & praises women?"
I was reluctant to answer.
after a hesitant answer, the man
said "It was reported that just as
many college men are pressured
into having sex as. women."
Peer Pressure is different than Rape.
Rape leaves no choice to the
person. Rape is unforseen &
unexpected & life changing.
This is why books like these
need to exist. — To inform
people who have a misconstrued
idea of rape. — for people
who think rape is comparable
to a choice.

CPSIA information can be obtained at www.ICGtesting.com
Printed in the USA
LVOW01s1531130114

369231LV00023B/1394/P